ARTFUL CREATION

LEARNING-TALES OF ARTS-IN-BUSINESS

To Adrian with thanks
for your enthusiasm
and the wonderful story
about Stickey!
Best wishes-
Lotte

Lotte Darsø
Artful Creation
- Learning-Tales of Arts-in-Business

1. edition 2004 Samfundslitteratur

©Samfundslitteratur

Cover: e-types
Typeset: e-types and Samfundslitteratur Grafik
Illustration layout by e-types:

p. 4:	original photo by Isabelle Demangeat
p. 11:	photo by Adam Philp
p. 24:	photo by Adam Philp
p. 38:	photo by Adam Philp
p. 56:	photo by Adam Philp
p. 58:	letter procured by Creative Leaps International
p. 68:	material by Rich Gold, partly from his website: www.richgold.org
p. 76:	material from Bang & Olufsen's brochure on "Business Theatre"
p. 84:	photo by Titi Astono, Dacapo
p. 92:	artistic notes by Miha Pogacnik for Brahms' Violin Concerto
p. 100:	artwork by Michael Brammer
p. 108:	postcard series and 'positives' from 'Urban Fiction', Catalyst, Unilever Ice Cream & Frozen Food
p. 124:	from article in 'Børsen', April 19th, 2002 (article from Danish Newspaper, "Business can learn from Arts")
p. 134:	photo by Adam Philp
p. 148:	photo by Adam Philp
p. 160:	photo by Adam Philp
p. 174:	photo by Adam Philp

Print: Narayana Press, Gylling, Denmark

ISBN 87-593-1109-6

Published by:
Samfundslitteratur
Rosenoerns Allé 9
DK-1970 Frederiksberg C
Denmark
Telf: + 45 38 15 38 80
Fax: + 45 35 35 78 22
slforlag@sl.cbs.dk
www.samfundslitteratur.dk

ARTFUL CREATION
LEARNING-TALES OF ARTS-IN-BUSINESS

BY LOTTE DARSØ

A PLACE AND A PROCESS

Writing a book is a process of creation,
which takes place in a context.
I have found a place and a process.
The place is a summerhouse,
beautifully built and beautifully situated.
Quiet. With a fireplace.
No phone. No Internet connection.
The process is a structure, a habit, a discipline,
which helps me create a space for writing.
I work on setting the right mood.

Every piece of writing has its music.
For this book it was Bach's Goldberg Variations,
played by Glenn Gould, an original artist.
I arrive at the house, I light the fire, I put on Bach.

On the CD cover of 'A State of Wonder. The complete Goldberg variations 1955 & 1981,' Tim Page wrote about Glenn Gould:

"But Gould's Bach swung like mad. It was urgent, vibrant, strutting and downright *sexy*, quite unlike anything else around. ... The recording heralded a new approach to Bach's keyboard music – it combined the stark, separate contrapuntal voicings so easily delineated on the harpsichord with the tone color and dynamic calibration available from the modern piano. Never before had this music been played with such dazzling and incisive virtuosity. ...

Gould had a penchant for singing along – loudly – as he played. And he clearly had no interest in traditional stage decorum; his body shuddered and contorted at the keyboard while his expressive face, suffering and ecstatic, seemed to embody the essence of music in all its pain and exaltation."

ACKNOWLEDGEMENTS

This book is based on 53 taped interviews and includes many people's experiences and voices. When I started in April 2002 I expected that, after having talked to five or ten artists, I would get a lot of repetitions. This was not the case. Every person interviewed had a slightly different twist or perspective. Every person and every art form turned out to be unique. Every time I did an interview, I was in awe. I want to express my warmest gratitude to, and respect for, all the people I have interviewed. They are here listed in alphabetical order:

Nancy Adler, Richard Albagli, Paul Audley, William Ayot, Martin Best, Debbie Bird, Victor Bischoff, Eric Booth, Michael Brammer, Marijke Broekhuijsen, Bobby Brittain, Judy Sorum Brown, Ted Buswick, Jill Chappell, John Cimino, Bruce Copley, Alastair Creamer, Janet de Merode, Lily Donagh, Annemarie Ehrlich, Rich Gold, Adrian Greystoke, Stanley S. Gryskiewicz, David Guss, Hollis Headrick, James Hill, Piers Ibbotson, Karl James, Michael Jones, Mathilda Joubert, John Kao, Bernard Kelly, Isabelle King, Elmar Lampson, Dianne Legro, Paul Levy, Oliver MacDonald, Alexander Mackenzie, Alejandra Mørk, Linda Naiman,

Robert A. Nalewajek, Richard Olivier, David Pearl, Miha Pogacnik, Ashley Ramsden, Paul Robertson, Otto Scharmer, Milo Shapiro, Ellen Speert, Steven S. Taylor, Herbert R. Tillery, Margaret J. Wheatley, and Mads Øvlisen.

I would like to thank my wonderful colleagues from Learning Lab Denmark for their support: the directors, Marianne Stang Vaaland and Hans Siggaard Jensen for pointing out the melodic composition of the book and how to improve the rhythm; and the core people from The Creative Alliance: Michael Dawids, who conceived the project and has contributed with inspiring dialogues and great vision, David Barry for thoughtful questions and feedback, and Hilde Bollen for indispensable assistance with compiling lists, finding websites and checking information. I would also like to thank Camilla Mehlsen and Stefan Meisiek for their valuable contributions to two of the case studies.

I am grateful that Danish Centre for Management supported the research project from the beginning, Kim Steen Nielsen and Bente Wennerberg in particular.

I would also like to express my gratitude to my publisher, Tanja Verbik for professional editing, to Jens Kajus from e-Types A/S for brilliant layout and design, to Silje Kamille Friis for inspiring ideas and support in selecting the illustrations, and to Mary McGovern for skilfully revising and proofreading the English.

Finally, thanks to my family, Nickie, Perle, Lilie and Pelle for their loving support.

April 2004 – Lotte Darsø

ARTFUL CREATION
LEARNING-TALES OF ARTS-IN-BUSINESS
BY LOTTE DARSØ

CHAPTER 1

INTRODUCTION

"The purpose of art is not the release of a momentary ejection of adrenalin but rather the gradual, lifelong construction of a state of wonder and serenity."

Glenn Gould, pianist

➤ " ... So Izzy came up to me and said 'Can you do this thing?', which I had already briefly looked at and thought it would take too much time. But she said, 'Look, it would really help me out.' So I said yes. It turned out that it was this project called 'Sticky'. The idea was that for two days, fifteen Unilever staff were going to do a series of workshops with Improbable Theatre, some of the most fantastically talented, theatrical people in this country. And then for the rest of that week we would rehearse a show and perform it as the highlight of the Mayor's Thames Festival. I do not know if you have heard about 'Jerry Springer, the Opera', which is a big hit of the West End. You cannot get tickets for love nor money. And I was amazed because the guy I was working with on 'Sticky' was the creative director for Jerry Springer. So it was awesome to work with them. We did a lot of exercises, which were quite uncomfortable. For example, we were animating things, bringing things to life, and we had to bring newspaper to life. I was not the kind of child who played with newspaper and was very creative. I am not very good at painting or drawing, and personally I found it very challenging and I know that a lot of us did. It really pushed our boundaries as well as making us a new group of friends. We met a real mixture of people, all driven by that same, I-want-to-just-experience-life-to-the-maximum mindset. In an office environment, experiencing life to the maximum is not always easy, which is why I think people say 'I am going to take a year out and go and work abroad.' If you can have the same intensity of experience in your job, then that is what matters. 'Sticky' was almost like a dream. I look back, and it went so quickly, as these things will, and I can hardly believe it was me. Everyone afterwards was so jealous, and, as I said, I just fell into it. I said yes without thinking about it too much. Again, I think that is a good part of our company culture, which Catalyst has encouraged..."[1]

This is just one example of Arts-in-Business, probably not very typical at this time, but I profoundly believe that this is the type of story we will be hearing in the future. Do you have art in your business? Of course you do, though you may not be asked to perform a piece of theatre in front of 15,000 people in the open air in central London. But surely you have art in your organisation, at least in the public places, like the reception, the auditoria, the meeting rooms, etc. In your own office you may have posters, photos, reproductions of famous art, children's drawings or other items of your own choice, or you may have to put up with the choice others have made for you. Most people have some kind of art in their daily organisational life. Art, aesthetics and design also influence brands and the products businesses produce, e.g. in the design of labels, packaging and logos. Art plays a part in many internal as well as external business manifestations.

   The type of art, branding or design of these manifestations in many ways expresses the identity of a company. While some companies pay little attention to this fact, others are very conscious about the signals they send through their annual reports, their ads, their product labels and their brand. Still, most companies use art traditionally as decoration and therefore the role of arts and business remains the same, with the arts being *sponsored* by business. This role is, however, changing, as we saw already and as we will examine in the following.

TO USE OR NOT TO USE THE ARTS IN BUSINESS
Basically there are four options regarding Arts-in-Business:

1. Business uses the arts for *decoration*.
2. Business uses the arts for *entertainment*, either by giving the employees benefits such as tickets for selected shows, performances and arts exhibitions in their leisure time, or they invite artists into the company for performances at annual meetings, customer events or special occasions.
3. Business applies the arts as *instruments* for teambuilding, communication training, leadership development, problem solving and innovation processes.
4. Business integrates the arts in a *strategic process of transformation*, involving personal

development and leadership, culture and identity, creativity and innovation, as well as customer relations and marketing.

ARTS AS DECORATION

Even though the first approach of using the arts as decoration sounds very traditional the following two examples demonstrate that it is possible to use art as decoration in a strategic way. For more than 25 years Mads Øvlisen, as CEO of the pharmaceutical company Novo Nordisk, has bought art from young artists, who were not yet known or established. This art has not always been popular among the employees. Mads Øvlisen had, though, a specific purpose: "I hope that our art signals that this is a company where you are allowed to think differently, where you may make mistakes and learn from them" and "You do not have to like the art you see at Novo Nordisk, but I hope it makes you stop and ask a few questions."[2]

Once during the visit of an important customer and a very intense meeting with a heated discussion, the art on the walls became very provocative. The first painting they met on the way to the guests' dining room had a strip across it saying, "Be aggressive". The customer commented, "If that's the message from your CEO, then I better understand what is going on!" When the guests were seated, however, directly across from where they sat there was a painting with a ballet dancer, who gave his public the finger. The customer turned pale and said: "I hope you won't go that far!"

In an interview Mads Øvlisen explained that buying art was neither an investment nor sponsorship. Art was a management signal about the organisation to the organisation. It signalled experimentation, asking questions, contesting borders and limits, quality, originality and renewal. He hoped that the paintings and other art pieces would make people reflect and continue to wonder, and that it would help them not to get stuck in a groove of professional habits.

The next example concerns the company Raymond James Financial, Inc., who labelled their annual report from 1999 "The Art of Financial Planning" and explained on the first page that designing a plan is an art: "We instruct our Financial Advisors in the art of financial planning so that each one can design customised solutions to financial problems." This is later expanded, "just as an artist brings a canvas to life, the art of financial planning can bring our clients' visions to life." Apart from using art as a metaphor in their annual report, the company has a large art collection, supposedly one of the largest privately owned collections in the Southeast of the United States. The collection is maintained by a full time art curator, who regularly conducts art tours for clients and community members. At the same time he explains the vision and the mission of the company. The company's key goal is not simple investment, but rather customer-designed investment strategy and tax planning.

ARTS AS ENTERTAINMENT

Regarding using the arts for entertainment, many companies use the arts in this way as company fringe benefits. At Unilever Fabergé and Ice Cream & Frozen Food, however, not just any show will suffice. The entertainment has been carefully chosen, and is often very sophisticated. Marketing manager Lily Donagh explains:

➔ " ... but I think just having access to go and see the theatre and music is fabulous, ...new places and concerts, and that is kind of my main thing, getting involved in that, getting to see some really cool stuff that you would not necessarily be able to go to otherwise, so that is brilliant, I think, it is really good. We have relationships with the Royal Court, and I particularly like the sort of things they put on, because they are quite challenging and different and modern, they are thought provoking."

Art as entertainment can also be in-house, as was the case when Clifford Chance, the world's largest law firm, invited the London Musici into the company as 'chamber orchestra in residence'. Under their conductor Mark Stephenson, the London Musici "have become experts at putting on concerts in office atria and working with teams of business people to help them express themselves through music."[3]

ARTS AS INSTRUMENTAL
Applying the arts as an instrument has been applied by the pharmaceutical company Nycomed. Senior vice-president Alejandra Mørk tells the following story of how they were going to have a large team-building meeting for their project team of 50 – 60 people. They engaged two actors and a visual artist from ArtLab[4]:

➔ "... and they carried it out and it was very much about being present and about communication on many different levels. It was everything from the room being decorated to finding your own small rock among many rocks with closed eyes. There were exercises of improvisation, there was non-verbal communication in the form of papers, a lot of different things, and it ended by us creating a picture where everybody identified a space and glued the rock they had chosen themselves on to a glass plate – it was the visual artist who directed this – in an almost ceremonial event with candles on a set table. And we still have that picture today and I still know, whenever I pass it, which one is my rock and where it is, because you were to choose where to place yourself in relation to the others according to the significance you had for the project. So we still have this, and it is hanging very centrally just in front of the project office, and it was not an event. It was a meaningful process in order to make something function in a project group. And that is what this is about, it is real work and not something we do for fun."

ARTS AS STRATEGIC
Finally, integrating the Arts in a strategic process of transformation is apparent in project Catalyst at Unilever Fabergé and Ice Cream & Frozen Food, as we saw quite vividly at the

start of this chapter, where a marketing trainee was invited to participate in creating an improvisational theatre piece in central London. In fact, Unilever's project Catalyst applies the arts strategically by drawing on all four approaches, which you will hear more about in chapter 4. Unilever has focused a lot on expression and emotion, and one of the skills that are important for business is expression through writing. Isabelle King, Catalyst assistant, told the following story:

→ "So we have our reading group and we had a creative writing course, which was run by an author, Gwyneth Jones, and that ran 8 weeks. She was looking at lots of aspects of creative writing such as how you create atmosphere, how you develop your characters. She was looking at plots and structure and we were really keen to take this forward because, as I said, we looked at business writing and at creative writing and people can always be better at writing. Lots of people have not had anyone look at their writing skills since they were maybe 16, 17, 18, and we write all the time, so that was fantastic."

→ "Then we introduced reading in schools. People volunteered to do it, and our staff go out and read in local junior schools and help the children, who have fallen behind for some reason, whether they have learning difficulties or problems at home or simply do not have the interaction with an adult, that one-to-one time, which can make their reading a lot easier. And sometimes after a term they will have improved so much that they do not need that contact any more. Other children may need a whole year of that special time. And if they have difficulties at home, reading with them provides an adult they can rely on, who is supportive and in that way our staff act as ambassadors in the local community. We are a big company within this community and we want to give something back."

→ "... and then a final element of that program was to have literature events. We have had two events this year; one was where we invited all the children in the local community, who we had helped with their reading, and their teachers and our staff to Walton. The chairman James Hill awarded each child with a certificate to say congratulations, well done. After this we had a children's author called Marcia Williams come in and read to the children and she was absolutely fantastic. That was one event. And the other event was to mark national poetry day with a celebration. We had looked at business writing and creative writing, but we had not looked at poetry. That was an evening event upstairs where we had three poets come in and read from their work, which was fantastic. Then again, creating unique opportunities for people, lots of people had never heard a poet read out loud, it expanded their literacy horizons. We got the poetry books here, which people have bought, and as a result of the creative writing program we launched a competition for staff here. We wanted them to write a children's story aimed at children between 9 and 11 because we thought children are some of our most important consumers, we have got all these products for kids; captain Birdseye, kids' ice cream, kids' food and actually how do we connect with them, are we good at communicating with them? We wanted to find out what it is that makes them tick."

The point here is simply to show that everybody has art in their business, but how do they apply it, and do they get the full use of it? If you have art in your business, what is the role of art? And what could it be?

This book will tell 'real-life' tales of Arts-in-Business, where artists apply artistic methods to facilitate change, development and learning in organisations. The tales are based on an international research project, conducted during 2002 and 2003, by Learning Lab Denmark[5] and Danish Centre for Management[6]. The goal of the research project is to map the field of Arts-in-Business and describe what is currently going on internationally through snapshots and case studies of both successes and failures. The intention is to provide a coherent theoretical framework for making sense of this new development and at the same time help this new field advance.

The research data include 53 qualitative interviews with artists, business people, researchers and people interested in the field from Europe, North America and South Africa. The data also involve participant observation, action research, collective reflection and explorative experimentation.

The guiding research question is: *What can Business learn from the Arts?*

The purpose of this book is to demonstrate the potential and variety of new artistic methods available for business and, of course, to point out in what ways business can learn from the arts, and why it is important. The message of this book is *not* to promote a new magical instrument, a new 'quick fix' for business. It is an attempt to define the contours of 'artful creation', a new paradigm that draws on our full human potential (body, mind, heart and spirit). Artful is here defined as a quality of expanded consciousness that evolves through profound personal experiences, and often facilitated by artistic processes. The emergent field of Arts-in-Business is one of the signposts of this new paradigm of 'artful creation' and could have an important and positive impact on future business and society. The book will tell tales of how it worked and how it did not work, of the difficulties and barriers that arose, and of the conquests and successes.

I am very aware that poverty of language is one major challenge in trying to pass on lived artistic experience. How can the dynamic quality of these engaging tales be kept alive? In the text I have tried to meet the challenge by giving room throughout the book for the interviewees to speak for themselves, in particular in the case stories, and by including photographs of artists and artistic products as well as artistic notes. Even though this cannot replace the real experience, I hope that the tales will inspire you to experiment and try some of these methods for yourself.

The book consists of eight chapters interwoven with tales of Arts-in-Business. The organisation of the book is as follows:

In **chapter 1**, the introduction, the basic ideas are presented together with the purpose and background. Here we introduce the four main levels of using Arts-in-Business, with a few vivid examples to bring the subject to life. In this chapter you can also find an introduction to the chapters.

In **chapter 2** we paint the 'big picture', a brief analysis of the historical development and current trends. By introducing the framework of Ken Wilber we try to understand the recent development of business, from engineering models, Taylorism, rationality, efficiency, bottom-line economy towards a more ethical, sustainable, triple-bottom-line, aesthetic and even spiritual dimension. Next we discuss the role of the arts, from the sacred, through beauty, inspiration, provocation, anarchy, and industry, to becoming social. This is followed by some deliberations on the artistic process and a definition of the concept of artfulness. The chapter ends with some thoughts on the organisation of the future by trying to understand the current trends of Arts-in-Business as the beginning of a new integration into the 'creative economy' of the future.

In **chapter 3** we discuss and develop the theoretical frameworks. The main framework is the *Arts-in-Business framework*[7], a matrix model, based on two parameters: the degree of ambiguity and the degree of involvement. Combining these characteristics produces 4 arenas: Capabilities, Metaphors, Events and Products. The four arenas will help us to describe the case studies and to understand the learning processes and outcomes. As learning is a focal point of the study, we discuss individual and organisational learning by introducing Crossan & Sorrenti's model of organisational learning followed by Cowan's concept of "Rhythms of Learning". Both complement the Arts-in-Business model and help to refine our understanding of the learning that takes place. A third framework is a model for social innovation, developed in my PhD, which facilitates understanding the dimensions involved in creating new knowledge. This process can evidently be energised through the arts.

Chapter 4 contains seven case stories and an illustration of how governmental initiatives can influence and help to develop a new field. The chapter starts out with the "**Creative Leaps of Bureaucracy**", a tale about the musical group, Creative Leaps International, who opened the George Washington University 'Center for Excellence in Municipal Management' program in August 2002. It is a story about how music and song can enhance leadership development. The main aspects of learning concern the potential for inner transformation, so rare in ordinary leadership programmes, which are usually based on theoretical and intellectual discussions. Secondly, we can learn from this case study how music facilitates deep and almost immediate bonding (creating "common ground") in groups. This story leads to another tale of music, "**Creative Leaps of Learning**", which was basically the same process, carried out by the same group with 35 schoolteachers at Norwalk, Connecticut.

The second tale poses the question "**What happens when you PAIR a scientist with an artist?**" It concerns the Xerox PARC PAIR Artist-in-residence programme that went on for 10 years. We briefly tell the story of this visionary project, which had no other goals than to create better scientists and artists, but which, in fact, has produced important learning and spin-offs. The narrative is based mainly on interviews with the late Rich Gold, director of PAIR, and partly on the book "Art and Innovation".

After this we examine the metaphor of "**Business Theatre**", carried out at Bang & Olufsen, a leading company that designs televisions and audio equipment. Since 1999 this company has applied artistic metaphors in their processes of training, development and change. In particular they have used a theatre metaphor for making their shops attractive and for making their products alive and 'applaudable' all over the world. The problem they faced was not only the challenge of making a shift from a technical approach towards a more visionary one, but also a high turnover in sales people. The theatre metaphor has proved helpful in their international training concept on "performing exciting sales" as well as in keeping their sales people.

After this we move into "**I carry with a smile. Organisational theatre for domestic helpers**". The Dacapo Theatre is a corporate theatre group, who has existed for more than 10 years. Their work is inspired from the Forum theatre developed by Augusto Boal, the founder of "Theatre of the Oppressed". A large municipality in Denmark decided to invite all their 'domestic helpers' to participate in 30 Forum theatre events with Dacapo. The goal was to bring to the surface concerns and complaints regarding funding cuts and future reorganisation, and to improve the working culture through involvement in theatre. The goal was achieved, but it is uncertain whether this was caused by the theatre sessions. What we do know is that the plays started a lot of good conversations.

From here we will go on to describe "**Art and Business for European Identity**" by telling the tale of one of the drivers of the Art & Business vision, Miha Pogacnik, virtuoso violinist, cultural ambassador of Slovenia and business consultant. We will describe how Miha Pogacnik works with his violin and great classical masterpieces in order to help the audience sharpen their senses. The key words are deep reflection, transformation and new capabilities. Miha's interpretations of musical masterpieces enlighten universal human archetypes, which are profoundly meaningful to individuals as well as to organisations. Miha Pogacnik has started the initiative of IDRIART and his mission is to create "practical Utopia".

"**Why not catapult a brand new Volvo?**" is the story of a one-year partnership between artist Michael Brammer and Volvo Cars Corporation. Catapulting a brand new Volvo into a red heart was Brammer's idea for the world exhibition of cars in Detroit in 2003. The idea was both provocative and controversial, but what was to be learned from this? People learned from this that, among other things, the organisation should have been better prepared for the 'disturbance' to make it fully effective, but also that there are different ways of marketing and of getting into the media. This was definitely a story that the media swallowed whole.

"**Catalyst for change through personal development**" describes a project at Unilever, UK, which started in 1999 and has continued since then with a lot of successes and some good failures. Unilever Fabergé and Ice Cream & Frozen Food seem to be not only the corporation that has experimented the most in this area, but also the only corporation in the research project that has applied the arts strategically to a process of transformation - for building an 'enterprise culture'. Unilever has employed actors, directors, clowns, stand-up comics, business writers, novelists, poets, play writers, painters, drawers, perfumers, circus, fashion designers, fabric designers, electronic designers, musicians, filmmakers, bookbinders, multimedia artists, cartoonists, library services, cooks and reading agencies. We have chosen to tell the tales of 'Urban Fiction' (a photography course), 'Sticky' (a live performance in London) and 'Live & Direct' (a feedback project, based on theatre rehearsal techniques, involving 80% and 50% of the two organisations).

We end this chapter by discussing "**How Governments matter - The snowball case of Denmark**". In year 2000 the Danish government decided to make an effort to try to understand and develop the interplay between Arts & Business. A joint effort between The Ministry of Culture and The Ministry of Trade and Industry resulted in a white paper and, as a result of that, in the creation of three initiatives: NyX, a meeting place and market place for connecting Art & Business; The Creative Alliance, a research consortium under Learning Lab Denmark, focusing on exploring the learning potential between Arts & Business; Louiz, a cultural entrepreneurial start-up organisation. Since then there has been great focus on the development of this field in Denmark and many projects, organisations and companies have been created. Even though it is too early to evaluate these initiatives, this story may inspire other municipal or federal governments.

In **chapter 5** the main idea is to weave the threads of learning from chapter 4 into new insights on transformation and into a theory of 'artful creation'. The main analysis is accomplished by applying the 7 steps of Otto Scharmer's model of 'presencing': Downloading, seeing, sensing, presencing, crystallising, prototyping, and embodying. Each step is analysed and illustrated with several examples from the case studies and interviews. This forms the basis for building a new and more differentiated Arts-in-Business framework around a centre of 'artful creation'.

In **chapter 6** we try to answer the research question: What can Business learn from the arts? This is done through two lenses, first by introducing the revised Arts-in-Business framework and explaining the new insights for each of the four arenas; secondly by applying Ken Wilber's four-quadrant method for answering the research question from both a subjective perspective and an objective one, as well as from both an individual standpoint and a collective one.

Chapter 7 recaptures the discussion on transformation by distinguishing between two distinct approaches to Arts-in-Business, which leads to the introduction of an icon that symbolises a paradigmatic shift from the old instrumental management towards the birth of a new: 'artful creation'. The chapter contains both recommendations and admonitions, as artistic processes are extremely powerful and should not be used by all organisations. The recommendations include a catalogue of suggestions for people who are considering applying the arts to business as well as a list with guiding questions and some practical advice about how to get started.

In **chapter 8** we outline the visions for the future role of Arts-in-Business and for an artful society. We speculate on the future of capitalism, on the future role of business, on the future role of the arts, and on the future type of career path. Will capitalism become compassionate? Will business get a heart? Will the future career path be double? Joseph Beuys has said that the real art is the creation of social relationships. If that is the new role of the arts, what will the future look like?

Finally, some practical information regarding the artists, researchers and business people who have been interviewed for this book. At the back of the book there is an alphabetical (by surname) reference list of the interviewees including their titles, type of work, contact information (websites), and date/place of interview. This list has been created in order to avoid too many footnotes in the text.

The powerful real-life tales told by these artists and business people are woven throughout the book. Enjoy the journey!

1   Interview with Adrian Greystoke, marketing trainee at Unilever Ice Cream & Frozen Food, London

2   Knud Aunstrup: Mads Øvlisen's use of Art at Novo Nordisk A/S, 1998

3   David Butcher (2003:38 – 43): "A Fruitful Union", article in Management Today, August 2003

4   ArtLab (now MAB) is an education for out-of-work artists training to become consultants in business, www.artlab.dk, see also chapter 4, 'How Governments Matter'

5   Established by the Danish government in 2001, Learning Lab Denmark is a centre for research on learning, affiliated to the Danish University of Education. Learning Lab Denmark aims at solving urgent societal problems related to learning, through experimental and practice-oriented research and development activities. This is done with dedicated partners from different societal sectors. Learning Lab Denmark consists of a secretariat and six research consortia, working with both the educational sector and business. www.lld.dk

6   Danish Centre for Management is an association of 1200 public and private corporate members. It is a meeting place for developing holistic leadership in practice www.cfl.dk

7   Lotte Darsø & Michael Dawids (2002): "Arts-in-Business – Proposing a theoretical Framework", presented at EURAM Stockholm, May 2002, at The 5th Art & Business Conference, Borl, Slovenia, June 2002, and at The Art of Management and Organisation, London, Sept. 2002

CHAPTER 2

THE BIG PICTURE

The purpose of this chapter is to provide an overall context for understanding the development of the field of Arts-in-Business. What is happening and why is it happening now? What is the role of the arts and how is it changing? Ken Wilber offers an answer to some of these big questions in his four-quadrant framework, which will be presented in the following and later applied to summing up the analysis of the case studies. In this chapter we will also briefly discuss the artistic process and define the concept 'artful creation'. Finally we will look at some of the challenges and problems, which the majority of corporations and organisations are facing at the beginning of the 21st century as this can help us to understand why art is becoming a catalyst for organisational change and development, the subject of this book.

The task of providing a brief historical overview is, of course, an impossible one, as it will evidently be fragmented. Nevertheless, I will try to draw out some historical elements that are important for understanding the big picture. According to Ken Wilber, evolution takes place in steps of differentiation followed by integration. We can find several periods of integration in history. If we look back a couple of hundred years, we can see that, during the Renaissance, art was obviously not separated from business and society. Leonardo da Vinci, who was both an artist and a scientist, demonstrated the unity of art and science through his combination of studies of the human body, mathematics, architecture and art, e.g. expressed in his masterpiece "The Vitruvian Man" ("Homo ad Circulum")[1]. Today Martin Best, a musician, a specialist in the art of the troubadour and the founder of The Corporate Theatre, says: "As a student of the Renaissance I do not at all see the separation between commerce and arts. The Medicis were business people and bankers and they were the greatest encouragers of art. And the artists felt quite at home with the Medicis in the court of Florence." Thus art was an inseparable part of life. It was, however, still a question of sponsorship, as the artists were being sponsored by the great banking houses and the great merchants of the time, just as artistic endeavour was patronised by the royal houses and the church.

We do not have to go back in time to experience art as an integrated part of life. According to anthropologist Dr. David Guss[2], who lived for several years among the Yekuana tribe by the Orinoco river in the jungle of Venezuela: "Arts is integrated in every aspect of their society, whether it is the hammock they sleep in, it is a baby sling to carry a child in, or it is the food they have hunted and manufactured. They don't have a category of art. Among the Yekuana there is no art, because everyone is an artist and everything in the culture is art." Thus, at the present time differentiation and fragmentation appear to be predominantly Western phenomena.

But likewise we can find several historical periods of differentiation. The Renaissance was followed by the period of Enlightenment, where reason and logic became the focus and ruled out everything else, including arts and ethics. "The Big Three collapsed into the Big One of flatland" (Wilber, 2000:116). The Big Three, the Beautiful, the Good and the True[3], were introduced by Plato more than 2000 years ago. A similar classification is illustrated in Ken Wilber's Four-Quadrant model:

The left side of the model is subjective, the right side objective. The upper part symbolizes the individual and the lower part the collective. By crossing these axes four categories are produced: Upper Left subjective-individual (intentional), Upper Right objective-individual (behavioural), Lower Left intersubjective-collective (cultural) and Lower Right interobjective-collective (social), or 'I', 'it', 'we' and 'its'. When talking about the Big Three, 'I' stands for the 'Beautiful', 'we' represents the 'Good'; 'it' and 'its' symbolise the 'True' as both deal with the objective exterior world. In "A Brief History of Everything" Wilber demonstrates how natural science, as well as the social sciences, has conducted research from one quadrant only, and how it has thereby been blind to important aspects that could have been understood from a different quadrant. Wilber's main point is that we need to examine the world from an all-quadrant approach, and we will take up this suggestion in chapter 6.

The real split of the Big Three seemed to happen with the second industrial revolution

FRAMEWORK BY KEN WILBER, 2000

	SUBJECTIVE		OBJECTIVE
INDIVIDUAL	I		IT
COLLECTIVE	WE		ITS
	INTERSUBJECTIVE		INTEROBJECTIVE

when management became 'scientific'. From then on *only* pure objective reasoning (the True) was appreciated, and the Good and the Beautiful were neglected. In the name of efficiency Frederick Taylor took an important step towards 'scientific management' by separating planning (management) from doing (the workforce). An epoch of productivity, efficiency and profit was underway with the organisation symbolised as a machine, and this symbol of modernity lasted more or less throughout the 20th century. This industrial development brought Western society tremendous wealth, but it also brought about the feeling of fragmentation, which, according to David Bohm[4], is "man's essential illness today". The problem is that man "cannot assimilate his whole field of experience into a totality felt to be beautiful, harmonious and meaningful."[5]

In the last decades of the 20th century a new paradigm evolved, labeled 'knowledge society' by Peter Drucker (1993), signifying a value shift from the material towards the immaterial. The implications of this shift are immense, but it seems that organisations are too busy with 'business as usual' to really take it seriously. When knowledge and competencies become the main asset, the real value of organisations is no longer material products, controlled by the business, but knowledge in people's heads and bodies. Product innovation is still important, but as Peter Drucker stresses (1993), in 'knowledge society' at least 50% of innovation is social and concerns new ways of collaboration, new constellations (involving new types of people, e.g. artists) and new processes of learning and knowledge creation.

In organisations the classical research by Burns & Stalker (1961) offered a new metaphor besides the machine: the organisation as an "organism". Margaret Wheatley (1999) took this idea further and applied the principles from living systems to organisations. Furthermore she pointed out how organisations are desperately driven towards moving at "the speed of light" (the hoped-for speed of machines) and how the real need is, indeed, to find "the speed of life". Concepts like identity, meaning, relationships and values became subjects on the western agenda as well as ecology, sustainability, the triple-bottom line, ethics and spirituality. By the turn of the millennium most would agree that the industrial age was ending and that the western world was by now a global knowledge society with, however, strong roots in industrialism.

THE ROLE OF ARTS

"Should art educate, inform, organize, influence, incite to action, or should it simply be an object of pleasure?" (Boal, 2000)

This book primarily deals with the arts and artists getting involved in business. Obviously it is linked to the field of organisational aesthetics, pioneered by Antonio Strati. Strati[6] distinguishes aesthetics from art through its etymology by pointing out that aesthetics concern "knowing on the basis of sensible perceptions" (seeing, hearing, smelling, touching and tasting), whereas the original meaning of art is "the transformation of raw materials with ability and intelligence". Strati outlines eight categories of aesthetics[7], but this book will not go into a discussion of the concept or role of aesthetics[8]. It is more concerned about the evolving *role* of the arts in relation to business. I have identified seven different roles: sacred, beauty, inspiration, provocation, anarchy, industry and social.

Art as sacred: Since ancient times art has been used to invoke and worship the spirits and Gods through offerings, amulets, symbols and ornamentation of sacred places, such as temples, churches and pyramids. Findings from ancient burial places uncover exquisite artwork in wood, stone, clay, shell, gold, silver and all sorts of precious stones. Furthermore music, song and drums often accompanied religious and spiritual ceremonies. Originally art was sacred.

Art as beauty: When art became more mundane the most important quality was, in many people's view, its visual and sensory value. Art must be beautiful, or it is not art. The idea of what is beautiful has, of course, changed over time, but the role of art is to lift us away from our daily life into a world of wonders and beauty. This is the popular and universal function of art.

Art as inspiration: Inspiration is a two-way quality of art. The idea of a muse visiting the artist is archetypal, since the artist must be inspired in order to create, but 'true' art also inspires the receiver in various ways, for instance to change mood or to think new thoughts. Art can make us recall who we are and who we want to be. Art calls on our feelings and our humanness.

Art as provocation: Art has always been potentially provocative, but the type of provocation has changed. Earlier the fact that artists were often messengers of renewal was enough to provoke. Impressionism was a provocation when Monet showed his first impressionistic paintings – simply because it was a new style. Later we have seen much stronger provocations, e.g. Duchamp's urinal[9] at The Tate Modern in London, Manzoni's[10] can of human faeces, Evaristti's gold fish in a blender[11], Brammer's stuffed puppies[12], and lately Feiler's "Snow White and the Madness of Truth"[13]. Arts can be revolutionary when taking on the role of questioning our daily life and the status quo of society. From this to art as anarchy is only a small step.

Art as anarchy: In postmodernism art is deconstructed and this often leads to a lack of meaning and a certain sort of nihilism. Ken Wilber provocatively says (2001: 87), "With the death of the avant-garde and the triumph of irony, art seems to have nothing sincere to say. Narcissism and nihilism battle for a center stage that isn't even there; kitsch and camp crawl all over each other in a fight for a representation that no longer matters anyway; there seems to arise only the egoic inclination of artist and critic alike, caught in halls of self-reflecting mirrors, admiring their image in a world that once cared."

Art as industry: The industrial age has, of course, had its influence on the arts, and works of art have been mass-produced (e.g. Andy Warhol, Per Arnoldi) and sold to a wider audience. The aim is both to communicate to a larger group and, of course, to harvest a larger profit. We can buy posters of famous paintings, photos, etc. and some artists have sold their artwork on calendars, T-shirts, umbrellas, etc. (e.g. Hundertwasser). The music and film industries are examples of highly successful business adventures.

Art as social: Joseph Beuys, the German avant-garde artist, who was related to the 'Fluxus' group, advocated for a transformation of the sculpture from space to time in order to show the world that the time-based sculpture is, in fact, a social sculpture. According to Beuys, real art is not the creation of objects, but the creation of social relationships. This is also known as the extended notion of art, indicating that basically every human being is an artist.

It is evident that the arts are at a crossroads, and a lot of the interviewed artists express great concern regarding the future of arts. Martin Best, founder of The Corporate Theatre, expressed it this way:

➜ "I think artists are in a much more dangerous place than business, because we are becoming incredibly confused about our ideas of what art is for. We are losing our ability to distinguish between good art and bad art, between high art and low art, between art that is of the spirit and art that just has to do with the profane."

THE ARTISTIC PROCESS

Once upon a time the emperor of China ordered a drawing of a rooster from a famous artist. "Come back in four years, then it will be finished," said the artist. But when the emperor came back after four years, the artist needed another four-year period. This repeated itself and finally after twelve years the emperor anxiously returned to see the rooster of his dreams. After a cup of tea, which the emperor could hardly swallow for anxiety, the artist took out a piece of white paper, dipped his brush in black paint and in one graceful movement drew a rooster more alive than any rooster. The emperor was deeply moved, but was also a bit resentful that the artist had put him off for twelve years when it took only a few seconds to draw the roost-

er. The artist then led him into the back, which was covered from floor to ceiling with piles of drawings of roosters.

The many drawings at the back represent the artistic process of the composition 'rooster'. The years were partly used for understanding a rooster entirely and to experience it from within, partly to find the minimum of expression for the maximum quality.[14]

This tale illustrates the general misconception that the artistic process is about inspiration only, whereas, according to the artists themselves, it is also a lot of hard work and a lot of practice. Secondly, little is known about the actual process, as, in general, artists prefer to conceal it and are hesitant towards articulating it. The interesting point is, however, that it is the artistic process that is becoming the artist's business. Artists are beginning to reflect on their own process, and the artists in business are ahead in that sense, as they are actually selling their process – not their product. The key ingredients of the artistic process, which are valued in business, are: asking questions, energising oneself and others, working with intuition, daily practice and discipline, stamina and determination, expression and reflection.

Strati[15] pointed out that the etymological meaning of art is about the transformation of raw materials. Actor and assistant director Piers Ibbotson expresses it this way: "Art is entirely about doing and making, and if it isn't, you are not doing art, you are doing something else, which is why all the talk about creativity is an alarming and dangerous red herring, it misses the point to go on about creativity. *Art is about practice.*" If that is the case, in what ways is the artistic process similar to or different from creativity in corporations? Actor and programme director Marijke Broekhuijsen from Nyenrode University, Netherlands, says, "The arts refer to a concrete world, it is not about concepts, it is about acting in a sense of doing something. Most of the creativity professors and people active in that field deal with *creative thinking*, whereas I think the arts is a help for *creative doing.*" Artists themselves, in fact, never talk about creativity; they are more pragmatic and tend to leave the talking to talkers; and meanwhile the artists get started, doing and creating. It is thus important to distinguish between the business conception of creativity and authentic artistic creation.

As for the secrecy of the artistic process, Piers Ibbotson explains:

➜ "Artists generally don't like to articulate their practice, and when they are working they tend to do it in secret. Nobody watches concert pianists practising, nobody really observes composers composing, nobody gets into artists' studios to see what they are up to or into rehearsal rooms or whatever. This is essentially mysterious to people who don't do it for a living...The assumption is that art is a God-given gift, and creativity is an inspiration - that's like people having an extra leg or something – combined with a complete ignorance of the fact that this is work, it is a job."

There are, however, some obvious reasons for artists to protect themselves during their process of creation. According to visual artist, author and idea developer, Kirsten Dietrich[16], who also applies art to organisations, the artistic process involves four main phases: emptiness, silence, faith and outcome. The most difficult part is the first phase of emptiness as it involves an identity crisis and fear of failure. The clue is to surrender, become quiet and have faith that something will emerge. Then, when the process of creation really gets going, it involves a high degree of vulnerability, which means that the artist must protect herself from external interference. Deciding when the artwork is finished is the final challenge.

At least this offers one explanation of why artists 'hide' their process of creation. There may be many other explanations since, according to my research, the artistic process is quite idiosyncratic, both in relation to each specific individual and each art form. There are, of course, some fine examples of descriptions of the artistic process such as Betty Edwards' book 'Drawing on the Artist Within', Julia Cameron's "The Artist's Way", Dick Richards' "Artful Work" and Shaun McNiff's "Trust the Process". McNiff (1998:2) accentuates the unique quality of the process in the introduction to his book: "When approached through explanation, the creative spirits fly away beyond our grasp." His point is that the artistic process is destroyed if articulated. It is a unique space - beyond words. McNiff highlights an interesting characteristic of the artistic process, which he describes as a knife-edged balance between structure (planning, training, skills, craftsmanship, pre-conceived visions and ideas) and chance (unplanned expressions, taking in the immediate signals and inspiration of the environment, and interacting with the physical qualities and available materials). In their book, "Artful Making", Rob Austin & Lee Devin distinguish between 'industrial' and 'artful making' (2003:xxv-xxvi). The former is described as "detailed planning, as well as tightly specified objectives, processes, and products", whereas artful making is "any activity that involves creating something entirely new" and "a process for creating form out of disorganised materials." The distinction identified by Austin & Devin is significant, but the concept 'artful'[17] is more encompassing than that. Thus, apart from distinguishing business creativity from the process of creation, we need to make a differentiation between artistic and 'artful'.

ARTFUL CREATION

What, then, is meant by being artful? Explained in a very simple way, artful means 'full of art', i.e. art experiences that initiate an inner transformation, which again opens up for a special kind of consciousness. This type of consciousness can be developed only through direct experience, experience that involves feelings and that touches the person profoundly. The concept of artfulness encompasses body, mind, heart, and spirit. Thus, it is not a concept that can be understood from a theoretical perspective alone. It is rather a quality of consciousness that modern man has forgotten in the overall process of specialisation and differentiation. If we listen to the wisdom inherent in the ancient American Medicine Wheel[18], which "reveals the relationship and integration of all things created", we will hear the following words (Storm 1994:202):

→ "You are not just a body, mind, spirit and emotions. You are a Self. You are directly responsible for your own care your entire life long. How you balance your Self – Spiritually, Emotionally, Physically, and Mentally – is the challenge you must accept and answer while you live here on Mother Earth."

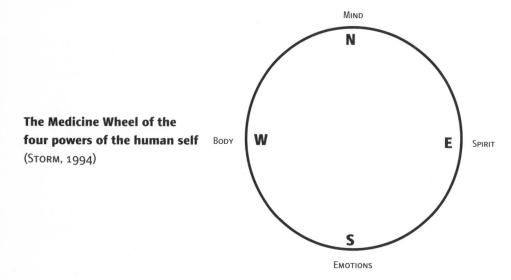

The Medicine Wheel of the four powers of the human self (STORM, 1994)

Artfulness feeds from an inner reservoir of experiential knowledge, which is similar to the concept of "artistic intelligence" developed by David Cowan[19]. Cowan distinguishes between knowledge and wisdom, arguing that "knowledge derives from the past, wisdom illuminates the future". According to Cowan, artistic intelligence is the manifestation of the energies of the Medicine Wheel that corresponds to each direction: envisioning, improvising, introspecting and including.

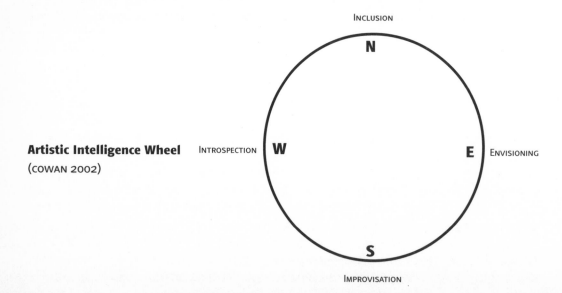

Artistic Intelligence Wheel (COWAN 2002)

The qualities of the Medicine Wheel have an interesting correspondence to the empirical observations of Carl Jung, e.g. applied in the Myers-Briggs Type Indicator: Starting in the East and moving clockwise, Jung's four functions of human consciousness are intuiting, feeling, sensing and thinking. Cowan's framework, which we will return to in chapter 3, emphasises the complexity and the dynamic interconnections and levels of different ways of knowing, thereby capturing what we consider fundamental to artfulness (or "artistic intelligence"): "... artistic intelligence emerges through a particular level of development of these intelligences in concert."[20] Another quality of 'artfulness' can be understood through the concept of field reality by Otto Scharmer (2002:7[21]), whose presencing model will be introduced and applied in chapter 5:

➤ "The noticeable outcomes of this process include a heightened level of Self, energy, and commitment; significant long-term changes; and *an ongoing field reality that can be tapped and activated later*".

The profound experiential knowledge obtained through the arts (or other deeply meaningful experiences) enables individuals to 'tap into the field' of inspiration and energy more easily, i.e. to go back into the experience or into a similar kind of experience. This consciousness enables the individual to be more intuitive, and thus wise, in the sense that Cowan describes. The concept of artfulness, just as the artistic process, is not easy to pinpoint and articulate. In the following we will apply artfulness in relation to the process of creation, when the experience of the people involved has been so profound that it entails expanded consciousness, sensitivity and wisdom.

CREATING THE HUMAN ORGANISATION OF THE 21ST CENTURY

At the beginning of the 21st century many corporations are stuck in the industrial paradigm. Some are naturally so, because their products are industrial. Others are stuck because they dare not leave the command-and-control approach, even though their products are mostly knowledge, services or experiences. In between is a large group of organisations that outwardly pretend to be engaging in new approaches and processes of change. The problem is that inwardly they are still under the spell of scientific management, still hierarchical and controlling, with little freedom and a lot of anxiety. In April 2003 I interviewed Margaret Wheatley, author of "Leadership and the New Sciences" and "Turning to One Another", about how she saw business and art:

➤ "What business is best at right now is numerically based methods for planning, measuring and managing. ... It is not just the analytic aspects of business that are dominant, but also the belief that you can actually make the world work according to what you want, if you are smart enough, if you can see far enough ahead, if you can produce at certain levels, if you can be innovative and know what the future customer wants. It is interesting to think how much of business is based on, in a sense, playing God with the world, and thinking mathematics is the key... And then you put all of that expertise in the modern world, where the future is unknown, the environment is turbulent, nothing works according to plan, actually it never has. ... So where I see business, in the United States especially, is in a major mistake right now. Instead of looking for how to work with chaos, they are actually still seeking how to control chaos, and so they are just using old business methods more badly, more desperately than before. And yet the opportunity here is to really explore more of the dimensionality of life, more of our emotions, more of our human spirits, because humans have gone through periods of darkness and chaos before, and we do not have to fix it, but we do need to know how to go through it. And for me that is where music, poetry and deep emotional expression will save ourselves. I do not see this as a casual need to say, well the arts should come into business. I see this as: Is it possible for business leaders to realise that the dilemmas in question they are facing cannot be solved by their traditional management behaviour, their traditional management tools? And that they are going to need to really be able to dwell in the deep domain of human experience and things like faith, courage, friendship, love, compassion, all of those emotions, grief, loss, which are only expressed in the arts. ... I think there is a need for our whole Western culture to start to explore, not our emotional intelligence, but our full being as humans and the only place I know how to find that is in the arts."

The same reaction is reflected in the institutions of the educational systems, where the arts have generally been 'down-sized'. According to my interviews, this concerns Europe as well as the US. It seems that school systems have turned to the same kind of trying-to-be-in-control systems that many governments and corporations cling to. They strongly believe that the primary needs of children are factual knowledge – instead of the acquiring of tools and approaches that would help them to get hold of any kind of knowledge and would furthermore help them to create new kinds of knowledge. This very one-sided view is not benign for the many types of intelligence needed in the future.

In my interview with John Kao, a musician, an entrepreneur and the author of "Jamming", he also expressed his concern about the current state of business:

➡ "A lot of the thinking now is about whether the decision-making environment can be a lot more like a theatre, a lot more like a media centre where people interact with each other and with knowledge, and build and create knowledge collaboratively. Using tools where some come from media and filmmaking and storytelling, storyboarding and scriptwriting and disciplines like that - which is quite interesting. It points out also the fact that this is not soft stuff, it's not just 'artsie' stuff. The arts actually have a very muscular, strong contribution to make to business...
Business is challenged all of the time to think about the future, think about customers and strategy in different ways. Many of the tools that are available now for these purposes are just not that good. They are of limited power in terms of engaging a lot of people in the most creative way. And they are of limited power in terms of explaining things in a way that changes people's behaviours. Most of the problem with the way people communicate in business is that it doesn't change people's behaviour. It is very easy to put a piece of communications in a filing cabinet and forget about it. You have these big companies and

they are going to die, so they have to change, but the situation resembles somebody who has throat cancer and a hole in their throat and they are still smoking cigarettes, because you can't change their behaviour. A lot of these companies find it very difficult to change and they need these new kinds of communication tools. Aristotle said the purpose of drama was to profoundly change the way you saw the world. That's the purpose of drama, harnessing the power of transformation, because changing your point of view without being able to change your behaviour is not so valuable."

For organisations that want to take part in the creative economy of the future there seems to be an urgent demand for a fundamental rethinking of management theory and corporate practice. What is needed are new experiments for creating social innovation. The new economy will be based on human fantasy, passion and inspirational social encounters. For this we need new types of processes, new frameworks to be guided by, and as you will see in the following, there is a lot of inspiration and new knowledge to be gained from Arts-in-Business. During the last decade a diverse range of visionary and explorative meetings has taken place between arts and business. Xerox PARC, Washington DC Federal Government, Unilever, Volvo Car Corporation, Nycomed and Bang & Olufsen are just a few examples of major organisations that are already seeking to stimulate organisational change and product development through artistic interventions and partnering. A profound change is taking place in the organisations that are seriously concerned about the future of business and society, as they are realizing that 'rational man' is giving way to 'artful human'.

While many have obviously been working in this field for years and are convinced that these ideas make sense, there is still a startling lack of research studies and theoretical frameworks to portray and attest the learning dynamics of these very real meetings between arts and business. No one has yet delivered a comprehensive description[22] or a coherent theory of this new field. In this book we will make an effort to do that.

In this chapter we have outlined the different roles of the arts associated with the sacred aspect, the beauty, inspiration, provocation, anarchy, industry and the social aspect. In the following we will deepen the social aspect of the arts by showing that artists are trying out new roles as catalysts for organisational renewal and change, and in the next chapter we will introduce a framework consisting of four arenas that the arts are beginning to orchestrate: metaphors, capabilities, events and products.

1   From 2002 'The Vitruvian Man' has been immortalised on the Italian Euro
2   Interview with David Guss, Boston, August 2002, see also David M. Guss (1989):"To Weave and Sing. Art, Symbol and Narrative in the South American Rain Forest", University of California Press

3   In Plato's "Politicus" (Statesman), written 360 BCE

4   David Bohm (1998:30): "On Creativity", edited by Lee Nichol, Routledge

5   Ibid.

6   Antonio Strati (2000:18): The Aesthetic Approach in Organization Studies, in Stephen Linstead & Heather Höpfl: The Aesthetics of Organization, Sage publications

7   The eight categories are: beauty, the sublime, the ugly, the comic, the gracious, the picturesque and the agogic, the tragic and the sacred.

8   There is a helpful survey of the field of aesthetics in Steven S. Taylor & Hans Hansen (2004): "Finding form: Looking at the field of organizational aesthetics" (work-in-progress)

9   In 1917 Marcel Duchamp sent a "work" called "Fountain" to the New York "Independent Show", signed with the name "R. Mutt", it was nothing but a common urinal. Today it is exhibited at the Tate Modern, London

10 Piero Manzoni wrote about this: "In the month of May 1961, I produced and tinned 90 tins of 'artist's shit ' (30 grams each) naturally preserved (made in Italy)."

11 In 2000 the Chilean artist Marco Evaristti presented a couple of gold fish in a plugged-in blender in an art museum of Kolding, Denmark. If any person of the audience wanted, they could turn on the blender – and kill the fish.

12 In 1994 Danish artist Michael Brammer included 4 stuffed puppies on an art exhibition in Copenhagen. No one took notice until Brammer himself notified the press that he had killed and stuffed the puppies solely for the exhibit. Because people got angry they started coming to the exhibition and it ended up being well attended.

13 An exhibit in Stockholm showed a picture of a woman on a small raft floating in blood-coloured water. The woman, who was presented with an angelic smile, killed herself and 21 Israelis in Haifa in 2003. On the opening night Israel's ambassador to Sweden, Zvi Mazel, angrily pulled the plug on three spotlights and plunged the exhibit into darkness. "Given what passes for 'art' these days, perhaps Mr. Mazel could claim that his outburst should also be classified as art – performance art, so to speak." The Wall Street Journal Europe January 20, 2004

14 Freely translated from Peter Bastian (1987:120-121): "Ind i Musikken. En Bog om Musik og Bevidsthed", Gyldendals Bogklub (ed: Into the Music. A Book about Music and Consciousness)

15 Antonio Strati (2000:18): The Aesthetic Approach in Organization Studies, in Stephen Linstead & Heather Höpfl: The Aesthetics of Organization, Sage publications

16 At an Arts-in-Business session at Danish Centre for Management in 2002, Kirsten Dietrich presented the themes "Processes of Creativity" and "Silence – a Necessity for Creativity"

17 Artful is, in fact, an old concept with a new meaning. A well-known Dickens novel, Oliver Twist, uses the word artful about a thief, where the meaning of artful is cunning and deceitful. This is very far from the definition of artful in this book

18 Hyemeyohsts Storm (1994:192): "Lightningbolt", Ballantine Books

19 David A. Cowan (2002:6): "Artistic Intelligence and Leadership Framing: Employing the Wisdom of Envisioning, Improvisation, Introspection, and Inclusion", The Art of Management and Organization conference, London

20 Ibid.

21 Claus Otto Scharmer (2002): "Presencing: Illuminating the Blind Spot of Leadership", draft of the introductory chapter to a forthcoming book (2004) "THEORY U: Leading and Learning from the Future As It Emerges", Berrett-Koehler Publishers

22 A good survey can be found in Nick Nissley (2003): "Art-based learning in management education". In B. DeFillippi & C. Wankel (Eds.), "Rethinking management education in the 21st century". Greenwich, CT: Information Age Press.

CHAPTER 3

THEORETICAL FRAMEWORK

This chapter is meant to be the prelude of a theoretical framework, which will gradually be informed by the empirical case studies throughout the book. The outcome, an empirically based theoretical contribution, will be presented in chapter 6. In this chapter four frameworks are introduced, all of which contribute with distinct qualities towards making sense of this new field. The first is the Arts-in-Business framework developed at The Creative Alliance[1], Learning Lab Denmark. The next two concern individual and organisational learning, and the last is a framework for social innovation.

My colleague, Michael Dawids, and I started the research project in February 2002 with explorative conversations, and I started travelling and interviewing in April 2002 and finished my research in December 2003. In that period the field expanded immensely - or was it just the network?

From the beginning the main research question was: In what ways can business learn from the arts? Gradually another question was added: 'What can business learn from the arts? Both are interesting questions, the first concerns 'how', i.e. the process, the second 'what', i.e. the content and outcome. A third question concerns 'why' business would want to learn from the arts? What makes art special? In the following chapters we will try to give some answers.

As we had both been interested in this area for some time we decided to spend a couple of 'full' days on developing a model or framework that could help us and others begin to understand this emerging field. At the time we even doubted if we should call it a field. We knew what was happening in Denmark, which was quite a lot (see chapter 4), and we knew about some artists abroad doing interesting work with business, but the activities seemed rather fragmented, and we had no idea what we would encounter. After many trials and iterations we developed a matrix, which was presented at three European conferences[2] during 2002. The matrix is based on the two dimensions, which we found most relevant for this particular study as well as for the field in general: the degree of ambiguity and the degree of involvement.

AMBIGUITY

Ambiguity is an important signifier of society today, both for the arts and for business. For business, however, ambiguity and uncertainty is uncomfortable and in most cases something that must be reduced or controlled. Business people prefer to work with specific goals, detailed plans and accurate measurements. But nobody can avoid ambiguity in this rapidly changing world and business, like it or not, must face and deal with a lot of unknowns. The question is whether corporations are equipped for this?

For the arts and artists ambiguity opens up for immense possibilities, different perspectives and new approaches. This concerns the artistic process as well as the finished artwork. One of the discerning features of art is indeed that it can inspire multiple interpretations. Ambiguity is an invitation to the freedom of changing perceptions and forms, whereas from an artistic point of view, the frozen target of business will often feel like a straitjacket. As ambiguity thus expresses a pertinent condition of society as well as an important value - whether perceived as positive or negative - it is significant for the construction of our matrix.

INVOLVEMENT

We chose the second signifier for a different reason, which had to do with the current development of the field. The new trend seems to be that artists are now getting directly involved with business, whereas the relationship used to be a more distant one, based on philanthropy and sponsoring. Thus one option for business is to use the arts as a role model, in which case people can read or hear or talk about art and artistic processes. The other option is real interaction between artists and business people, as e.g. in Forum Theatre, where members of the audience are invited to try out different roles on stage from their everyday work life, or in 'painting-as-teambuilding' sessions, where people, in groups of 4-5, literally paint together on the same canvas. The variety of this arena is enormous. In order to be able to distinguish activities according to this recent development, we chose the degree of involvement as the second characteristic.

THE ARTS-IN-BUSINESS MATRIX

In the model below, the vertical axis displays different degrees of ambiguity, going from high ambiguity towards the well-defined. The horizontal axis moves from non-involvement, art as a role model, towards direct encounters and interaction, art in action. These combinations create four arenas: metaphors, capabilities, events and products.

THE MODEL
ARTS-IN-BUSINESS

WELL-DEFINED

ARTISTIC CAPABILITIES   ARTISTIC PRODUCTS

LEARNING

AMBIGUOUS

ARTISTIC METAPHORS   ARTISTIC EVENTS

ART AS A ROLE MODEL   ART IN ACTION

ARTISTIC METAPHORS

Combining art as a role model with ambiguity brings our focus to the arena of artistic metaphors. A metaphor is "a way of thinking and a way of seeing that pervade how we understand our world generally" (Morgan, 1997:4). Metaphor draws our attention to specific features and is, in fact, a powerful tool for communication – even manipulation, because metaphors, at the same time, as Morgan points out, can also prevent us from seeing certain aspects. When the world appears utterly ambiguous, metaphor allows us to focus on some particular aspects, but it is still ambiguous; metaphor does not make the world well-defined. Interestingly, if you look at the evolution of language discourse in business, business has gone through different epochs of preferred metaphors within the last couple of decades: war metaphors, sports metaphors and now art metaphors. Artistic terms, such as setting the stage, improvising, jamming, orchestrating, rehearsing, performing, conducting, resonance, beat, ensemble etc., are now being adopted by management language. The title of a special issue of Organisation Science (1998) was "Jazz as a Metaphor for Organizing in the 21st Century". Other examples are "Jamming. The Art & Discipline of Business Creativity" by John Kao from 1997 and "The Experience Economy: Work is Theatre & Every Business a Stage" by J. Pine & J. Gilmore from 1999. In Austin and Devin's book from 2003 "Artful Making. What Managers Need to Know About How Artists Work" a comparison between theatre rehearsal and software development is carried by the metaphor "artful making".

Mads Øvlisen, former CEO of Novo Nordisk A/S, at times used metaphor very deliberately in his communication:

➜ "On one hand I am very careful about using metaphors, because there is a certain risk that it will become a cliché, but I once used a zen poem that said "clouds gone, the mountain shows". I used it in a period where we had had a lot of problems with some very important procedures and I used it to describe how we had been strengthened because of the crisis, because it had made some clouds disappear and we could now see where we stood. But it had also shown us how huge our task was, looking at the mountain. I used that to say that we need to keep climbing, and that by acknowledging our weaknesses we would also become stronger and stronger in achieving our objectives. ... I used that for an international meeting, and I had also procured mountain climbing images and photos, which I used. ... One of the advantages of a metaphor is that the right metaphor, used the right way, conveys a lot of associations, which means that you don't have to hammer the message through, but that you also leave something for people's imagination to work with."

In the following we will look at more examples, e.g. Bang & Olufsen's use of "Business Theatre" for training their sales people.

ARTISTIC CAPABILITIES
When combining art as a role model with the well-defined, we talk about artistic capabilities and skills. A capability is a psychological resource, developed through practice. A skill is the actual physical capacity, developed through practice. The third concept, related to these, is competence, which involves the mastering of capabilities and skills in relation to the situation and the people involved, i.e. the context. Competence concerns knowing when and with whom to apply which capabilities. Certain artistic capabilities

are important for business and can be taught by artists, such as presentation and communication skills, listening skills and storytelling. The same goes for teambuilding and collaboration inspired by ensemble and rehearsal techniques, as these are used by musicians and actors. A variety of business people, from managers to human resource consultants, can benefit from these approaches.

Recently there has been a tendency to move into more complex capabilities implicated in leadership and personal development

The conductor Peter Hanke[3] has developed a concept about the "conductor as the visible and listening leader", in which he works with a professional choir that is trained in the concept. The idea is to show how a conductor must communicate non-verbally, using only eyes, body and gestures to 'lead' and how s/he receives immediate feedback from the choir, as they react promptly to the smallest gesture. Peter Hanke starts by demonstrating how it works and then invites people from the audience to come up and conduct. This experience is rich in learning as the choir mirrors the degree of clarity (or the opposite) in decisions, body language, precision, authenticity and the will and capability to inspire. The 'conductor' gets a couple of trials, and after each 'audition' there is feedback on how it felt to conduct as well as how the choir felt being conducted by the person. Of course, this type of session also involves the arena of 'events', as we shall see in the following.

At present many artists are working from this arena. Annemarie Ehrlich, eurhythmy trainer from Holland, who has worked with corporations for 15 years, explains the kind of capabilities she is trying to call forth in business:

➡ "I have learned that we as facilitators have to translate the process into their language. Every person can experience that they need a quality in their work, a quality we can develop through eurhythmy. It is what you described in your model about the capabilities. I try to develop the eurhythmic capabilities, which the businessman needs in his work, for example overview, awareness of much bigger processes - of the entire process - and not only of the result. *Eurhythmy is gymnastics for your soul instead of gymnastics for your legs. When you are moving, you make your consciousness physical and everyone can see it.* In the process you find out if you can give yourself directions and when we work with balls, it makes a huge difference if you watch to see which hand is free, where can you put your ball. It is your inner thoughts, but from outside people can see it. So it's not only for yourself you can see it, everybody can see it. Do you give yourself directions or not? And this is very necessary in your own performance. If you speak to a group, how is your position, how are you standing, who are you directing. You are facing each other. Show you have something to communicate, point with your eyes and think while you are speaking. This sort of arranges consciousness. You can learn from your experience. .. I can always guarantee only two qualities. One quality is that people become more independent, and the other quality is that they will have another social togetherness. I can guarantee this if you do four to six weeks of eurhythmy (e.i. $1/2$ - 1 hour a day). All the other possibilities are very individual. So I can't say everybody will do this or will get that. But some of them can get the overview. If they have the capability for it, they can develop it. But not everybody has this awareness, not everybody can do it. So this is very individual. ...And one of the things I work very hard on is self-management. I don't correct from outside. I try to form the thing from outside, but everybody will notice whether you can do it or you can't do it. What can you develop, so that you can do it next time? So self-knowledge is for me very important. But there is no guarantee, I give lessons without people getting self-knowledge."

Marijke Broekhuijsen, originally from the theatre and at present programme director at the Executive and Management Development Centre, Nyenrode University, Netherlands, uses many types of arts for self-development and self-management:

→ "During that time, in 1980 exactly, I started as an independent trainer in management development. Shell was the first big company I worked for, and in the beginning I was explicitly asked as a theatre professional. I made use of mime, acting and many other forms of performing arts, mainly theatre. Nowadays people talk about theatre in management development as if it is quite new, but it isn't. But I was in the pioneer group I think. ... We (performers) were used to use whatever means available to get to the audience, so we didn't think about our work as special or new at the time; it was just a challenging new group of people to reach. In the various companies I worked especially in programmes that were orientated towards personal development, development of competencies and of self-management. At Nyenrode I often use arts in the context of leadership issues."

In the next chapter we will examine more examples from this arena, in particular in "Catalyst for change through personal development".

ARTISTIC EVENTS
Direct contact with art or artists is really a meeting. It can be a detached, reserved meeting, or it can be a genuine meeting, a social embrace. A painting on the wall will often speak to someone in a different way than if the person sees a photo or reads about it. Likewise being in the same room with a theatre group and listening to live music is totally different than watching it on TV. But both experiences allow multiple interpretations. Each spectator will see the painting differently, just as each participant will understand the theatre piece or the music differently. For lack of a better term, we labelled this arena 'artistic events', which combines arts in action with ambiguity. This arena covers everything from strategic use of arts in business (as the Novo Nordisk example from the introduction) to highly interactive events such as Forum Theatre, painting as teambuilding, concerts of ideas, learning from musical archetypes, drumming and making music together and setting up an entire opera and performing it. This arena is currently expanding - and full of interesting examples, each different from the other. David Pearl, opera singer turned 'business arts pioneer', London, tells this incredible story:

→ "In the middle of the 90s I was phoned up out of the blue by one of the world's leading

management consultancies. They were organising an off-site for their top directors and loved ones, over 1000 people in all, and wanted to use the arts in some way, not for entertainment but as the central theme. Culturally, they wanted their people, who are flung all across the globe, to interconnect in new ways. Commercially, they were looking for new perspectives and possibilities for their problem-solving and the service they offer their clients. They talked to a number of people in the arts about what they might do, and even though I didn't have any formal training in this area, or maybe because of that, they liked my idea. I was then presenting a music series on BBC TV, but this seemed fascinating so we went for it. My idea was that we build a skeleton-theatre on a cliff in Portugal in the Algarve, and then we would take 400 people at a time for five days each, and they would work through a process of creating a one-off piece of spectacular, collective music theatre. They would do every aspect of it, lighting, sounds, composition, text, design, costume - with top class practitioners to guide them through the process. Then they would do a performance, whether they were 'ready' or not. Very helpful for people stimulating a certain spontaneity in these otherwise rather perfectionist executives. For inspiration, provocation and outline structure, I suggested we use the Sufi-poem *The Conference of the Birds*, a metaphor for a group of these international directors all flying together in search of the secrets of leadership.
It was really an extraordinary success. Most people in the business in England know about it, because it could almost set a new kind of standard for these things. As you know, conferences are very often very dull, very expensive, very one-dimensional – or at best – two-dimensional. This was completely interactive, completely participatory."

Oliver MacDonald, self-taught musician from RedZebra, London and South Africa, explains how the arts can support creating relationships that are conducive for real meetings:

➡ "Often we get brought in at the beginning of a conference to prepare a group to really work effectively together, so what we will do is to start the process... It is not about having good fun, but the actual connection that they feel and the support they feel. Often people go into conferences without knowing each other or have not seen each other since the last conference. We work with them on getting them in contact with each other. The communication that goes on through music is quite individual, because you are giving and receiving simultaneously, you are creating sound, you are receiving that sound and in good examples of music there is a harmony, there isn't one person who is more essential to that kind of equation. Because of the way we focus on that in a group discussion, there is no difference between creating music as a band and having a really excellent meeting. Can you recall a meeting where you really came around? Usually when you look at what actually went on at that meeting, it is that people have felt that they have really been heard. Not that they have been doing all the talking, but it has been a dialogue, which has been two-way. And that is what we're interested in, it is how much more satisfying it is to not just be heard, but to listen actively and to really feel that you are part of it even when you are silent, even when you are maybe not being so obviously productive, and we believe that listening as well is being very creative. It is something you are creating."

The above examples give a taste of the potential of this arena. In chapter 4 we will examine "The Creative Leaps of Bureaucracy", "I carry with a smile. Organisational Theatre for Domestic Helpers" and "Art and Business for European Identity", which all start from 'events'.

ARTISTIC PRODUCTS

Finally, the combination of arts in action with the well-defined leads us to the arena of artistic products. This arena covers everything from creative industries[4], such as film and music business, architecture, decoration and design (e.g. the Bauhaus movement of the 1930s), art curators, to assigning artists for creativity and innovation development in business settings (the Idea factory and IDEO). Corporations may ask an artist to help them to express their company values in the interior decoration, in the annual report or in their 'branding'. This is a well-defined task and the company will use the time needed to help the artist understand the aim and purpose, but, of course, the artist will still often surprise the company in the solution to the task – and that is, in fact, why they asked an artist to do it. Ashley Ramsden & Bernard Kelly, storytellers from Storytelling in Organisations, London, describe two specific tasks:

➡ "We worked with a task team of a major bank whose task was to change the culture within the organisation. They had spent a year together working as a team and they were speculating on how to feed this back into the organisation, particularly into the board. We came in at the latter stages to look at their journey as a team and use the work they had done to create a story about it and tell that within the organisation.
Another task was working with a major oil company that wished to pursue some work in an African country. There were various ethical issues they wanted to examine before they did that piece of work. We were brought in to find a story in which they could explore some ethical dilemmas. And for this piece of work we found an African dilemma story. There is a whole body of African stories about dilemmas. They don't have endings, they end on a question of choices, and this African story was essentially about what happens when one individual becomes wealthy to the detriment of the many. So here the story was a kind of vehicle for looking at difficult issues."

The pharmaceutical company Nycomed has used artists from Artlab[5] more than 20 times within the last couple of years for various small, well-defined tasks and has had many good experiences and results[6]. The first time the task was to support the selection of a formulation for a medical product for colds. The project manager arranged a meeting with three artists in order to explain the challenge. The artists asked a range of questions regarding the problem until they found out that the essence was the decision-making process, and consequently their task would be to encourage resolution. The artists went away to plan the meeting. They were not at all interested in the medical problem of formulation. The day of the meeting, which was scheduled for two hours, started out with various choice situations. A table had been set with different types of cups, different coloured napkins and small presents in front of every seat, some wrapped, others not wrapped. Every participant then had to make a decision about where to sit. After this the project manager introduced the topic and the objective of the meeting. Before making the decision on the future formulation, the artists conducted a physical exercise involving all the participants. They each received a stick and were instructed to stand in a circle with the stick in front of them, balancing it vertically by slightly supporting it with one hand. Without giving signs or talking they were all to move one place at a time around the circle concentrating on keeping all the sticks standing. After this had been accomplished, the choice was made on the formulation. The company has been very satisfied with the decision, but that is not really the point here. Much more important was that the participants had a very different and a fully concentrated and resolute decision-making process.

The types of tasks for artists are manifold. In chapter 4 we will look at one of the new directions the arena of artistic products has taken through the case study "Why not catapult a brand new Volvo?"

THE CENTRAL THEME IS LEARNING

The first purpose of the matrix was to be able to clarify and classify this new and some-what messy area of Arts-in-Business. Categories help the human mind understand over-whelming input by adding structure. Categories also facilitate communication, which is vital for an emergent field of research. Another important purpose of the matrix, how-ever, is to enable us to examine the learning trajectories that cross between the arenas and to understand what happens at the centre of the model, which we at first called the 'solar plexus of learning'. The solar plexus in our body is where the nerves meet; it is related to performance and consequently also to fear of performance. It is vulnerable, and in order to protect this vulnerability it often 'knots'. We saw it as the 'solar plexus of learning', because learning, which touches our feelings deeply and opens a 'knotted' solar plexus[7], feels painful – and so does real transformation. Therefore we need to examine the concepts of learning and transformation more closely.

A FRAMEWORK FOR IMPROVISATION AND ORGANISATIONAL LEARNING

With so many existing theories on learning, it can be difficult to identify the most adequate frameworks for informing and elucidating the research findings. We found a relevant framework for organisational learning by Mary Crossan and Marc Sorrenti[8], which will be complemented by David Cowan's concept of "Rhythms of Learning", based on the Ancient American Medicine wheel. Crossan and Sorrenti set out to make sense of improvisation, which according to them has two dimensions: Spontaneity and intuition, and they define improvisation as (2002: 29): "intuition guiding action in a spontaneous way." We are, however, interested in their framework for other reasons than making

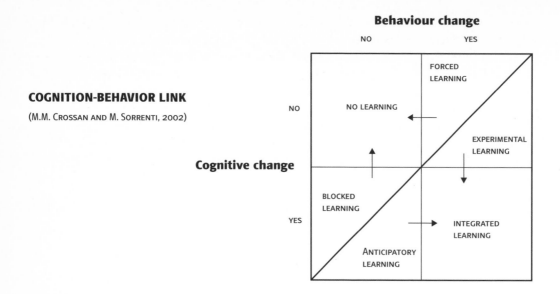

COGNITION-BEHAVIOR LINK

(M.M. Crossan and M. Sorrenti, 2002)

sense of the concept of improvisation (even though we will use that later). We see it as a refinement of the learning aspects of the Arts-in-Business matrix. Let us start by explaining their figure.

The underlying assumptions of the model are simply that learning is based on changing at least one of the two dimensions: cognition or behaviour. If there is no change in either of these, there is 'no learning' (top left). If there is change in both of these, we can talk about 'integrated learning' (bottom right). If there is cognitive change, but no behaviour change, this is 'blocked learning'. A person may know something, but this is blocked either by former learning, sheer laziness or by culture and habit. It has probably happened to all of us that after having attended a course and having cognitively picked up new learning, we return to work on Monday morning and put aside the new knowledge until later because of a pile of work waiting to be done. Eventually the course and the learning seem to evaporate into 'no learning'. In other cases, where people learn about cooking, drawing or driving by getting some theory and some instructions, this is 'anticipatory learning', which little by little becomes 'integrated learning'. On the behavioural side, if there is change in behaviour, but no cognitive change as yet, we can talk about 'forced learning'. It is forced because it is required by rules and regulations, but as soon as there is no control, the behaviour stops, as there is no cognitive understanding and consequently no learning. If, on the other hand, new behaviour is tried out in a non-judgmental manner and the cognitive understanding comes with reflection, we talk about 'experimental learning' moving into 'integrated learning'. Crossan & Sorrenti's point is to show that one of the ways to work with experimental learning is through improvisation. What we find most interesting in the present context, however, is that the difference between 'anticipatory' and 'experimental' learning corresponds closely with the two lower arenas of the Arts-in-Business framework, 'metaphor' and 'events', respectively. The characteristics of 'metaphor' are that it is a mental process and that the first change is usually cognitive; and the challenge is to actively resist being blocked by habits and instead turn the ideas in the direction of 'anticipatory learning' and 'integrated learning'. In the arena of 'events' the characteristics of the interaction between artists and business people are often both behavioural and experimental – sometimes also improvisational. Here the major challenge is to have time for reflection and dialogue afterwards.

INDIVIDUAL AND ORGANISATIONAL LEARNING

The above framework is organisational, but what about individual learning? Individuals learn all the time, whether they are aware of it or not. Learning is a fundamental process of life. People, who are good at learning, are open-minded, curious, and eager to take in information. Learning is thus often assimilated and integrated non-consciously, but most is gained when there is also time to think and reflect. When we are not aware that we are learning, it is rather smooth and painless. We learn a lot from the daily bombardment of information, experiences and challenges, but we usually do not notice it until, perhaps coincidentally, we read a note we wrote some time ago, or others notice the change in our behaviour or skills. With reflection, however, we can become more conscious of this process.

I remember when this suddenly became obvious for me. In 1992 I was teaching and facilitating innovation processes on a course for unemployed academics. We were nearing the end of a nine-month course and I looked forward to hearing people's feedback on the course and in particular on their own progress and learning. A person, whom I really thought had advanced and changed, said, when it was his turn, that the course had not made much of a difference to him and his development, and I could not believe my ears. He was a totally different person than when he came – and he could not see it! My immediate reaction was to introduce logbooks to the next course and make people write diaries from the first day regarding their present state, what they wanted to learn and what was important to them. And that made a difference. The experience, however, has stayed with me, and it suggests that we should not underestimate the subtle evolutionary transformation of daily learning. According to the teachings of the Native American Medicine Wheel we continually learn from life:

➥ "In the wheel, a learner is continually enmeshed in the process of learning from life's teachings, rather than expecting learning to occur at only particular times and places, such as at school or by reading a book."[9]

But there is a different form of learning, which is more sudden, hits like a lightning and almost hurts. This type of learning is cognitive and changes our underlying assumptions, our world picture.

The above example is, in fact, an example of this type of learning, because it shows a situation where somebody is provoked, moved and shocked in such a way that her underlying assumptions have to change. This can be quite painful (it was!), because earlier knowledge has to be revised and changed. Evidently this is also transformation, but of a much more direct and revolutionary type. Profound transformation often involves some kind of a crisis leading up to it and is followed by a painful discarding of previous learning and habitual thinking (untying the knot of the solar plexus). On the other hand this change can result in intense renewal - even the feeling of being reborn.

Can organisations learn? In principle, they can, but we hear more about the lack of learning than success stories. One of the most influential theories of organisational learning was formulated by Chris Argyris (1992) and Donald Schön. According to this, there are two ways of learning, single-loop and double-loop. Single-loop is adaptive and works by correcting mistakes. It is often 'forced learning' and does not question the underlying structures, if e.g. the same type of mistake happens over and over. Double-loop learning, however, questions which variables direct people's behaviour and aims at changing these instead of just correcting errors. The Argyris framework was inspired by thermostats in the field of electro-technology[10] and is consequently a rather linear and instrumental approach. It has been very influential in the academic world, in spite of the fact that there is little evidence of double-loop learning happening in organisations. Why is that?

In the 1990s Peter Senge launched a systemic approach with "The Learning Organisation", but in spite of its popularity and all the literature that followed this book, organisations still have great difficulties with learning and transformation. Why is organisational learning so difficult?

David Cowan has managed to combine individual and organisational learning. By re-examining "the landscape of individual-organisational learning in a more multifarious, circular, longitudinal and integrative manner",[11] Cowan (1995) suggests an alternative approach, "Rhythms of Learning". It builds on the Native American Medicine Wheel, which sees life and learning as dynamic and evolving cycles.

➜ "The medicine wheel facilitates conceptual development by establishing linkages to personal experiences, by attempting to increase rather than to decrease context, and by representing learning as a lifelong path traversed uniquely for a single person yet in concert with others."[12]

David Cowan expands the learning concept from cycles of ever-increasing levels into spirals of learning. This way he portrays organisational learning as individuals located in different directions on the wheel as well as on different levels of development.

A cycle of learning usually begins in the East with new ideas and visions. The eagle's quality is to watch from above and perceive future patterns. Bringing these visions to the South for curious inspection, the sense of the mouse is to try to translate the visions into concrete action by finding ways to help. When the orientation shifts to the West, it indicates a move from outer to inner examination. This gives the person involved strength (the bear) to take responsibility for the implementation. In the North the learning is integrated into wisdom, and shared (the quality of the buffalo) in compassion with younger

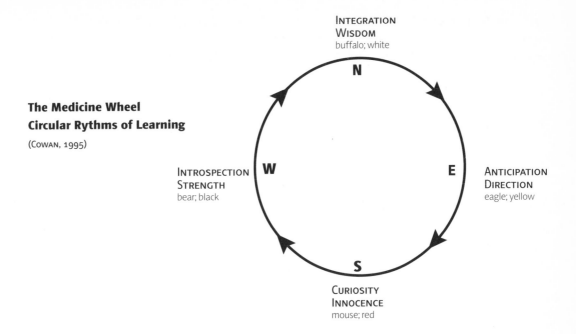

The Medicine Wheel
Circular Rythms of Learning

(COWAN, 1995)

INTEGRATION
WISDOM
buffalo; white

N

INTROSPECTION
STRENGTH
bear; black

W   E

ANTICIPATION
DIRECTION
eagle; yellow

S

CURIOSITY
INNOCENCE
mouse; red

travellers. The wheel continues towards the East, where new ideas and new visions are conceived.

Seeing organisations as being dynamically created through individual learning journeys in shifting partnerships at different levels and turns of a spiral is powerful:

➤ "As derived from the medicine wheel, the potential for learning lives within every performance and every relationship. This conceptualisation makes every person in an organisation continually responsible for activating their part of the wheel – both in performing and improving. ... Relational concepts such as sharing, listening, and caring become accentuated in every organisational process and are central to our understanding of learning. The design of organisation becomes primarily the design of partnerships, with everyone owning a role within "networks of expert novices"."[13]

These two frameworks complement each other in encompassing both an artistic focus and a comprehensive individual-organisational outlook on learning and transformation. Our main questions will primarily concern the possible learning trajectories in relation to the matrix: How can an event be transformed into change processes or new capabilities? How can an artistic metaphor generate a new product, a new process or a new capability? What kind of learning can be accelerated or catalysed through artistic processes? After the presentation of the case studies in chapter 4, we will revert to the themes of learning and transformation in chapter 5 and 7. We will conclude this chapter with a framework for social innovation.

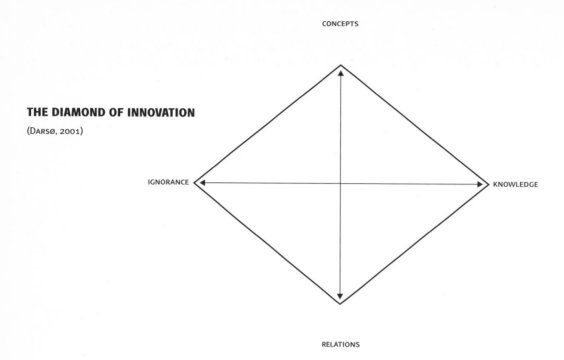

THE DIAMOND OF INNOVATION

(Darsø, 2001)

SOCIAL INNOVATION

In the experience economy, the knowledge society, the age of creativity, the society we live in by whichever name we want to give it, one of the key competitive differentiators is the competence for social innovation. But what is social innovation and how can it be accomplished? From 1996-99 I worked in a pharmaceutical company on a research project, "Innovation in the Making" (Darsø, 2001). I studied the very early processes of innovation, the conception and crystallisation of concepts. The research resulted in a model, the diamond of innovation, which can be helpful for understanding the social aspects of innovation (2001:336).

The model should be understood as a process field of dynamic innovation processes. Four parameters were identified for enhancing innovation processes in heterogeneous groups: knowledge, ignorance, relations and concepts. These parameters should not be seen as opposites, even though they may appear so at first. Knowledge and ignorance can co-exist. Concepts and relations are often intertwined. What is interesting in relation to the present theme, however, is the findings that relations of trust and respect form the basic requirement for reaching out into the area of ignorance, and this is where innovative crystallisation is triggered. Most groups prefer to work in the safe and certain field of knowledge, but unfortunately this alone does not create innovation. Therefore, creating 'common ground' and preparing the group for accessing the field of ignorance become primary concerns and attractive competencies. And this is where the arts enter the stage, as one of the learning aspects we have identified in several case studies is the powerful relationships and the immediate bonding created through artists or artistic processes. Another important feature concerns how the arts can invite people into the unknown, into improvising, into questioning the habitual and ordinary and into the process of creation. A third finding, relevant for the theme of this book, was that conflict can be generative for innovation, but only when it takes the form of a creative tension, not a clash. Creative tension can be generated by new perspectives, odd questions and intriguing provocations, and this happens to coincide with the key competencies of the arts.

Thus, the first and basic building block of social innovation is a high quality of relations between people, the next input consists of people's knowledge and competencies for sharing what they don't yet know, and thirdly an element of creative tension can advance the process towards innovative crystallisation. Hence the most important ingredients for social innovation are not technological - but genuinely human. In the terminology of Joseph Nye[14]: we are moving into an era of "soft power".

1   The Creative Alliance: In 2000 the Danish government made an effort to understand and develop the interplay between Arts & Business. This resulted in the creation of the research consortium "The Creative Alliance" at Learning Lab Denmark in August 2001. The consortium's task is to explore and accentuate the learning potentials of the interplay between arts and business. It is the world's first research centre to have this as its main focus. See also chapter 4: "How Governments matter"

2   Lotte Darsø & Michael Dawids (2002): "Arts-in-Business – Proposing a theoretical Framework", presented at EURAM Stockholm, May 2002, at The 5th Art & Business Conference, Borl, Slovenia, June 2002, and at The Art of Management and Organisation, London, Sept. 2002

3   www.exart.dk

4   Frederiksen, Siggaard & Dawids; "Speculations on organization, capabilities and learning in the creative industries" presented at the Third European Conference on Organizational Knowledge, Learning, and Capabilities, ALBA, Athens, Greece, 5-6 April 2002

5   ArtLab hosts MAB (Moving Arts & Business), an education for out-of-work artists training to become artistic consultants in business, www.artlab.dk, see also chapter 4

6   Interview with Alejandra Mørk, Senior Vice-president, Nycomed; supplemented by a phone call to pharmacist and project manager Lis Lønager Boesen, Nycomed, Denmark

7   Unknotting the solar plexus can be done through singing on a single note according to Githa Ben-David (2002): "Tonen fra himlen. At synge sig selv" (ed: The tone from heaven. Singing yourself), Borgen

8   Crossan, M.M. & Sorrenti, Marc (2002): "Making Sense of Improvisation", in Kamoche, Pina e Cunha, & Vieira da Cunha (Eds.) (2002): "Organizational Improvisation", chapter 3, p. 29 - 51

9   David A. Cowan (1995:227): "Rhythms of Learning. Patterns that Bridge Individuals and Organizations", Journal of Management Inquiry, Vol. 4 No. 3, 222-246

10 Chris Argyris (1992): "Organizational Learning", Blackwell Business

11 David A. Cowan (1995:223): "Rhythms of Learning. Patterns that Bridge Individuals and Organizations", Journal of Management Inquiry, Vol. 4 No. 3, 222-246

12 Ibid. 1995:229-30

13   Ibid. 1995:234

14   "Soft power" and "soft balancing" are new concepts developed by Joseph Nye (2004): "Soft Power: The Means to Success in World Politics", Public Affairs

Tales and Trajectories of Arts-in-Business

collaborations and experience working with the arts and artists. Wherever possible it is
composed of seven case studies, and opens with an example of the important role
government initiatives can play in developing a creative environment. This
addition has been requested by many of the people interviewed, as they hope that it
will inspire new initiatives in other governments. After each case study the main
trajectories of learning are outlined in the Arts-in-Business framework and the key
learning aspects are summarised. The journey begins in Washington DC in August
2002.

CHAPTER 4.

TALES AND TRAJECTORIES OF ARTS-IN-BUSINESS

In this chapter we bring the theme to life by acquainting the reader with a variety of organisations and corporations that are working with the arts in new ways. The case studies demonstrate how some artists have chosen alternative spaces for working with art – outside the traditional institutions – and how the artwork itself has given way to emphasising the artistic process – at times omitting the artwork completely. In this chapter vivid tales are told - as often as possible by the people who have been directly involved. The chapter is composed of seven case studies, ending with an example of the impact that a new governmental infrastructure can have on developing a creative environment. This addition has been requested by many of the people interviewed, as they hope that it will inspire new initiatives in other governments. After each case study the main trajectories of learning are outlined in the Arts-in-Business framework and the key learning aspects are summarised. The journey begins in Washington DC in August 2002.

Creative Leaps International
Thank You

Dear John, Paul, Jon, Dianne, Donna and Richard,

There are absolutely no words that would describe the gratitude we feel.

Your visit and performance at St. Joseph Convent profoundly touched our hearts, souls and being. If I could package all the love and energy that has transpired due to your presence and performance, it would only be transported through the tunnel of God's loving and profound care for all of us. So, I can only say this. Every once in awhile people come here and they do what they come to do, they move on and leave us with a memory. It was different when you came. There was a transformation that took place in a deep part of our being. You have made such a difference in all of our hearts.

In the present moment, the fire of love and hope prevails for us even in the midst of our profoundly broken, unjust and unkind world.

Thank you is such a simple statement. We hope the blessing we gave and the heart blessing we send your way will be a means of conveying lasting grace and profound love to hold you as you journey around the world. You round out the rough edges and leave imprints that transform the heart and soul of all those you meet.

We believe that you will be back with us, giving us the best you have and are. And we will return the gift by being loving present to receive and give from our deepest heart space.

May you be abundantly blessed on your journey and may you always feel the presence and power of the love and goodness we shared in our time together. You will never be forgotten.

We all look forward to a return visit. And we will do all we can to make that a reality.

Blessings love and gratitude.

Gloria Peterson

Gloria Peterson– Continuing Education and Events Manager and all the Sisters at St. Joseph Convent

CREATIVE LEAPS OF BUREAUCRACY. MUSIC AND SONG FOR ENHANCING LEADERSHIP DEVELOPMENT

WASHINGTON DC, AUGUST 26, AT 5.17 P.M.

"The mind is not a vessel to be filled but a fire to be ignited!" says John Cimino at the start of a "Concert of Ideas" as he invites participants to re-discover the inner stories that make leadership personally meaningful and worthwhile. His group, Creative Leaps International, launches this journey of exploration with playful musical exercises ("snippets") challenging listeners to engage their imaginations and add a creative dimension to their listening: "What did you see in your mind's eye?" "What *feeling* does the music give to you?" and participants respond sharing their vivid visions and candid emotions. The "Concert of Ideas" is a compact 90-minute experience filled with dynamic musical performances, poetry and stories, after which people are offered an extensive de-briefing for reflection and sharing of their thoughts, insights and ideas. These discussions become a forum for municipal, corporate and federal public administrators to open up to new perspectives and learning opportunities in leadership ....

What is happening here? Who is there? Why are they there? What is the process?

It is the afternoon of the first day of the George Washington University "Center for Excellence in Municipal Management" programme, a 13-month graduate-level program designed around the core competencies that are needed for municipal and federal government agencies. The 30 participants are public administrators and managers, such as captains of police, fire chiefs, managers from public health, family and mental health services, procurement, budgeting, office of personnel, etc.[1] The performers are Creative Leaps International, a company created by John Cimino and Richard Albagli, who in 1972 founded the parent company Associated Solo Artists Inc. Richard Albagli recalls how it all began:

➜ "I was a member of a fraternity at Rensselaer Polytechnic Institute in Troy, New York studying physics, and I began to get very frustrated about the fact that I wasn't playing much music - the marimba had always been an escape for me. So I decided that I would put on a concert and described it in this way that the first half hour I would play music that people wanted to hear, and the second half hour I would play music that I wanted to play. The next year, when I was at graduate school, there was a poem by Stephen Crane called the "Tongue of Wood" and that became the theme for the concert. And by the third year it had become an annual event – that had 'always' been done. And I think that John jumped in on the fourth year – and over the course we wound up at 27 of them. It became a creative outlet for a lot of people."

THERE WAS A MAN WITH TONGUE OF WOOD
(1899)

There was a man with tongue of wood
Who essayed to sing,
And in truth it was lamentable.
But there was one who heard
The clip-clapper of this tongue of wood
And knew what the man
Wished to sing,
And with that the singer was content.

(STEPHEN CRANE: FROM "WAR IS KIND & OTHER LINES")

➜ John Cimino: "At the time we were both young scientists from Rensselaer Polytechnic Institute in Troy, New York. But we believed that science, as much as we loved it and were fascinated by science, it was not enough. I had a love of poetry and music, but I was a very young person, 18-19, and Richard was a graduate student in physics. And he introduced me really to the possibility of me being a performing artist. I didn't know that I had a singing voice, and eventually I would be trained and become an opera singer. And through this poem called the "Tongue of Wood" we recognized that inside of each one of us there is a voice that wants to come out - whether it's in dance or song or poetry. Richard's "Tongue of Wood" concerts created a forum where the young scientists, including myself, could let our heart and poetic side come out somehow in performance. So that's how our friendship began. And by the time I finished my undergraduate work we had this idea that we would found a non-profit company that would bring art and science together. Assist with the integration of the two. At the same time we saw that the arts bring in energy, curiosity and vitality to the learning process. *So we had two ideas, how to leverage and energize learning through the arts and how to connect art and science in an interdisciplinary style*. Those two ideas were the premise of the company we founded, the Associated Solo Artists. And through the first 20 years, from 1972 – 1992, we brought our programs - many, many dozens of different programs - to schools at every level of education from first grade through high school, connecting art and science and finding ways to energize learning, using art as a catalyst. It was only *after* we had worked for twenty years with students and teachers that we found our way into the corporate sector and founded Creative Leaps International in 1992. All our most important methodologies originate from those early years."

Creative Leaps has four principals besides John Cimino, award-winning operatic and concert artist, and Richard Albagli, principal percussionist and timpanist: Dianne Legro, opera singer, cabaret artist and recitalist; Paul Spencer Adkins, leading tenor and Pavarotti prize-winner; Donna Wissinger, world-known flautist and top athlete performer; Jon Klibonoff, soloist, chamber musician and the company's leading musical advisor and orchestrator. Other top musicians, actors and teaching artists are ready to step in when any of the principals are unable to attend due to their many other activities.

It was the fifteenth time Creative Leaps opened the leadership programme with a concert of ideas and the reader might wonder *why*? We have asked Herbert Tillery, former director of the Center for Excellence and Municipal Management at George Washington University, now deputy Mayor for operations in Washington DC.

➼ "What we are trying to get people to understand is that transformational leadership, out-of-the-box thinking, is the kind of thing that truly transforms governments. And we focus on local governments, because we think that that's where the real service delivery is. I think, and this is purely my perspective, having the arts integrated with the leadership program clearly identifies an out-of-the-box kind of approach to leader development. So the Concert of Ideas and Creative Leaps, I think, is an example of how you use advanced thought to create new paradigms of action. .... And I've never seen anything else that so clearly demonstrates what you're talking about when you're talking about out-of-the-box thinking. Introducing arts into a leader development forum – it's just so bizarre. But everybody that I've had go through this experience has liked it. There are a few people who have not adjusted, and the reason they haven't is because they have not broadened themselves to thinking creatively. And those are people that I have found to be those who are not very good leaders, because they haven't allowed themselves to be immersed by the concept and to open their minds to new thoughts. Therefore there really is a correlation between out-of-the-box thinking and how people transform governments. People who are not able to do that are not able to move their organizations that much. I would say that 95% of the people who have had the experience of participating with the Creative Leaps program have been really impressed with this concept. So I'm a big fan."

WHAT IS THE INTENTION AND HOW IS THE PROCESS?
➼ John Cimino: "The Concert of Ideas places art as a catalyst in the service of creative thinking and renewal inside of people, to awaken their sleeping knowledge, the tacit knowledge that reconnects them with their values, to activate their imagery, to get some cross activation of their internal senses, for instance when you listen to music it is possible

also to connect with visual imagery. One of our goals is to energize and activate perception, the different modalities of the senses and whatever capacities are linked to the numerous forms of intelligence that we seem to possess. And the concert of ideas is designed so that each moment, each piece of music or theatre or poetry is working with one or two different modalities. That might be music by Robert Schumann, quietly playing, and we are tuned into Robert Schumann and his wonderful gift and then, layered on that, we might hear the words of a scientist like Albert Einstein."

WASHINGTON DC, AUGUST 26, AT 5.15 P.M.

We are sitting in front of the stage at the Chapel of the Bolger Center for Leadership Development, Potomac, Maryland. The sound of a flute from the back corner of the room makes everyone turn around in surprise. Donna Wissinger, like the playful God of Pan, dances through the room, making a few stops, talking to people with her flute and her gestures and with her flute inviting the programme director to come up on to the stage. The programme director smilingly accepts the invitation and stands up to welcome Creative Leaps and the audience, 30 federal and municipal managers and the invited guests, among them a few curious people from companies wanting to get acquainted with the work of Creative Leaps, me, the researcher from Denmark, and some Board members from Creative Leaps International. Now John Cimino comes forward and says: "We are here to celebrate you and the important work you do." He talks about how the concert of ideas is built in such a way that the music can evoke and awaken something inside every individual, shake up things and bring surprise as well as old stories forward, and he asks everyone to give their full attention both to what happens "on stage" and, even more importantly, to what happens inside themselves. Creative Leaps will inspire, stir and provoke ideas, reflections, images and feelings, but the real work is up to each individual of the audience. The repertoire covers a great variety from classical music to cabaret and spirituals, as well as poetry, recitations, questions and tasks. During the concert, we are activated in many ways, people contribute their images and thoughts, we stand up to sing and move – and we are moved. At the end of the concert the energy is soaring.

DEBRIEFING

There is a break for dinner - and rejoining at 7 p.m. for a debriefing. The first part concerns reflective writing on the questions: What thoughts, impressions, recollections or ideas surfaced for you as you experienced the Concert of Ideas? How did the performance make you feel – what emotions did you experience, how are you feeling now?

The second part consists of small group discussions of 45 minutes, sharing personal experiences from the Concert of Ideas within the group, trying to connect these experiences to leadership, personal development, values, innovation and change, and using the Creative Leaps' leadership style, performed on stage, as an inspirational role model for discussing leadership. This is followed by a short creative presentation in plenum of each group's discussion. Among the things said are: the possibility of many interpretations, motivator, to elevate your spirit, shared leadership is partnership, being rekindled, feeling important, a dawn of the new horizon, respect for differences, keeping the passion, leaders also have to make it look effortless, art gets everybody moving, exhilarating feeling, spiritual calling, thought provoking, opened a lot of doors, left us vulnerable, a sense of sincerity, and to see what you do in your everyday life as an art form. There is a lot of applause and laughter in the room. The atmosphere is relaxed on this first day of the programme.

John Cimino concludes by showing some slides on knowledge, leadership and the importance of relationships. By now it is 9.30 p.m. Everyone is exhausted, but also content.

INNER TRANSFORMATION

The majority of leadership programmes deal with leadership on an intellectual level. They provide the participants with great theory and helpful frameworks for understanding and discussing leadership and subjects related to that, but they rarely get personal. Theory, however important, does not touch people. Music, here in the form of a concert of ideas, well prepared and well carried out, is evidently able to reach an inner space, which gives rise to learning at a totally different level. Herbert Tillery says:

➔ "What is different about Creative Leaps is the mindset that they put you into, the thoughts that they cause you to think. Understanding yourself is very important, because you have to understand yourself when you're trying to be a better leader. And so this parallel of what they do with the music in terms of *getting you in touch with yourself*, and then the way that they take you into the classroom and cause you to think about the feelings, the things that you have sensed, and applying that to the way that you deal with people. That has been the powerful message for me in my involvement with Creative Leaps. ...

I think, from a spiritual perspective, it really does cause me to get in touch with feelings and sometimes the feelings have been feelings that I haven't had before, and it causes me to question why I haven't had them and then try to evaluate what life experiences have caused me to either suppress a feeling or deny a feeling."

Similarly, Janet de Merode, member of Creative Leaps' board, says:

➔ "First I think for the individual - I guess I've always believed that man makes his dreams, it's not history makes man - but for the individual you feel that stretch. You feel you have been transported to a place where, in your thinking, that you have not been for a while or that you have never been. And so there is liberation in that, I think, for the individual. They feel empowered to think on their own instead of saluting to the bureaucracy or to the company's encouragement. *They feel encouraged themselves within themselves.*"

It is evident that the performance of Creative Leaps has had a deep impact on the reflective quality of the participants' inner thoughts. They seem to experience very profound and meaningful feelings related to their most authentic selves, their spirit. For real leadership development, assessing yourself is important.

➡ "You can't effectively lead others until you effectively know how to assess yourself. And be willing to assess yourself. So often we don't want to look at ourselves. And I think that's what it would do for other people, enabling them to see there's another way of accepting themselves and then try to transfer that to other people."[2]

This effect corresponds with the intentions of Creative Leaps. John Cimino said in his interview:

➡ "I most especially feel that this approach creates kind of optimum conditions for persons to re-examine themselves, to be in dialogue with another person, to address problems or agendas in their life or their profession. So we activate, we prepare what we like to call inner readiness inside the person. And art as our vehicle, as our instrument has this catalytic capacity. And we don't have to twist and reshape it, all we do is bring life to the art, place it in the same room with our people, and because human beings are what we are – homo sapiens – sense-making beings, we like to make meaning around everything. Each person will make his or her own meaning, call up their own emotions and respond in a beautiful, aesthetic way."

Thus, on a personal level we can denote inner transformation, but learning is also taking place on a more collective dimension.

BONDING

More and more authors seem to discover that in a creativity economy relations are the building blocks for groups, organisations and society. For innovative crystallisation, building 'common ground' between the members of a group makes a huge difference, because strong relations enable people to endure chaos and ignorance and come up with bright new concepts (Darsø, 2001). Relations create conversations and conversations create relations. As Margaret Wheatley (2002) expresses it: "You can't hate somebody whose story you know." Bonding thus becomes an important (future) competence and new ways and approaches for forming relationships become highly relevant. Music can do this in various ways. Herbert Tillery explains what took place: "We do it (listen to the Concert of Ideas) on the first day, and we do it in groups of 25-30, and these are people who haven't known each other in the past, but using this concept you very quickly get past that point of trying to introduce each other and get them to warm up to each other and all of a sudden they are beginning to bond, because they are not just listening to the music, they are interacting with the music."
According to Robert Nalewajek, a board member of Creative Leaps, a similar thing

happened when Creative Leaps participated in a conference on Human Issues and Management in 1993: "Right after the music – boom! People went together. It accelerated that bonding and relationships - and got people interacting at a level that normally takes much longer into the conference."

As we shall see later, bonding can also be supported through other art forms such as organisational theatre and painting processes.

CREATIVE LEAPS OF LEARNING

On the following day, August 27th, we all met in front of the hotel at 5.30 a.m. as Creative Leaps had agreed to do a Concert of Ideas for a group of 35 teachers at a school in Norwalk, Connecticut at 11 a.m. The Norwalk performance is the start of an educational experiment that will be observed carefully by a lot of educational specialists. The two-year programme consists of three seminars with all the teachers, and ten classroom workshops with the kids. The guiding questions are: "What role could the arts play in teaching and how can the arts improve the overall creativity and school performance?"

A little bit of background may be necessary here concerning the presence of arts in the schools. I interviewed Hollis Headrick, executive director of Center for Arts Education, an organisation in New York City, which started in 1996.

➜ "The center is a public-private partnership whose goal is to restore arts education in New York City public schools after about 30 years of system-wide cutbacks in the arts. ... Chauvinistically we say we are sitting in the arts capital of the world - but kids here don't have arts education. And so that is a crime, I mean, that can't be! The school system here in New York City is the largest in the country. There are over 11,000 schools, 1.1 million students, 80,000 teachers and a budget of about 13 billion dollars! So that is the reason why our organisation was created. It was to try and stimulate this activity and support programs that could be looked at as models. We have a whole group of schools that are being funded, and they should share programs so that other schools can learn from those schools about what works and what doesn't. ... There is a lot more data now reporting about how there is beginning to be a transfer of arts learning into other areas. It is an emerging area – there is still a lot of research that needs to be done..."

The Norwalk school system, via Creative Leaps, has committed itself to this *arts advantage in learning*.

The overall process at Norwalk was the same as with the public administrators in Washington DC. First the Concert of Ideas (with one piece of music being exchanged for another) and secondly the debriefing. The difference was that the teachers knew each other well, and that could be felt through the level of noise (talking) and interaction. The spirits were good in the group of public administrators, but at Norwalk it really took off and set the place roaring. I briefly interviewed a couple of teachers afterwards and asked about the quality and duration of this exhilarating feeling, and one of them responded: "Oh no, this is not just a one-minute high, this energy will last for a long time." The words used to describe what they felt were: revitalised, energised, renewed, unleashing of creativity.

As the procedure was very similar to the Washington DC process above, it will not be commented further here. The story is included because it appears that many of the interviewed artists work with *both* educational and corporate organisations.

TRAJECTORIES
The Concert of Ideas clearly belongs to the arena of 'events'. It is interactive, it is inspiring, provocative and engaging. But with the debriefing it becomes more than that. Herbert Tillery emphasised:

➡ "To debrief and put it in leadership context, *that is where the connection is and that is what* lasts. I mean you go to a concert and you just listen to music; over time you forget it, but if you put it in context and you have a lesson on what you were supposed to get from it, that is what stays with you. I have been through 12 of the 15 concerts and I have listened to the same music and I have learned something different every time. And to me that is what leadership is all about, in terms of looking at yourself introspectively and finding out who you are – I have been in leadership positions now for 27 years of my life and I still do not say that I am a leadership professional, I am a student of leadership, I learn something from every experience."

The above citation suggests that debriefing takes the process from the arena of 'events' into the 'solar plexus of learning', an inner very personal and vulnerable space. With the present data it is difficult to say what kind of effect it will have on that specific group of leaders. We do, however, have the testimonial of the deputy Mayor of Washington DC that is has had a lasting effect on the 300 federal and public administrators, who have been through the program so far. This indicates that the learning trajectory either moves into the arena of 'capabilities' or 'products' – or both, depending on whether the learning concerns new capabilities or implementation of change processes. In the perspective of the organisational learning framework (from chapter 3), this poses the question whether the 'anticipatory learning' gets 'integrated' or not.

If we look at the role of art here, it is obvious that inspiration is in play together with beauty, but also the sacred and social aspects are involved. The two most important aspects of learning are inner transformation in relation to leadership development and 'creating common ground' through bonding and meaningful relationships with others.

IN DISCUSSION WITH RICH GOLD
WEDNESDAY NOVEMBER 13

artist

scientist

During the lunch students have the chanc to take part in a discussion with Rich Go what he calls "The Junk Tribe".
Rich Gold is in town for the "Engineering is Magic" symposium.

designer

engineer

Also for MSc. Students

The 4 hats of creativity I have worn.

I have worn four hats of creativity in my life time. Each hat is different, each sees the world in its own way, each has its own methodologies and each ends up making different kinds of stuff. There are perhaps 10,000 individually bought and sold pieces of stuff in the average home and these four professions, combined in various ways, created 98% of it. The wearers of all four hats believe in something which they consider quite good called creativity which can be defined as the making of new stuff, stuff that didn't exist before. In some cultures one tells the same story over and over for millennium. In our culture, this is illegal, it is called copyright infringement. Every year we need to make new stuff, never seen before stuff. In fact, we have to make 3.5% more stuff this year than last year, or it is considered a recession. We make so much stuff that every Christmas we simply have to give it away. And most importantly, we have almost no way to make a living without making more stuff. I call the culture we live in, The Junk Tribe, not because the stuff we make is necessarily junky, but because it is designed to become junk to make room for the next wave of stuff that we have to create in order to make a living. It is an interesting culture and an exciting tribe to be in. I personally greatly enjoy being creative, that is, making new, never seen before stuff. But our tribal ethos also creates certain problems: half the world's population lives in poverty; we continually lose sense of our moral compass; and of course we are in the process of destroying the planet on which we live. I am open to solutions.

ENGINEER
MAGIC

mo

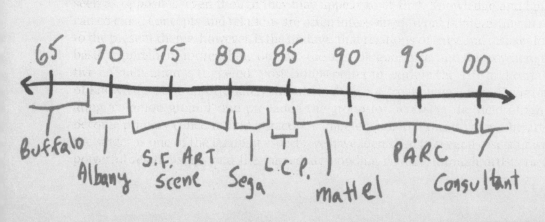

WHAT HAPPENS WHEN YOU PAIR A SCIENTIST WITH AN ARTIST? KEEPING UP INNOVATION THROUGH PARTNERING WITH ARTISTS

The PAIR project of Xerox PARC (Palo Alto Research Center) is the story of a 10-year adventure. The idea behind PARC Research Center was that innovation would naturally emerge when you put creative people in a hothouse setting.[3]

➔ "PARC started in 1970 when Xerox decided to create a research center. The guy who headed it was a physicist, and in physics you also build your own experimental equipment. Computer people don't seem to build their own computers when they experiment. What if we brought in people who both created new kinds of programs and new kinds of computers? So that was the beginning of Xerox PARC. In the first five years they created everything we now call computers, they created Windows, the mouse, the icons, the first drawing package, the first word processor, etc. Because of that it became famous. But they saw themselves as scientists not as engineers, and they had this very scientific view of things. They weren't making products; they were discovering new ways of interaction."[4]

One of the challenges of such a setting was to keep researchers creative and innovative. The PAIR (PARC Artist-in-Residence) programme was conceived by Rich Gold, artist and director, to have this aim by inviting artists who used new media into PARC, and pair them with scientists who used the same media, but who perceived these mainly from a technological perspective. As Rich Gold was at the same time made head of his own laboratory RED (Research Experimental Documents), PAIR became a part of that, and obviously 'documents' became the main focus and technology the common language. The idea was to use these new partnerships as the point of departure for discovering new types of documents, new applications, new ways to create documents, new features for documents, etc.

The PAIR project was not the first Artist-in-Residence programme in the new media arts. In 1966 the Experiments in Art and Technology grew out of the work of Billy Klüver, a scientist from Bell Laboratories, who was already then exploring the potentiality of collaborations between artists and scientists (Harris, 1999:9). The PAIR design, however, distinguished itself by being specifically interested in the learning potential of these collaborations, the language, the methods, the creative process, the design process and the interaction per se – or as Rich Gold very simply put it: "The idea wasn't originally innovations or patents; it was kind of intellectual experience. Just to make better artists and better scientists, not to make better art or science."

The team was multidisciplinary and among the artists were: a video-artist, a documentary filmmaker, an interactive novelist, a radical vocalist and professional gesturer, a net artist, an interactive sound sculptor, a sound artist, copy-artists and installation artists. Craig Harris sums up what others can learn from PAIR (Harris, 1999:34):

➡ "The strength of the PAIR paradigm is in PARC's understanding of itself and its goals, in PAIR's inclusive approach to activating the surrounding communities, in its willingness to take risks when no clearly definable outcome is evident, and in its acknowledgment that it is setting in motion a process and allowing the collaborations and intersections to evolve on their own. These fundamental premises are indeed portable, with each context creating its own ecology and therefore its own unique nature and impact."

THE PROCESS

Most of the collaborations were designed to take 6-8 months but lasted more than a year, and some went on for many years. The artists were selected from the San Francisco area (in order to support the local community) by the PAIR External Advisory Panel. Probably the only unifying feature really is that every collaborative pairing has been different, some with successful artistic expressions, some with mutually inspiring interactions, some with frustrations and basically no outcomes, and some with acquired new competencies. The process has in many ways been extremely messy, but also fruitful in a lot of unexpected ways. The projects had outgoing names such as "Oh Night Without Objects"; "Deep Creek School"; "The Snake Pit: SIGGRAPH 95"; "Forward Anywhere". These names indicate a rich conceptual and metaphorical content, which have had a unifying influence on the projects.

An unforeseen spin-off effect was the extreme number of visitors that came to PARC because of the PAIR project, for instance family members, who had never seen PARC before and who suddenly got curious. This way PAIR "acted as a strange bridge to their own families."[5] Another unexpected effect was the effect PAIR had on sales:

➡ "We could have 3-4 sales people come in with their clients to PARC and we actually had to limit it, because nothing closed the deal better than coming in to see the future – and they just loved it. When the customers came in they would present their problems to the scientist and the scientists love that kind of thinking; it was kind of top level and you got this interesting feedback. It helped them think about what they wanted to think about next."[6]

There were, of course, also some barriers. One of the difficulties, in particular at the out-set, appears to be resistance towards the PAIR programme, on the part of the scientists. As an example of this Paul de Marinis writes (De Marinis, 1999:168):

➜ "After lunch I did a tour of labs, talking with numerous researchers, trying to find a good fit. What seemed to surprise me then, but doesn't now, was that the researchers doing work in fields most related to my work (speech analysis, electronic design) appeared pro-foundly uninterested in my ideas and projects. ... As I spent time at PARC, I have tried to understand or at least accept this pattern. A few researchers are honestly enthusiastic about the PAIR program and artists. The majority are either benignly or actively uninter-ested in it, leaving a few who are probably hostile toward it."

Other barriers in the process have been related to the difficulties of language and the challenges of cross-disciplinary interaction:

➜ "The third mind – that incarnation of the collaborative imagination – doesn't just hap-pen automatically when people work together: it is an achievement, it takes time, and it requires effort. ... We were making headway on one of the pivotal accomplishments in col-laboration – the development of shared understanding" (Crane, MacDonald, Minneman & Winet, 1999:146-148).

OUTCOMES
Even though Rich Gold in retrospect lamented the lack of better documentation and gen-eral transfer of knowledge from PAIR, he acknowledged that it had generated many interesting aspects of learning:

➜ "I think for most of the scientists, they really appreciated how art was made. Many of them know a lot about arts and they go to galleries, but they never saw how it was pro-duced and I think many of them were surprised how similar it was to science, the start of the problem, the idea and the work through it and how thoughtful the artists were and philosophically based. I think that came as a surprise. For the artists many of them had already worked with science, and I think for them the biggest knowledge gain was what it is like to be inside a corporation and to discover that corporations, far from being these terrible awful cold places, were actually quite pleasant and warm and vital and friendly. I think that's what their biggest surprise was. For me it helped me re-conceptualise my life in terms of getting a clearer sense of what these different paths of innovation or thinking were, and it is what got me thinking about design and how it relates to art, things which I had never thought about deeply."

What is said above about the artistic approach links well to the discussion we had in chapter 2 about the mysterious quality and rare disclosure of artistic processes. The part we would like to examine a bit closer here is the point about science and art being similar, and about the relation between art and design. Fortunately Rich Gold elaborated on this aspect in a lecture the same day[7], where he drew the model displayed below:

→ "The scientist's mind and the artist's mind are about the same, they are thinking at the edges of thought, very complex questions, but I have not found that artists were able to ask any more interesting questions than scientists. Scientists are almost identically as creative as artists."

Both scientists and artists depend upon patrons and peers. The patrons, who could be foundations, universities or corporations, are the people who sponsor or invest in the creativity, knowledge and skills of the artist/scientist. And for both the opinion of their peers are much more important than trivial down-to-earth things like testing or selling. Designers and engineers, on the other hand, are more 'this worldly' and care about the functional side of the product. They primarily make tools and therefore designers care about user testing and engineers want spec(ification)s in order to know exactly what the task is. The main difference between designers and engineers is, according to Rich Gold, "that design works with aesthetics and engineering typically does not."

The most difficult challenge regarding communication and cooperation between these professions is the "wall" between art and science on one side and design and engineering on the other. "Arts and design don't work together easily. Artists think of designers as failed artists, and designers think of artists as people with their heads in the clouds. But in reality you need both."[8]

In corporate research laboratories the main challenge is to do cutting-edge research, turn

ART-DESIGN-SCIENCE-ENGINEERING

MATRIX DEVELOPED BY RICH GOLD, 2003

DEPENDENT UPON PATRONS AND PEERS

FUNDAMENTAL AND LONG LASTING TRUTH	ART	SCIENCE	TRUE / FALSE
COOL/UNCOOL	DESIGN	ENGINEERING	GOOD / BAD

DEPENDENT UPON CUSTOMERS AND CLIENTS

it into a product, produce it and sell it – and preferably at the speed of light. To do this you need to get the best out of people's creativity, knowledge and skills. Rich Gold came up with an interesting notion for 'bridging the gap' of a product cycle:

➡ "I call it the Swinehart 13, he is a researcher at PARC. He says that it takes 13 years to go from the gleam in the researcher's eye to profitable product, and that is very consistent. ... So there is this interesting problem which is: researchers only care about an idea maybe for the first four years, when it is still new and they can write papers. Corporations are only interested in ideas about three years out from the end, because that's where they can see the products arise. So there is this big time in the middle, where ideas fall through. What I have discovered is that this is where artists are most useful. ... It is the time after you have the concept, but it is not a product yet. The artist can step in there and make artwork and keep the idea alive. It keeps it in corporate memory; it helps show it and potential ideas for it. Then the marketing people can see that. Bringing artists in at the beginning is useless. By the end you need engineering and not artists. We have discovered that scientists like turning over their finished ideas to artists, while they begin working on their new ideas. So that's an interesting use of artists in a corporation – bridging the gap."

Finally we want to mention PAIR's use of EKO's:

➡ "Evocative Knowledge Objects, that's what my group began thinking we were doing, which are sort of like demos in a way, but they are deeper and they help evoke the idea in the other person - a way of crossing this difficult boundary between science and engineering. The scientists they just hand the paper they wrote to the engineer. So the engineer looks at it and says 'what is this', but if you construct this EKO, they look at it and say 'oh I know how to do that right'."[9]

What we see here is how prototyping an idea bridges the gap by making communication a lot easier and more concrete. Furthermore an EKO is much more likely than a paper to elicit prompt feedback. In his book "Serious Play" from 2000, Michael Schrage describes many corporate cases on how prototyping can encourage and speed up communication and thereby increase the potential for innovation. We will expand on the discussion of the potential of prototyping later and relate it to Forum Theatre, musical archetypes and graphical facilitation.

TRAJECTORIES

When I first got interested in the PAIR project it seemed like a perfect example of the 'product' arena in the Arts-in-Business model. As it turned out during our interview, Rich Gold's original idea was a different one, as he "wanted to work on the human level and not at the artefact one." This means that we should understand PAIR as an 'event' even though the project carries on for a longer time than we would normally expect of an event. The trajectory that Rich Gold outlined was thus one going from 'events' to 'capabilities'. And indeed, many participants, in particular artists, claim that the pairing has changed their lives and production enormously - indicating that the learning trajectory continues from 'capabilities' to 'products'. One concrete 'product', which was devised through the collaboration of a mathematician and a sculptor, was a bitmapped graphics editor, but, apart from that, no major new patents came out of PAIR. Other products were artistic installations accompanied by events, leading the trajectory back to 'events'. Regarding the arena of 'metaphors', as pointed out above metaphors have been a natural part of developing mutual understanding, because metaphors can cut across all sorts of differences and be interpreted from multiple backgrounds, professions, experiences, etc. In this way we can say that the PAIR learning trajectories involve all four arenas of the model. As the project was closed in early 2002 after the Internet bubble collapsed and the Xerox stock went from 64 to 4, only the people involved will know what is produced in the future based on the knowledge and capabilities, developed through PAIR. Sadly, its visionary creator, Rich Gold, died in early 2003, a great loss of human genius.

In the PAIR project the role of art was primarily one of provocation, as the idea was to stir the organisation and keep the innovative spirit alive. The experiment generated three main aspects of learning (both 'anticipatory' and 'experimental'). The first concerned individual learning on the part of the scientists, the artists, and for Rich Gold himself. The second insight was that artists were able to 'fill the gap' between research and marketing. And the third was the idea of EKO's, Evocative Knowledge Objects, which could help the transfer from scientist to engineer. Predominantly PAIR stands out for its bold and unbusinesslike approach with no specific goals and in total trust of the people and the process. The pairing of scientists and artists was an invitation to 'experimental learning' as it concerned a totally new experience, which was reflected upon only later.

INCENTIVES

Exciting Show · Exciting Sales

BANG & OLUFSEN

Business Theatre

TELLING   SELLING   RETAILING

BETTER BUSINESS SUPPORT

BUSINESS THEATRE. BANG & OLUFSEN USING A THEATRE METAPHOR FOR TRAINING AND DEVELOPMENT

In 1925 two entrepreneurial engineers started a small radio company in Jutland, Denmark. In 2003 Bang & Olufsen is a leading design company of sophisticated televisions, video and audio equipment. They employ 2,800 people at their Headquarters in Jutland, Denmark, have retail shops in 14 countries and have a market share of 1-2% in the world.[10]

B&O's aim is to sell excellent technology wrapped in beautiful design, which transmits sound perfectly. In many respects it is an outstanding company with many links to the arts. A lot of its history can be seen and read in their storytelling time machine, Beotime 2k.[11]

Since its start, B&O has had its ups and downs. In 1993 the company had a major economical crisis, but the then new CEO, Anders Knutsen, and his management team succeeded in turning the business around by applying a strategy under the name of "Break Point 93".[12] It involved firing 700 employees, restructuring the organisation and implementing a back-to-basics programme with focus on diligence, prudence and vision. The term 'break point' derives from tennis and describes the intense moment when one of the two players will win the game - and Anders Knutsen did win the game but the company had to go through some critical and difficult years to make the turn-around.

In 1997 a 'Culture Group' was formed. Two people from outside the company joined the group to help three internal managers tease out the company values (for internal use). Of the outsiders, one was an artist[13] and the other was a philosopher[14]. Not surprisingly, the values the Culture Group came up with were not the usual type of company values. The values, as they saw them, were Synthesis, Poetry, and Excellence. *Synthesis* stands for the ability to work in a diverse and conflictual environment and yet come up with outstanding solutions beyond expectations. *Poetry* indicates that every product that leaves

B&O speaks like a poet and has a 'message' that the client can 'read'. The products are a way for B&O to get into dialogue with the world, because the creators behind them are poetic. *Excellence* is in everything B&O does, into the smallest detail. There are no compromises – only perfection and quality. Synthesis and excellence were accepted by the employees and survived. Poetry as a value, however, did not 'digest' well internally and has today been exchanged for the values of originality and challenge.

The values often appear in marketing, for instance "Excellence and simplicity rediscovered" is used about the BeoVision 5 plasma screen television. In the process of designing this television, David Lewis, one of the top designers, was inspired by a piece of art. The story goes that one day on his way to work Lewis passed a gallery and saw some paintings on the wall, but he noticed that other paintings were still standing on the floor, waiting to be hung on the wall. From this Lewis got the idea of framing the BioVision 5 like a painting and designing it in such a way that it can be put on the wall or remain on the floor.

In the year 2000, two directors from B&O's International Training and Human Resource Development were facing an important challenge. They were to create a new international training concept for the B&O sales people and agents. The problem with the existing training programme was that it was very focused on technical knowledge about the products and did not incorporate the B&O vision of "creating experiences that surprise". Another problem was the turnover of sales people, which was quite high then. The general sales set-up is that B&O subsidiaries have contracts with each local shop regarding training, decoration and growth rate, but apart from that B&O shops are generally independent, which means that what comes from Headquarters cannot be dictated, but must be desired because it is relevant, appealing and motivating. The subsidiaries have a support system through a number of Retail Development Managers, who visit the shops (about 25-50) on a regular basis in order to support them and inform them of new possibilities regarding decoration, product information and training options.

The solution that came up to these challenges was 'Business Theatre', a training concept for the B&O sales people. In an interview[15] with Thomas Asger Hansen, the director for International Training and Human Resource Development, he explains how this came about:

➜ "If I think back to why we clung to this framework, which we developed in the first training concept and called Business Theatre, then it actually started with a discussion between me and some directors from our subsidiaries and a B&O trainer from Spain, who, for some reason, called his shops 'theatres'. The point is that we work on educating sales people. That is, we must make it work. It really begins with thinking of the customer: what do you as a customer want, when you enter a B&O shop? Then you expect a certain quality, and you probably also expect some aesthetics and some design. And then overall you expect a reasonably good experience out of entering that shop. There is a reason for entering that shop. Normally, it turns out, you don't just randomly drop by a B&O shop. You have kind of a mission or a desire to enter the shop.... So you can say that people who enter our shops must be given an experience. And that is the point of departure for the theatre metaphor. Because it developed when we discussed: what if we presume, just hypothetically, that the shop is a stage or a theatre where you will have a good experience, what kind of ingredients will there be? There are some set pieces, i.e. our vision merchandising, our big campaigns. They are stage wings. We also make changes of wings; they have to change. Between 4-6 times a year there will be new set pieces. Our concept thinking demands that we try to make a minimum of four campaigns, including windows and in-store walls. These must be exciting, so that we can make changes that make the shops dynamic and alive. What comes naturally after that is a discussion: Who are the actors? Who is the audience? Who are the directors and the instructors? And what was funny then was that when talking about this and when we asked our distributors and our organisation in general: Who plays which parts? Then you would very quickly get a response like "Well, the actors must be the sales people", because they are there to animate the show, to make it work. The audience will be our customers, etc. And the way this should be taken is actually that *it is the products, which are the actors, and the sales people, who are the instructors*, in my opinion. Because a sales person, who talks and talks, that is not exciting. That is not what you have come for. You have come to experience the products. *So they are the actors, aren't they? ... So this whole discussion gave us a new image of the role of the sales person. And that was really what I was after. Because everybody knows that it is the experience that is centre stage*. That is really important. The next step is then to find out how to create that experience in the best way. You do that by presuming that the products are the actors. They should become alive. They must be prepared to make themselves come alive."

The concrete result of this process was a brochure "Bang & Olufsen Business Theatre - performing exciting sales"[16]. On page 2 there is a picture of an old Greek theatre with three pillars, named "Telling", "Selling", and "Retailing" and on page 3 it says:

➡ "The change is from 'product only' to Business. Business training means integrating issues such as retail profit, shop performance, brand promise and vision & values into the training obligation. The idea of the Business Theatre is simple. Exciting sales are exciting performances. We deliberately stress a tight relationship between an exciting shop or service performance and the financial success implied in the wording: Exciting sales."

In 2003 the brochure itself is not in use any more, but according to the director the concept is firmly implemented in the overall framework of the Business Qualification Sales Education, and most specifically in step 2. B&O sales education step 1 includes theory, service and technical information, which is taught by distance and e-learning, and involves written web-based examinations. Step 2 is classroom training at B&O Headquarters. One of the ways the training is done is with this type of instruction: "Like, now you are going to make a role play, get that product to talk, become alive, without saying a word. You can do anything, you are just not allowed to talk."[17] The third step of the program involves simulated customer experiences through "mystery shopping", where the skills of the sales people are tested in practice. Afterwards the "fake" customer describes his/her experience, what was good and what was bad, and gives the sales people feed-back on their behaviour. This is the more practical examination. The concept of 'Business Theatre' is, according to the director, also strategically important for B&O's future growth.

➡ "From having been a bit of a 'sleeping pillow', because this was so far above what others could offer, there was almost automatically a story to tell, we will now have to focus on telling this story and transmitting it. The next thing that happens is – and I have no doubts whatsoever about this – that in 5 – 10 years the personnel's quality as facilita-tors of this stage and experiential thinking will be a parameter of differentiation which it isn't today. If we are skillful, then we will have a level in five years, which others can't reach. And we have the possibility of doing it, because the others, our competitors, within the radio and video industry, are simply too big to be able to obtain this shared leverage. They have other focal areas. They can't always allow themselves to go by quality alone, on the frontiers that we can. So if we are able to carry this one through, then the people and their own understanding of what their role is, will simply be the real task, and it will be a key factor in a five-year term."

REFLECTIONS

In this case study we see how a metaphor can bring about mind shifts. This is interesting at two levels, one concerning the overall generative power of metaphors, and secondly the more specific generative power of *artistic* metaphors. What difference does it make that the metaphor is artistic?

"Generative Metaphor: A Perspective on Problem-Setting in Social Policy" is a classical article by Donald Schön from 1986, in which he not only demonstrates how our percep-tion and framing of a problem often determines the solution to it, but also how framing a problem creatively or at least non-traditionally (in his example by regarding a paint brush as a pump) can provoke the creation of new concepts, i.e. innovative crystallisa-tion[18]. As discussed in chapter 3, a metaphor invites us to see new aspects of a theme, often something that we have never seen before, but when a metaphor profoundly changes the way we see the theme, we usually talk about transformation or double-loop learning[19]. This is fundamental to innovation.

But 'Business Theatre' is also an artistic metaphor. What difference does that make – if any? The difference is that an artistic quality (theatre) sparks a different tone, a different ambience, a different visual image than would, for instance, a war metaphor.[20] As we saw in the interview earlier, the theatre metaphor invited people to talk about scenery, wings, props, lights, costumes, actors, instructor, audience, experience, performance, applause, show, etc., which inspired a different, more artful, sales performance and to new types of relationships with the products as well as with the customers. In "The Beauty and the

Machine", the study this paragraph is built on, Camilla Mehlsen concludes by reminding us of the importance of how we construct our world by using metaphors (2003:87):

➤ "As the metaphor has been shown to have implications for how we understand and act, also in organisations, it is important to be aware of the metaphors that impress our language. For the metaphor forces us into its hidden patterns, no matter whether the metaphor is as mechanical as a robot or as beautiful as a symphony."

Another observation concerns using a metaphor as a 'conversation piece'.[21] Asking the questions about who were the actors, etc. evidently inspired important conversations about the role of the sales people, identifying and creating their new role – and even more so in relation to the products because of the surprise effect when people realised that the products should, in fact, be the real actors. In a recent workshop at Learning Lab Denmark[22], the director of the Royal Danish Opera used a very powerful expression to explain the overall purpose of the Royal Danish Opera, which was "to make people cry". This 'conversation fragment', in fact, generated a rich conversation. In her latest book[23], Margaret Wheatley suggests several 'conversation starters', which are strong and thought-provoking questions. This area has apparently a lot of potential for further exploration.

In addition to this came the realisation of the need for new artful capabilities, such as storytelling and new ways of communicating with the customers. Bernard Kelly from Storytelling in Organisations explains:

➤ "We talk about storytelling very much as a kind of active co-creation really, so it's about the person telling the story and the ones listening to it. And I think that's often very appealing in organisations; how does one create something bigger than the individuals involved?"

The aspect of co-creation is obviously important for building a good relationship. And 'soft' things like that, which are actually very hard to work with, are what the arts are good at and what business really needs. As the director mentioned earlier, this was not only the creation of a new concept for training. It was also an important strategic change of direction for the company.

TRAJECTORIES

The Bang & Olufsen case is a good example of the successful application of an artistic metaphor. It shows us very elaborately how a metaphor can generate new ideas and insights that have powerful implications. It also demonstrates how a good metaphor can raise important questions and start highly relevant conversations in organisations. In this case study we see a trajectory from the arena of 'metaphors' towards 'products', as the concrete outcome was a training concept, described in a brochure. But the trajectory continues into the arena of 'capabilities', because the "Business Theatre" concept involves developing and training a range of new capabilities, such as communication skills and building good relationships, and in particular, storytelling. This is, according to several of the people interviewed, a major change, both strategically and culturally. Thus, the role of art was here a mix of provocation and inspiration, and the major learning aspects concerned the mind shifts provoked by metaphor, the inspiration for starting new types of conversations, and the identification of the need for new and more artful capabilities in business.

We will conclude this case by pointing out a more general implication of the need for artful capabilities by quoting from Camilla Mehlsen's conclusion (2003:85):

➔ "The empirical data demonstrate that the values, expressed by art metaphors, in many ways are in opposition to industrialism's machine-like view of work and organisation, as they emphasise the sensuous, the ambiguous, the social interaction as well as other values and images that denote post-industrial thinking as regards management and organisation."

'I CARRY WITH A SMILE'. ORGANISATIONAL THEATRE FOR DOMESTIC HELPERS

➤ "Slowly the inornate hall fills with people. About a hundred chairs in eight rows, separated by a passageway, are waiting for the audience. The chairs are facing a mobile stage. It contains a bed, an armchair, and two tables. On the canvas behind we see the images of a person's living room: old paintings and statues are covering a flowery tapestry. The people entering the auditorium are predominantly women between 20 and 60 years of age. They all work in the home care organisation of a municipality. They are nurses, secretaries, cooks, drivers and so on. They are taking their places, maybe attempting to sit next to their favourite colleagues, talking to each other in low voices. When everybody is seated a female manager enters the stage together with a man, who is dressed all in black. Asking for attention, the manager begins to explain to the audience what is about to happen. They are informed that they are about to watch and, if they wish to, participate in an organisation theatre performance. This, they are told, is thought to help in the changes and developments that are at the moment troubling the home care organisation in the municipality. Then, after the manager has ended and left the stage, the man in black introduces himself to the audience as a "joker". That is the title, he explains, for a consultant who mediates between audience and stage. Next he describes what the organisation theatre that day will be all about.[24]"

Here we catch a glimpse of the introduction of the organisational theatre play "I carry with a smile" to a group of 100 domestic helpers at a middle-sized Danish municipality meeting. The background is a difficult situation that arose in this municipality, primarily caused by cuts in funding, which meant difficult changes such as downsizing, restructuring, and reorganising of the workforce. Among the home care workers there was a lot of insecurity, people were afraid of losing their jobs and of having to work longer hours and the changes meant that the system would be less flexible - to the disadvantage of both the home care clients and the employees. Consequently there was a lot of anxiety and a lot of 'murmuring in the corners'. Two managers of the municipality realised that something had to be done and took the initiative to suggest Forum Theatre as a way of facing the negative atmosphere. They had worked with the theatre group, the Dacapo Theatre, earlier and felt that through this approach it would be possible to bring up the home care workers' concerns and discuss them openly. Thus the goal was to start conversations about the various difficulties the domestic helpers were facing and hopefully to get a better understanding of the problems and concerns and possibly also come up with ideas and ways of improving the working culture. Management decided to include all the 3000 workers in such a way, that during one year there would be 30 performances with 100 participants in each. By inviting a small group from each of the 7 districts, they could keep up the daily work, which was highly practical, and by mixing the people from across the organisation they would get to know each other better and hopefully create a common understanding and shared knowledge. Most of the workforce consisted of women aged 20 – 60.

THEATRE OF THE OPPRESSED

Many of the theatrical forms applied today in Western organisations derive from the work of Augusto Boal, who developed the theatre of the oppressed through his work with illiterate and poor people of Latin America. Boal wanted to change the spectators into subjects, actors and transformers of the dramatic action. For Boal theatre was action, it was a "rehearsal for revolution"![25] Boal invented three theatrical approaches: Simultaneous Dramaturgy, Image theatre and Forum theatre.

In *Simultaneous Dramaturgy*, the theatre group creates a play, based on a story (with a problem) from the audience. When the story reaches the point of crisis or conflict, the actors, one at a time, asks advice from the spectators about how to handle the situation. The spectators participate by giving suggestions to the actors, thus 'writing' the play simultaneously as it happens on stage.

Image theatre is non-verbal and involves the spectators, who are invited onto the stage. The idea is to create an image of a situation or a concept by using the actors' bodies and expressions to visualize it. It has three steps: 1. establishing the actual image, 2. creating the ideal image, and 3. trying out a 'transitional image' in order to move from 1 to 2. An example of image theatre was given by Piers Ibbotson in his interview. Once when he was working with a department of a company that had problems with their management and culture he asked them to make an image of the work place. One of the images that came out of the exercise was very simple and powerful: One of the women in the group made an image in which all the men were standing looking to the front and beside each of the men was a woman kneeling on the ground. When asked for their responses, someone in the group said the image looked like a hunting party, with the women playing the role of obedient dogs at the command of the men. It turned out that women were treated in a humiliating way, their contribution to the functioning of the department was not fully recognized, which none of the men had thought of, but the image struck home – everyone recognised it, and the working ethic changed.

In *Forum theatre*, the spectators become actors. It starts with a story and a problem, which is played on the stage. The actors try to solve the problem in a way that would resonate with the spectators, but the problem is not solved; it may even get worse. The actors now invite the spectators to come up with better ways of solving the problem and to try them out on stage. This can be repeated several times with different people from the audience - a new version is tried out with each new spectator-actor until a satisfactory solution has been reached.

THE DACAPO THEATRE

The Dacapo Theatre[26] has existed as a professional organisation since 1995, but the idea of using theatre for creating focus and dialogue was already conceived by director Lone Thellesen much earlier. At the time she was in charge of internal health in a can factory with the responsibility for ensuring work security and health. She started to experiment with new approaches, such as inviting a trained art therapist into the organisation, who worked with drawing and painting and she also tried out theatre. She found that theatre had the strongest impact, as it encouraged a different kind of dialogue with more active participation. Around this time she met Lena Bjørn, actor and playwright, and together they decided to develop performances of forum theatre. They managed to set up two plays, which were performed by the employees for the employees of the can factory. These plays were so successful that they were shown not only at the can factory, but as the word spread, also in other factories. In 1995 the demand was so great that they decided to start professionally and so the Dacapo Theatre was established starting with four people full time. At the time of writing the group includes 25 people, consisting of actors (the majority), 'jokers' (consultants) and some administrative assistants. When they started in 1995 the plays were fixed performances, but as the demand has changed the performances are gradually becoming more tailor-made to meet the needs of each specific organisation. The Dacapo Theatre is inspired by Boal, but they have developed their own variant of organisational theatre by focusing on the exchange of perspectives rather than on the forces of oppression. The Dacapo Theatre uses conflict as a potential for change through dialogue, whereas Boal saw conflict as a weapon for freeing the oppressed.

SCENES FROM HOME CARE WORK

Regarding the project in 2003 with the municipality and the home care workers, the Dacapo Theatre adapted a play, which they had developed earlier. It was a special play for the health care sector, which had been performed in hospitals and at a health care fair. This play was modified so as to suit the world of the domestic helpers by interviewing them about their problems and concerns in order that the audience would be able to recognise what they saw on stage. It turned out that most of the problems concerned relationships, and specifically four types of relations were difficult: home care worker versus client; home care worker versus home care worker; home care worker versus manager; and manager versus manager.[27] To illustrate these problems scenes were played from the home of a client, where the main challenge for the home care worker was how she could be both efficient and at the same time kind and empathetic to the human needs of the client. Another scene showed two home care workers who were having a conflict because of their different approaches to dealing with the client, which finally left the client in despair, and yet other scenes were played about the home care organisation itself, showing the bureaucratic procedures of the organisation and the consequences and challenges this presented to home care workers and management.

After each scene the 'joker' would come forward and ask questions to the audience like "What did you see?" "What happened?" "Why did it happen?" "Could the people involved have done something else?" "What should they have done?" "Who is to blame?" These questions were discussed both in small groups and directly with the 'joker' as moderator. The suggestions of the audience were then taken by the actors and tried out and there was a lot of laughing. The audience was also invited to act out some of the suggestions on stage, but this was mostly declined. They preferred to stay in their seats, suggest different approaches and see the effects of their proposals.

OUTCOMES

What was the outcome of applying organisational theatre to the 3000 employees of a home care organisation? The general difficulty with measuring the effects of organisational change and development initiatives is that you can never be sure of what exactly worked. The managers of the home care organisation are convinced that the Forum Theatre sessions were very important for the increased employee satisfaction, which was seen in the annual employee satisfaction questionnaire at the end of the year. As pointed out in the analysis by Meisek & Dawids (2004), there are, however, other factors of possible influence, e.g. that there were no more funding cuts or downsizing during that year. To understand the effects better, questionnaires were sent out to all participants after the play, of which 30% responded. According to the response, the majority had enjoyed the performances, but as for the practical usefulness, this, at first, appeared quite low, as 84% said that they had not been able to use any ideas or solutions in their daily work; 12% had used something once and only 4% had used some of it several times. But judging from the response to a question concerning how much they had discussed the play afterwards with colleagues, the first interpretation might have to be revised. 95% had talked about it at least once; of these 58% had talked about it several times. Thus, the plays had started a lot of conversations in the organisation, and furthermore these conversations were kept going by the continuous performances (30 times during a year) involving new audiences. The conclusion was therefore:[28]

➡ "The organisation theatre performance reached the goals envisioned by the managers. However, there may be more after-effects. These seem to find their expression in the notion of the serious play that surrounds a conversation piece. The conversation piece is the play as it is presented on stage again and again. Around this conversation piece social action starts to spin, driven by the interests of the different involved employees. First this happens in the interactive part of the play, then it continues in the mundane talk that follows. To use an anthropomorphism: The conversation piece mediates social change. This means that changes in the beliefs and values of the employees may be happening, which are not directly observable on the surface of daily practices. These changes may be directly or indirectly linked to the theatrical performance. The diffuse nature of the development of such changes does not allow to establish a clear causal relationship. However, the empirical material collected during the study points into the direction of such a mechanism of action."

PROBLEM-SOLVING

Forum Theatre applied as a prototype for organisational problem solving is what Augusto Boal had in mind when he invented the term. Being spectators to relevant problems, illustrated in realistic interactions, gives an enhanced overall understanding of the complexity and interdependence of organisational life, and being able to 'manipulate' real human beings (actors) or would-be actors - instead of trying to imagine what could or would happen – actually makes problem solving more realistic. It is possible to test hypotheses 'live' and to understand that often it is not enough to change one person or one element; organisations work in more complex or systemic ways. The advantage of being able to 'rewind' the play is also evident. This way it is possible to try out many variations and solutions to the problem on stage, and afterwards the spectators can make sense of what happened and why. Organisational theatre thus essentially serves as a prototype for trying out and communicating about ideas and solutions.

Another quality of Forum Theatre is the blend of fiction and reality, which spurs new and sometimes provocative insights into the life of an organisation. Being a spectator of scenes from your own life in your own organisation also allows the distance that is necessary for reflection. In our daily lives we are swirled and whirled into constant thinking, acting and reacting, and when we are always involved as participators it is difficult to obtain space for reflection. When others play our life on a stage, it adds another dimension. We are taken out of our own subjective world and suddenly see the perspectives and problems of other parties, and we see how the action of each person is interrelated with the actions of the others and how it affects the whole.

Theatre is remembered vividly - in particular because it gets highly emotional when it deals with your own life. The idea that "I carry with a smile" acts as a conversation piece, and thereby sustains a gradual process of change, is feasible because of the collective experience of the large group. Having shared this enjoyable and emotional experience helps in building a common framework, which enhances mutual understanding and invites further conversations. It stands to reason that the quality and depth of communication is improved when using scenes from the play as common references, something that may, in fact, also occur on an individual inner level.

The municipality did not undertake any follow-up to enhance the conversations that were started in the sessions, except that they did create a card deck with scenes from the play, including important lines and challenges, which they gave to all employees and encouraged people to work on. It is important to look at the long-term effects of organisational theatre and, interestingly, the questionnaires present evidence that there are probably long-term spin-offs.

TRAJECTORIES

In the Arts-in-Business framework the obvious and classical trajectory for Forum Theatre is from 'event' towards 'product', i.e. a change process. Forum Theatre is a typical 'event' as it is live, interactive, and allows multiple interpretations. Boal's overall purpose with forum theatre is to provoke change and action - not just entertainment. In fact, he regarded theatre of the oppressed as a 'weapon'[29]. Boal's mission was, however, not the aim of the managers, when they decided to use Forum Theatre. Rather they wanted to face the frustrations of the workforce and bring things up into the open for reflection and possibly, but not necessarily, to start action. The problems were complex and involved many human relationships as well as some very bureaucratic procedures and regulations that cannot be changed by the home care workers. The idea was to recognise the problems of the home care workers and take them seriously without necessarily being able to do anything about it. Thus no direct changes followed from the sessions. If, however, we regard forum theatre as serious play[30], it suggests a second trajectory from 'event' towards 'metaphor', because even if the play did not result in direct change, the response to the questionnaires shows that the theatre sessions started some important conversations in the organisation that could eventually result in more subtle, gradual improvements. This indicates a trajectory from 'events' through 'metaphor' – possibly circling into an organisational reservoir of reflection and contemplation (the organisational solar plexus of learning?) – and eventually, like rings in the water, impinging on 'products'.

In 'I carry with a smile' the role of art involves inspiration and provocation in a social setting. Three aspects of forum theatre were highlighted here: the play as a prototype for problem solving; theatre being used as an organisational mirror for reflection; and the idea that the play and the shared experience can function as a conversation piece for continuous dialogue. Forum Theatre involves both 'experimental' and 'anticipatory' learning, but because of the shyness of the participants in this case, the changes that took place were probably mostly cognitive.

GIFT

TUNE! SARAJEVO ~ CRISIS ~ MEANING ~ ART/BUS

MY METHOD

"3" → EXPERIENCE ↓, (QUALITIES)

H·J, ="MAP"

SUPREME ORDEAL

ART AND BUSINESS FOR EUROPEAN IDENTITY. ILLUSTRATING MEANINGFUL EVOLUTIONS IN BUSINESS THROUGH CLASSICAL MASTERPIECES OF MUSIC

"Music, of all the arts, reaches the most, the deepest into our experience."

Miha Pogacnik

➤ "At a time when pressures for change are at their highest, from globalisation, new technologies, product and process innovations, successful business leaders need to be at their creative best just to survive. Creativity is the hallmark of art, and artists are increasingly a source of inspiration for entrepreneurs world-wide.

Miha Pogacnik's unique contribution stems from this new consciousness, the need for creativity, imagination and perfection in business. Time after time, his input in countless business conferences has been magnificent, unexpected and unique. Through music and art, Miha Pogacnik ignites a new force in us, the power of rising above our old selves in perceiving problems and opportunities in an entirely new light, and thus striking in new directions. Miha is truly at the leading edge of business as we move towards the 21st century."[31]

Marcello Palazzi, Co-Founder & Executive Director,
Progressio Foundation Rotterdam, Netherlands

Miha Pogacnik saw the potential of Art & Business long before anyone else and has worked in the field for more than 20 years. Today Miha Pogacnik[32] uses his violin to decompose and play classical masterpieces when doing his presentations around the world as a business consultant with many companies including: ABN AMRO Bank, General Electric, J.P. Morgan, Hewlett-Packard, IBM, Microsoft, LEGO, Mitsubishi, Nike, Nokia, Novartis, Procter & Gamble, Shell, Volvo, World Bank and World Economic Forum.

THE 'CALL'
How did Miha Pogacnik happen to pick such an unusual career? When Miha was growing up in the republic of Yugoslavia (today: Slovenia), he wanted to become a violinist.

After completing his studies in Germany he went to the United States as a Fulbright Scholar, but after an initial career as a soloist, he soon realised that he did not really want to pursue this further in the traditional way. He felt the limitations that established concert life imposes on an artist who wanted to respond to the monumental changes of the 80s. Instead he felt a strong interest for social change. Destiny led him to work with handicapped children, where his challenge was to teach them how to listen, so he learned to engage their attention in various ways, always with the goal of helping the participants become at one with the process unfolding in music.

IDRIART

In 1980 Miha Pogacnik started the IDRIART movement. Initiative for the Development of Intercultural & Interdisciplinary Relations through the Arts, and the following year 1200 people were gathered at a festival in Chartres, France. Since then about 170 festivals have been held in Central Europe, Russia, Estonia, East Germany, Australia, Mexico, Brazil, New Zealand, Mongolia, Tibet, and since 1984 annually in Slovenia in Bled and later at castle Borl, Ptuj.

➡ "From the beginning, Idriart concerts have striven to realize "the spiritual meaning of the unity of art, science and religion."[33]

➡ "Idriart may be said to have not a single goal but a number of equally important goals. There is, of course, the wish to bring forward the spiritual side of music and art as a healing force so particularly needed by our times and as a moral force for raised consciousness applicable to all areas of life. Then there is the desire to bring together people of many diverse nationalities in an atmosphere of artistic sharing, thereby transcending political boundaries."[34]

➡ "With IDRIART, we have set ourselves the goal to work in such a way that everybody involved participates inwardly so intensely that new 'vistas' may open for many in a lucky moment, and not just for the performer... When artists and all participants take on the responsible role of *performer*, the festival itself becomes a work of art. "[35]

In 1990 a Dutch consultant came along to one of the Idriart festivals to give a lecture on organisational development, and when he saw Miha Pogacnik in action, he said afterwards: "Do you realise that what you are actually doing is organisational development?" Miha realised that this was his 'call', and since then his main work has been in the field of management, business and organisational consulting.

THE ART OF LISTENING
It is difficult to capture in words what Miha Pogacnik is actually trying to do with his vio-

lin and his colourful illustrations of classical music. Among other things he wants to show people the art of listening. People are good talkers, but bad listeners, he says. Miha therefore tries to create a space where listening becomes possible. Most people's minds are so full of material that the created space quickly fills up with their own thoughts and images, and that is not the idea. The idea is to completely open up and to perceive the music, to become one with the process. Through that experience we can awaken and rediscover our senses in such a way that we sense the real quality of what it is to be human. We are suddenly totally present with a different intensity and in an awake state of mind. The music is actually a "detour" to take us to that state, because the classical masterpieces of music are so beautiful that we are easily enticed into this learning space. We can, indeed, learn a lot from the classical masterpieces. Miha always arrives very well prepared for a business session. He usually has a meeting or a long telephone conversation with the client about the topic and aim of the session before he selects a piece of music that he thinks will fit the purpose. Then he makes a sketch:

➜ "This is my sketch for the first movement of Brahms' Violin Concerto which I did with London Business Forum last March. I drew how the individual journey of the hero, or of a leader, is actually the opening statement. Here is where we are and these are the heavens we want to get to. Everybody would like to go there directly, but you realise that the music must take this painful, marvellous path downwards, below the threshold into another reality and actually die. And then start anew in this very turbulent way. And then cross the threshold again in a very dangerous moment of cadenza, the 'supreme trial' of the hero's journey. Then enter the 'coda', the final statement, which is truly heavenly for those who know the first movement of Brahms' Violin Concerto."[36]

In the summer of 2003, on one of the last days of the Arts & Business conference at Castle Borl, Slovenia, Miha played the Brahms' Sonata in D minor with Diana Baker on piano. The theme was finding the 'Coda' in music – and in life. Coda stands for the final meaning. He took us, the 80 participants, on a learning journey about death and beyond, about transformation in the dreamland, about life crisis and resolution – and most of all he taught us to listen - not only to the music itself, but rather to the inner meaning, which is the real music. Even though he dissected the musical masterpiece the 'Miha way'[37] in order to explain the pulse, the breath and the heart of it, the music grew on us incredibly intensely; it went straight to our hearts. When he and Diana finally played through the whole first movement, the atmosphere of the Knights' Hall was truly heavenly. When they finished, there was no applause, but a breathless silence, a holding of the sacred space, which lasted forever and which was a silence so completely full that nobody wanted to break it. Quietly people got up and hugged each other with tears in their eyes. Outside the hall, people stood silently in small groups, hugged each other and wept, and for the rest of the day peoples' eyes had a very serene and contemplative look.

Miha's own words regarding this masterpiece being truly heavenly were an obvious understatement. According to Miha, masterpieces always illustrate meaningful evolutions through archetypes, which can reflect lived experience of one's own life - and even not-yet-lived experience of the future arising after the masterpiece. Every person, who listens and understands the archetypes of the masterpiece, will recognise some spot where they will say "Aha, here I am in my life" or "Aha, that's where we are with our orga- nisation". Miha believes that experiences like that can gradually call forth new capabili- ties in people. People learn to see and listen in new ways, which may enable them to sud- denly see complicated social constellations in new ways and also to find new ways of resolving them.

SHARPENING THE SENSES

Regarding the sharpening of the senses, the first step is to wake up the senses, because they are both over-stimulated by noise pollution and the constant sounds of modern society and at the same time under-stimulated by lack of pauses, silent moments and focus. The next step is to sharpen the senses by differentiating the different parts and voices of the music. In my interview with Miha I asked him to expand on the meaning of the senses, and he literally did, when he explained that according to the insights of Rudolf Steiner, who has influenced Miha's thinking throughout his life, there are 12 sen- ses, not only 5. These are classified in three main types of preparedness: willing (the will to act and do), feeling (feeling perception) and thinking (finding meaning). I will men- tion the 12 senses here, but not go into a deeper discussion of them, except for the rele- vant few. Willing involves touch (to be versus not to be), life (growth versus decay), movement (speed versus form) and balance (deviation versus width). Feeling concerns smell (pure versus impure), taste (genuine versus false), sight (light versus darkness) and warmth (sympathy versus antipathy). Thinking includes hearing (harmony versus disso- nance), word-language (clarity versus cover up), thought (doubt versus truth), and the sense of I (confidence versus strangeness).

Steiner's classification helps to explain the link between hearing and thinking, which is one of Miha's underlying assumptions. If we take another small digression into the Steiner universe, we find some interesting insights in relation to the effect of music, as illustrated in the model below.

According to Steiner[38], the centre of music is harmony, and harmony goes directly into human feeling, the centre of total human experience. Feeling passes into thinking and willing. The melody carries feeling into thinking, because melody makes the head of the human being accessible to feelings, whereas rhythm directs feeling into willing. Accord- ing to Rudolf Steiner, tone lies at the foundation of everything in the physical world.[39]

→ "The secret of all great music is that it is the carrier of ideas which embrace all of humankind. Through trained listening the process of this perception can be raised to con- sciousness and applied in other areas of life. Music is the only art form, which fully embraces the human condition through the visceral or body element (rhythm), heart and soul (harmony), and spirit or intellect (melody) and also is the only art form whose foun- dation lies in the spiritual rather than the physical world.[40]

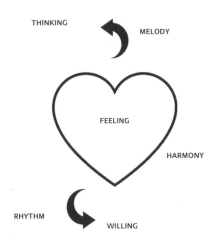

THE EFFECT OF MUSIC
(BASED ON RUDOLF STEINER)

This explanation can help us understand the first two aspects of Miha's mission and the plausible connection between them. Sharpening our senses, especially by listening to music, can set off inner journeys of reflection, which helps us make sense of our lives. As for music being an archetypal language, interesting research is being done on the effects of music on cognitive development. In an interview Paul Robertson[41], leader of the Medici Quartet, says:

→ "Another important aspect is the role of music in education and learning. We are now beginning to understand and appreciate the neurology of the musical response and its fundamental place as a basic building block that underlies complex cognitive development. Through this work, it is possible to appreciate the role of the arts, and music in particular. Because of its evolutionary history and its anatomical significance within the brain, musical response and the development of musical skill and musical language has a key role in developing other skills for us."

It is not the focus of this book to investigate this, but only to point out that apparently music has abundant potential[42]. A third aspect of Miha's work is the idea of bringing cultures together by grounding conversations in art perception. Art can educate us in such a way that we are able to enter into conversation on a deeper level than we normally do, and the artistic experience creates strong relationships and a feeling of connectedness. The kind of bonding that took place between the participants of the Brahms' sonata described above, transcends every aspect of separation and enables people to hug and truly feel love even for total strangers, because this shared experience takes us to a different level – to the universal quality of being human. The idea of Idriart is strongly grounded, but Miha's mission does not stop here. His "call of the times" is Art and Business for European Identity.

"PRACTICAL UTOPIA"

The vision is to identify and examine the most creative artistic individuals of the past 1000 years (or more) in order to discover the "formative" principles of Dante, Shakespeare, Goethe, Beethoven, Mozart, Rembrandt, Gaudi, etc. and through that process recreate our European identity for all of European society, including politics and business. A different and grounded European management style is needed for the future and this must be a very deep and meaningful co-creation between arts and business. Miha calls this project for "practical Utopia".

➤ "We are seeking to create a context in society, a context where art would provide a space in which problems would be dealt with. And of course, it would be important to create this experimental inspirational space in the middle of corporate and organisational development and reality. The art would get a chance to renew itself in its process, which means that artists will learn to look at what they do in a new way. So artists would grow and so would our hosts, who would discover that the process of immersing oneself into artistic activities would help them to grow new organs, new capacities to deal with the difficult future that is coming. We do not get equipped for leadership at conventional business schools or any other education as they are today. Artists should be where the most important decisions are made. And the artist is the one who is making the decisions – in other words, the artist within. So every human being can in some way be awakened to become an artist in a particular way."[43]

TRAJECTORIES

When Miha Pogacnik performs and interacts with people it clearly belongs to the arena of 'events'. Miha's intention, however, is to develop people's existing 'capabilities' through music - and to grow new capabilities ("organs"). These capabilities are primarily to sharpen the senses, especially the art of listening, but also the ability to focus and to be part of the process. His aim is to initiate a continuous inner transformation by sending an arrow of music into the 'solar plexus of learning'. Miha's second aim is to unite people across cultures (as in the many Idriart festivals) through great masterpieces of music.

The qualities expressed in this case study clearly demonstrate art as beauty, inspiration and sacred, but also involve elements of provocation and of social bonding. The case study points to the intriguing allegation that music is a different language for understanding and coping with life.

WHY NOT CATAPULT A BRAND NEW VOLVO? BUYING AN ARTIST TO STIR AND PROVOKE NEW IDEAS AND CONVERSATIONS AT VOLVO CAR CORPORATION

For a year the artist Michael Brammer has been on the payroll of the Volvo Car Corporation. His job was to meet once a month with Peter Rask, then global marketing director of Volvo Car Corporation, and to come up with new ideas that sprang to his mind, which would somehow challenge and develop Volvo's business. The immediate outcome was that the employees were both disturbed and provoked and furthermore the Volvo Car Corporation received a lot of media attention.

→ "If you look at it from the low end, then it has been good business for Volvo. It has been in the press so much that, when you evaluate it in relation to the cost of advertising, the price has been paid several times. That is not, however, where the value should be placed. The value should be appointed to some of the things Peter Rask says, e.g. that he becomes a better leader."[44]

Michael Brammer is an example of a goal-oriented artist, who works strategically with the media and with key people, both public and corporate, for promoting his artwork.[45] Two prior projects led to the cooperation with Volvo. The first was a film project, called Mr. Who, which involved 50 companies.

→ "The film is about the shortage you are born with. You can get irritated because the surroundings are so influential that it is difficult to see what is actually interesting. From I started in kindergarten until I went to school, I recall my parents' attitudes – and it is not very strange, I suppose, that I was influenced to become an ordinary fool, where life is only about getting a good education and buying a house as nice as that of your schoolmates - and all these things. That life is about going to work in the morning and going home and having weekends off; that your life, if you draw it in a diagram, is a straight line from 20 to 70. I don't think that is satisfactory... The intention is to show this in the movie, where there are 6 episodes of Mr. Who. What he is best at is mowing the lawn. He lives according to the precepts, so to speak. One section is called Mr. Who at work, one is about Mr. Who washing his car, one is about Mr. Who coming home from work, one is about Mr. Who playing with his children while Mrs. Who cooks, etc. Totally normal episodes and they live in a fantastic house, a dream house. They have a dream car, he has a dream wife and two dream kids, he has everything and would therefore never disappoint his teacher or his parents in any way. The film is then seen by a pixie - all families and persons have a pixie - and Mr. Who's pixie is very very enthusiastic about products. The whole world and our way of thinking is a product mind-set, we use 90% of our energy on either thinking or talking about products, no matter who we speak to, the subject is always prices or a loan you are about to deal with. You go to work and produce, and you go home and use. Everything is centred around this, at least 90% or more. There is nothing else. So every time Mr. Who takes out a product, the pixie hides and as we see the logo, we jump into an advertisement, which we have borrowed from the participating companies. We have cut the advertising film into several bits and glued them together randomly. Advertisements are already terrible, but this makes it worse. The intention is to try and ask some questions of the spectators' imagination. What can you use it for?"

The other project, which received a lot of attention from the media, was the cooperation between Michael Brammer and Hanne Beck Hansen, chief of police, and Tryg, a Danish insurance company, who sponsored the project. The three parties met once a month during a year regarding the decoration of the internal courtyard of the Copenhagen police headquarters. Michael Brammer recalls:

➜ "I knew, of course, that I couldn't be 'granted a safe-conduct' in decorating the internal police court yard. But how far could I go? I was interested in going as far as at all possible. Just creating something they thought was nice was not interesting. So I contacted some young people who made graffiti and stuff like that and found people whom I thought had a good sense of humour and who were skilful at drawing and were associated with the Academy of Fine Arts, but who also had a personal relationship with the police. They were not exactly paragons of virtue. … I had ideas and they had ideas, it took four months and we made a masterpiece. In my opinion it was really good and it would take two hours to read through all the bubbles. It was a five-metre tall painting, 126 metres long and there were a lot of details, e.g. mice, who had conversations, police mice, who arrested other mice. We had all of Copenhagen in it, the harbour, the space above, under water, the whole city in a painting. … The police [in the painting] were very hospitable to all, they were so nice, and they all had their penises sticking out of their trousers. There was a demonstration and they gave paving stones, which were hash cakes, to the demonstrators. I really tried to make them understand that this form of humour was young humour, and that their own humour was more like a soap opera, because they were over 50, and asking them whether it was the people over 50 they wanted to speak to or the young people who see Beavis and Butthead? When they saw the artwork, they said they would cancel the exhibition. … But I wasn't that stupid; I had made another painting, because I knew that they might reject it. So I had painted a painting where the police danced boogie-woogie all the way round with their hands on each other's shoulders. So I said that I would be happy to come up with a new suggestion and that I could produce it in 2 – 3 weeks. So I brought it in and there were a lot of people from Tryg, the sponsors; we had a PR company, an advertising agency and an Internet company there. There were about 20 of us. So they dared not reject it once more, and they accepted it. If I had brought this painting in the first time, they would have said no, that dancing boogie-woogie is ridiculing the police; some people would have been offended. Instead it would have ended with a floral decoration all around the courtyard. So those were the tactics."

Michael Brammer finds that his role as an artist is to stir and provoke in order to make people ask questions about the way they live and to make corporations conscious of their self-glorification and complacency. After the two projects, mentioned above, he thought up the next project, which was to be a partnership between him and a company, where he would generate ideas for the company triggered by his own irritation. With this in mind Brammer kept his eyes open towards potential companies, and one day in a Danish newspaper he read an interview with Volvo director Peter Rask. He called him and explained that he wanted to show him a piece of art that he had made earlier. He also explained that he was collaborating with the Copenhagen police on an art project. It took six months to set up a meeting, but they finally met, first in Sweden, then in Copenhagen and that was the start of the partnership with the Volvo Car Corporation, which ran from May 2001 to May 2002. Brammer's first idea, which was implemented, was building a small wooden house in the main foyer. In the house he placed a jazz guitarist, who should serve herbal tea for the employees that were invited into the house for two minutes. Outside he made an artificial lawn with a fence made by a garden hose, and he bought two remote-controlled racing cars. Brammer himself challenged the employees to race against him, sitting under a big sign "Don't stress my friend".

➔ "He [the jazz musician] was to go out of the house, and when somebody came he was to say: 'Hello, would you like to hear a little tune? It only takes two minutes.' 'Shall I sit in there?' 'Yes, you are to sit in there and listen to it and drink a cup of tea.' 'That is nonsense.' 'OK, it only takes one minute, have you got a minute? Then half a minute?' And then, of course, they could not help it at last, so they went inside and he played for 30 seconds and asked: 'Do you want the next $1^{1}/_{2}$ minutes?' Yes, then they wanted it. After two minutes he stopped in the middle of it and said: 'And now you will go back to work, and the next one can enter.' Regarding the racing field, when I got someone inside to drive, he would push forward, driving way too fast so that the car rolled over the water hose. Then I said: 'You have to sit down.' 'No, that is not for you to decide.' 'Yes, they are my cars, it is my project and I am the artist who made it all, so I decide and I invite you to race with me, and this is an art project that deals with relating to stress, so if you want to be part of it, you have to sit down.' Then they would sit down. 'And if you will please try to relate to your capacity. I have just seen you drive, you race way too fast, you do not have the capacity to go that fast, so you must try to act according to your ability. Have a try at driving at a speed that allows you to drive it for a whole round. It can actually move very slowly.' Then I tried to show this. 'After five rounds you can easily manage it and then you can lean back and then your hands don't sweat anymore, then you don't make mistakes.' That is a way of relating to stress, isn't it? The main point is that you relate to it. After I had been sitting there for a week I could race around the course without mistakes. Some people were very insulted by this project. It had nothing to do with art ... So I insulted some people and that was very good, I thought, because then it created a debate."

Brammer's most controversial idea was, however, the Volvo-catapult. It came out of a conversation regarding how Volvo should introduce their new 4-wheel drive Volvo at the big car exhibition in Detroit. During the conversation, they came up with some very traditional ideas, at least according to Brammer, and as he challenged them they challenged him back to come up with a better idea. And even though Brammer at first said no, his imagination started working and he constructed the Volvo-thrower.

➤ "It (the car) has to land on something soft, it must not crash, it is not a destructive act. I am not interested in creating something destructive. So it can probably drive afterwards. That is even more remarkable, I think, if they want their security stuff to work. But actually it has to be a big soft heart with a target on it and with a hole in it, so the car will hit love. That is what it is all about. Then there will be a competition in which they choose 10 participants, and then there must be a steering chair. You could invite CNN, BBC and other media to choose the personality who will shoot. CNN and BBC would compete on this project. The basic idea of the project is to ask: 'What is the most irritating thing about cars?' There are two things in my opinion, the first is that you can be killed by driving them, and the second is that cars are a status symbol that can be used for only one thing, that is, to crush other people. .... Therefore we want to do something silly with the car... talk about why cars are irritating. Can you imagine how much press Volvo would get?"

The idea has remained an artistic prototype. The Volvo Car Corporation would not go through with it, but it certainly gave them a lot of publicity in Denmark and Sweden. Michael Brammer is now working on making an art exhibition instead, with realistic scenes of the implementation. There will be drawings made by engineers with exact measurements regarding the thickness of the iron plates, how much force is needed, precisely how far it will fly, how it will land and how it will move through the air. People can try it out (with the model) and try to hit the hole in the big heart, and when it hits the target there will be a fanfare with a Volvo song "Throw your Volvo, because in a Volvo you can let your mind go." The other part of the exhibition, "Don't stress", will consist of a discothèque for cows cut out of big pieces of wood. The cows are dancing with drinks in their hands, and the discothèque is full of smoke, steam and hay, and disco music that goes "moo" and "oink".

ART AS PROVOCATION
Michael Brammer's work is a compelling example of art as provocation. The spectrum of provocation begins by stirring, disturbing, then provoking, and ends by insulting.

Michael Brammer deliberately went all the way. This might have worked if the conditions had been different. As it was it seems that more people were insulted and rejected than constructively provoked. In retrospect Peter Rask, the initiator of the project on the part of the Volvo Car Corporation, replied as follows, when asked what he would have done differently: "Taken more time to explain the project. Not forced it, but let it work organically, from within. If there is no understanding from the staff, it won't work." The staff was highly sceptical. Michael Brammer explains: "You can say that neither Peter nor I had tried this before, so we had no practice in how to introduce this project to the employees and how important it was to bring them in on this. It turned out that it was very important to introduce it to the employees. It was done over their heads, and this insulted them. They were told nothing, and suddenly I appeared; who was I, why was I there?"

So the first learning lesson is that a proper introduction is very important, stating the visions and goals of the project and explaining the role of the artist.

If we compare this collaboration to the PAIR project, there is a difference regarding both duration and being artist-in-residence versus artist-ex-residence. The Volvo project lasted 1 year, whereas PAIR lasted 10 years. Furthermore Brammer never became part of the Volvo organisation, as he visited once a month and stayed only for the events. In the PAIR project the artists were invited inside the organisation, and the scientists were therefore exposed to the artistic process, which enabled much more learning and interaction.

In neither of the cases was a follow-up process carried out after the events, which could have helped an organisational learning process towards 'integrated learning'. There were no facilitated meetings with discussions about what the events had brought up, e.g. on stress in the Volvo Car Corporation. There were no reflections, no sharing, and no conversations for gathering the fruits of the project.

Other learning opportunities apparently emerged. Brammer's Volvo-catapult prototype prompted the collision between two different ways of thinking. In fact, this offered a rich opportunity for innovation, but evidently this was neither seen nor seized. When great differences of perspectives meet, it can lead to two opposite trajectories, disruptive or constructive[46]. The difference that makes a difference is, according to my prior research, the quality of the relationships, as introduced in chapter 3. There was no common ground to build on, and the 'antagonistic dialogue' became a clash instead of innovative crystallisation. As the project had neither been properly introduced, promoted internally nor been made a part of a strategic conversation, the opportunity was not apprehended. It seems that in this case the artist was more strategic in his thinking than the corporation, at least in relation to the media. He brought the project into the media and through that both Michael Brammer and the Volvo Car Corporation had a lot of publicity. Maybe the Volvo catapult was considered controversial, but Volvo stood out as 'courageous' and the project as 'unique'.

On a more personal level, however, the meeting between opposites succeeded. Peter Rask has expressed the following: "His ideas [Michael Brammer's] have always had a lot of energy. They have always made me laugh! Personally I felt that it made me a better leader, I became better at stimulating and motivating."[47] This was perhaps an unintended spin-off effect, but nevertheless an outcome that could give rise to proposing new types of mentorships or coaching. This has, in fact, already been done by Art & Business, UK[48] and is also part of project Catalyst at Unilever.

TRAJECTORIES

Michael Brammer's task was rather well defined: to come up with new ideas that could shake up the organisation and inspire the employees towards more creativity. The hope was that this would also have an effect on customer relations. In the framework of the Arts-in-Business matrix, the project evidently starts in the top right arena of 'products'. The Volvo Car Corporation hired an artist because of his creativity and his mind-set. From the top right corner the project creates several trajectories into the three other arenas. The first idea that is implemented is the little house in the foyer, which belongs to the arena of 'events', as it concerns a direct interaction between artists and employees. It must have made at least some people reflect on the role of art, on their work and on stress. The idea of the Volvo-catapult was created as a prototype, which started a debate about marketing in the organisation, but also became a good story in the media because of its provocative nature. Prototype and 'metaphor' are similar because both raise important questions and start relevant conversations - in this case about values and marketing. Finally Peter Rask has stated that he became a better leader, because he learnt something about how to stimulate and motivate the employees, which points to the arena of 'capabilities':

➙ "Signing a contract with no content has no logical explanation – but then again, as head of Volvo's Marketing division it is my job to think outside the box. This gives me the opportunity to be inspired by talking with Michael Brammer – and this inspiration can be used in my leadership to generate creativity."[49]

We thus identified three aspects of learning. The first concerned the element of artistic provocation, of challenging people's values and attitudes, or bringing disturbance into the organisation. This disturbance was both cognitive and behavioural. The second perspective was the new and very provocative ideas about marketing, which led to important debates on the marketing strategies and media coverage. The third was the individual learning process that took place during the monthly meetings, where Peter Rask was exposed to an artist's way of thinking.

All in all, this project has generated a lot of learning, from both the mistakes and the successes, from the intended outcomes as well as the unintended spin-offs. It is a unique example of art as provocation and anarchy, of a corporation deliberately buying uncertainty, challenge and discomfort in the hope that this will add new creative energy to the organisation.

Urban fiction

a new wave of photographers

I used to only take black and white – now all I want to take is colour

The longer I looked, the more I saw

CATALYST FOR CHANGE THROUGH PERSONAL DEVELOPMENT. APPLYING A VARIETY OF ART FORMS FOR A STRATEGIC PROCESS OF TRANSFORMATION

➜ "We are a food and ice cream company and we have a great impact on people's lives through the very fact that we all need food. But I would like us not only to give people the basic food and calories. I would like there to be a magic in the food and ice cream, for it to enrich their lives the way that great brands do. Levi's jeans are not just a pair of trousers, they give you a whole other set of benefits. They make you feel better about yourself, about your clothes, about your life. I want our food to be more like that and that requires my people to think much more creatively about the way we do things, the way we advertise, the packaging designs, the way we communicate with each other within the company … *and I also want us to have that magic ingredient, which our competitors may not have and which allows us to do things in a more radical and creative way, a more joyful way, a more positive and inspiring way. I want to have a greater sense of adventure in the business, in the way we serve our customers, a bit of a surprise element, and I think that the Catalyst creative programme has helped to contribute towards that and I think it still does.*"

(James Hill, CEO of Unilever Ice cream and Frozen Food, Walton)

Unilever's project Catalyst is the most strategic, long-term and encompassing example of Arts-in-Business I have come across in my research. Strategic because Catalyst was conceived as part of an imperative strategic shift at Unilever, bringing a new 'enterprise culture' to life. Thus the timing was perfect when chairman James Hill met Alastair Creamer, the architect and producer of Catalyst:

➜ "…the reason it came about was that Unilever as a whole around 1998 and 1999 was going through a tough time. Their shares were dropping and it rethought through its whole strategy, its global strategy and as a result of that it emerged smiling in early 1999, this is the new strategy, there were 6 parts to it, it is called 'path to growth'; we are going to grow faster than we have ever done before and part of the key areas of that growth is our people, and the way we choose to express that is through this strategic thrust called 'enterprise culture'. … And this is where the brilliance of James Hill and Keith Weed came in because they saw immediately that they had to find ways to bring this to life. It was a moment of serendipity. We came into each others' vision - if you like - at that point."[50]

Catalyst has already been running for 4 years and is still being expanded to more Unilever companies. Unilever[51] was created in 1930 when the British soapmaker Lever Brothers merged with the Dutch margarine producer, Margarine Unie. Today Unilever employs 247,000 people and is one of the world's leading suppliers of fast-moving consumer goods. Unilever's corporate centres are London and Rotterdam. Project Catalyst started in London in 1999 at Lever Fabergé, Kingston (400 employees), in 2002 it was introduced to Ice Cream & Frozen Food, Walton (400 employees), and in 2004 it will be extended to Unilever UK (250 employees). Catalyst is all encompassing, firstly because it involves the arts on four levels: as decoration, as entertainment, instrumentally, and, most importantly, as a strategic process of personal and organisational transformation; and secondly because of the variety of the arts applied: actors, directors, circus, clowns, stand-up comics, business writers, novelists, poets, play writers, painters, drawers, cartoonists, perfumers, fashion designers, fabric designers, electronic designers, musicians, filmmakers, photographers, bookbinders, multimedia artists, library services, cooks, and reading agencies.

CATALYST

Catalyst is a project applying the arts and creative industries to facilitate organisational transformation in order to create an "enterprise culture". "It's about *igniting* your *passion*, unlocking *creative potential*, being inspired and *sharing* these experiences with your colleagues."[52] The project was conceived by Alastair Creamer, multitalented artist and arts manager, and Alastair is still the main driver and idea generator, but he has been assisted since 2001 by Isabelle King (at Walton) and now also by Katherine Mellor (at Kingston). They have an annual budget of £240,000 for activities, which is supplemented by funding for specific projects according to proposals, e.g. from Art & Business or from central Unilever UK. Catalyst maintains a high degree of autonomy but is, on the organisational chart, a part of Human Resources. Catalyst is a real experiment, which, in the words of chairman James Hill, means: "Like any creative process there are some failures, so Catalyst has produced maybe 200 or 300 specific activities over the last 3 or 4 years. Of those, probably 25 per cent were not really good at all, we wished that we had not done them." Permitting failure[53], however, sends an important signal to the organisation and James Hill praises Catalyst for having "a significant impact on the boldness of the people in the company." Catalyst is thus successful - also in its failures, because people learn from them – and, according to chairman James Hill, the success concerns personal, business as well as organisational and societal development:

➤ " … and I think that by exposing people to the visual arts, to the theatre and to poetry, the skill levels in design, video and therefore advertising and personal communication, both written and verbal, have gone up. People are being more challenged. Then I think there is something about working in a company, who do more things than just make 'Short' (washing) powder and fish fingers, a company that has a broader vision of society and on how it can enrich the lives of the people in it, so if I take the impact on people, a significant number of people have involved themselves in mentoring schemes with arts organisations or give a couple of days a month to be involved in a local theatre or a dance group. We have had competitions, people have written short stories, we had a wonderful short story competition and the levels of achievement there were very, very high, and I myself have my own story about how it has enriched my life, but I think there are many people, whose lives, I believe - you can ask them - have been significantly enriched by their participation in this program."

Obviously there are a lot of interesting tales to tell about project Catalyst. I have chosen three projects, which were important to the people I interviewed, and which at the same time are representative of the many. The first, 'Urban Fiction', is about photography and new ways of seeing, the second, 'Sticky', is about experiencing life to the maximum by exceeding boundaries, and the third, 'Live and Direct', is based on theatre rehearsal techniques and aims at team development and culture building.

URBAN FICTION

According to Alastair Creamer the core elements of 'enterprise culture' are expression and emotion. This also happens to be the profound expertise of the arts and, in fact, the very elements, which the business of Unilever is about. People have an emotional connection to most of Unilever's products, not a technical one. As for expression, this is mainly done through advertising, "but you also need to give people permission to express themselves as well, and express THEMSELVES and not just 'I am an employee at Unilever and therefore I have to talk in this tone of voice'." Photography is connected to expression through what you choose to focus on and how you compose the image to express your personal view.

The following story is told by Alastair Creamer, who participated in the course himself:

➤ " ... So the idea was to work with the photographer about ways of seeing. How do we look at the world? We sat down with the photographer Rut Blees Luxemburg[54], who is a well-known German art photographer. We had worked a lot with her in the past and she struck me as being someone who had a unique approach to photography. She takes a lot of photographs at night, and there is no one in them. She uses natural light, very long exposures, and creates incredible atmosphere, *but it was the process, the ways she worked that fascinated me the most*. She basically takes one or two photographs for her image; she does not take 35 or a 100, clicking away the whole time. She edits in her mind until she has got it absolutely right and of course, at night there are less variable factors, but all the work is done in her mind, and then she takes one or two final photographs. And that as a process fascinates me. Here we work the opposite way..."

➡ "The first thing she said was: "This is great, absolutely fine, but I want a couple of rules. One is that I do not want this to be about the technical side of photography. So there are no 'boys' toys', I do not want blokes coming up with their highly sophisticated cameras; everybody is going to have the cheapest disposable cameras. I do not really care whether people have taken photos professionally before, everyone gets the same equipment, so it is really a level playing field. What I am interested in is helping people how to look at the world, and that will be very much through the big reflection of how I work." So that was a really interesting idea. We then constructed 3 workshops that started about 4-7 pm. One was here (Kingston), one was in her studio and one was at a gallery....

You had to go to them all; that was the deal. So there were 12 places available and we got about 38 people applying and we ended up with 15. So we did these three workshops: two at the end of last year, one at the beginning of this year. And they were on different topics, one was on essence, one was on chaos and one was about choice. These ideas came about through conversations between Rut and me. Essence is a very important thing to us, how do you get the essence of a product in a photograph? So she spoke about essence and then she spoke about chaos, which was about mistakes really, how you can fail, and then the final one was about choices, because by then we had taken the photos, and then it was how do you choose?"

➡ " ... It was her eye leading her to say, I know the story you want to tell and have you thought of telling it in this way? And it was just the most invigorating, exciting moment for everybody, and she was posing mistakes with photos that we did not think were very good, or suggesting a propping or a way in which you might choose to place them in order to tell a story. She would start asking us questions and it was just a really stunning moment, and then she would go off to the next person. And each of us would sit down and think about it, maybe go back - and almost invariably she had chosen photographs in a combination that everybody was excited about. It told their story better, she managed to tell our stories, and basically, all she was doing was telling us to keep our mind open. Just because that is out of focus, just because that has not got what you thought it had in it, it does not mean to say that it is wrong. It was a great set of simple lessons in life and the magic, magic is maybe the wrong word because magic indicates that I do not know how I have done it, and she told us how she did it. As a result of that we then photocopied all the works downstairs, we mounted them on foam boards like the 'Sticky' project, it was quite simple and then we held an exhibition of these photographs here in early February and it was stunning. People were really proud and it was a big thing for the business; we invited a lot from outside as well. It was up here for three months and then it went to Blackfriars, Unilever's office and it also went to Walton, so it has done a little tour. And what we decided to do was to accompany the exhibition with a series of postcards.... Obviously with photographs you usually get negatives, we call these positives ...."

➡ " ... this was a project that was a way of seeing for marketers but we focused it very clearly on treating everybody as creative individuals. We are doing this for you. The fact that it has got a link into ways of seeing and you are a marketer will mean that it will have a payback to business. But it is purely for you to desire to turn up to these three workshops, and then to come in and hang the exhibition over the weekend; give up one day of your weekend to help us hang up the exhibition. .... So that is the way we did it. And it was just the most fantastic success, and it taught us a lot about the way we used the gallery downstairs, it taught us a lot about the kind of things people want to see, I think we probably have to do a photography project in one way or another every year. I think Rut got a lot out of it. We, the individuals, got massive amounts out of just being close to her and working with her."

→ " ... The relationship was extended without commissioning her to do the work, so we have got four works by Rut in our collection, and we have given her a lot of help and support in the various things she has done, so it is a really good new tool for creating a relationship, and I think we will continue to work with her and she now understands the way in which we operate, so it is a very good relationship."

→ "... so that is Urban Fiction. It is quite a small project, 15 -17 people but it had a huge impact. Very visual and I think one of the interesting things that we learned as we went through it was the real significance of photography."

STICKY

Sticky was the project you encountered on the first page, where Adrian Greystoke, a 23-year old marketing trainee from Unilever, highlighted how much it meant to him to be able to experience life at its maximum through work. The background for this project was a live outdoor performance that was rehearsed by a group of very talented English theatre directors, Improbable Theatre and World Famous, and presented at the Mayor's Thames Festival in London. The show travels around the world and involves 15 volunteers, such as people who have been in prison, people from a local community, local actors, etc. In 2003 they wanted to try to work with business people, which they had never done before, and the Catalyst people seized the opportunity to involve 15 volunteers from Unilever. One of the participants, Eileen McLennan, wrote a diary[55]:

→ "A group of 15 people come together to put on a show - STICKY. They will be participants in its production and staging. STICKY is a 45 minute piece of outdoor theatre in which various tableaux and images are created using sticky tape. These tableaux are created by the team. At the end of the show the tower is set alight. It is spectacular.

Monday: Rob and Julian have put this show together out of sheer love of theatre and spectacle. When you tell people about Sticky there's always a reaction: it sounds bizarre - a show made out of sellotape and newspaper, using pyrotechnics - and Improbable Theatre did face considerable resistance, but persevered. There is no particular financial profit to be had and the result of Sticky is difficult to quantify - a week's work by a whole team to give 45 minutes of joy to an audience. Tens of thousands of people have seen the show and loved it.

Thursday: We then take a tour of the set - a steel structure with a tower which will emerge from beneath the stage; four "goalposts" which, at the start of the show, are where we bind sticky tape into a web type structure, and a crane from which the "fly" lady will do just that from an alarming height. I immediately feel envy – I would love that job! Rob points out all the hazards: limited space to work in and lights, wires and equipment everywhere. He points out again that we have to "look out for each other".

The Show's Structure

Rob then explains the show's structure: a complex sequence, which involves all fifteen of us working closely together.

The key to the show's success is a sense of transformation

Opening: Phase I

Weaving a web around "goalposts" at four corners of the set. Do this with an increasing sense of urgency.

Pick up spider parts - at this point not identifiable as such, they look like pieces of pagan imagery.

Walk "ceremoniously and majestically" (Rob's words) with these, weaving in and out, and onto the stage.

On stage, gradually shape into the spider creature with wings.

The whole transformation is against a hybrid of music: house, techno, classical and new age.

Phase II

In the distance the audience sees a tiny, fragile, fly: a flying ballet artiste dangled about 300 ft in the air from the end of a crane. She is gradually levered on to the spider, who is going berserk at the thought of easy food; she disappears into the back of the spider; it appears she has been eaten.

The spider gradually disintegrates - we leave the stage and leave our spider parts.

Phase III - the Tower

An articulated steel structure rises in the middle of the stage, transforming the back of the spider into the top of the dome of a 200ft high tower. It is lit, and given life, colour and energy with pyrotechnics.

We will be part of the pyrotechnics (cool!) we will take our places and are handed our nine-foot bamboo "chestnut" lanterns, which are lit and surround the tower.

They gradually will go out, then the team will place them backstage.

We enter the dome structure and it will gradually rise, whilst we will attach sticky tape in what sounds like a complicated way. The sellotape will become the lines of the windows and, cleverly lit, this will give a spectacular stage effect. Quite tricky and dangerous, because the steel structure rises to become a 200ft tower, with us inside it, stretching rolls of sellotape! We will then clear, and go into Phase IV.

Phase IV Cogs and Machines
We go backstage and collect our individual parts of the machine. Again a transformation takes place. We carry these to the front of the stage to make the display, and then hand them to the crew and a machine structure is built. Already the parts suggest this looks like something out of the Industrial Revolution.
It is lit and there is a wonderful firework display!

Phase V
Out of the darkness flies the tiny fly who has survived the ordered chaos.
Rob explains that the structure is an archetype, which allows the audience the freedom to enjoy the show on a number of levels:
- For the sake of spectacle alone
- Seeing nature triumph over machinery (as this stops grinding, the fly is seen to emerge, still alive)
- Man's spirit victorious over industrialisation - the fly serving as a symbol of organic life
- As a comment on the events of September 11th – an inevitable comparison with the Twin Towers"

Saturday: THE SHOW: At 7.45 we hear "ten minutes please". We don our boiler suits and protective gear and walk out to take our opening positions. There are THOUSANDS of people in front of us!

The music starts and we start to wind the sellotape. We suddenly hear a panic on our side from our audience - our goalpost is falling down! Adrian keeps his cool and calmly walks with his sellotape and holds it up until a stagehand gets to it. We carry on. We perform the spider animation, and I can hear the audience's reaction - they are excited by the spectacle and sheer audacity of the show - they keep cheering, they are a fantastic crowd. When we get to building the tower I feel amazing, I look out and see hundreds of cameras flashing, not only from the crowd but from the London Eye as well! As we hold out our lanterns and the pyrotechnics kick in, they roar their approval. I'll never forget how this all felt. The haunting Gorecki music makes me want to cry. We start the cog sequence and I'm gutted, it's nearly over, and it's all happened too soon. Everything just goes so well, the team really works, what a buzz, what a joy!

We watch from our places the outrageous fireworks and for me the thrilling thing is that the crowd just can't believe their luck, that they've turned up and this is for them, this imaginative, daring piece of drama. I can hear kids behind me - Look at that! Wow!

Then we take a bow and it's all over. We go MAD and throw our arms around each other, laughing, shouting. We've done it. Yo! If that's not experiencing the joy of a team, I don't know what is."

Back in business: "What can I bring back? Well, my aim is to bring the colour, daring, contrast and innovation that is "Sticky" into my work and my life. I got the opportunity to do something really different, and it has stimulated my thinking. .... Just a small thing, but this company is partly about the FUN of Ice Cream, which we seem to forget! At a meeting the other day as a guest with a nervous looking sampling agency, I changed my attitude. I went in and said how delighted I was to be at the meeting, we had great new products, shall we try some. Adrian, another person on the Sticky week, immediately picked up on what I was trying to do, he said "Yes, Uncovered is gorgeous, I'll get the samples". We explained to them why the product was different and new - the cracking chocolate - how would we sample such a thing and make it live for consumers? The whole spirit of the meeting changed, the thinking flowed, we had fun. It was pure "Sticky".

This is the way I want to work, and work with people, from now on. On two projects I am currently working on, I have deliberately pushed out and extended the thinking. Good results have come about from this: things we "can't do" suddenly became things we can do!

The key thing that Sticky has done for me is it has broadened my point of view, and now I am striving for more and more. That week has made me challenge myself that much more, and always ask the question: - can I, or this team, do this better?

Thanks to the Catalyst team for making this happen for me, and to Improbable/World Famous for opening their door to us. A wonderful experience."   *Eileen, September 2003*

LIVE + DIRECT

This project aims at supporting teams in giving and receiving feedback by applying theatrical rehearsal techniques. Earlier Catalyst had been working with actor and director Fiona Lesley on communication issues (16 two-hour workshops around lunch), where she brought in a musician, an actor, a coach and a director. This relationship has now been strengthened by having a whole group, the MAP, of actors, directors and facilitators involved, in fact, in-residence for three months. The process has been designed by Alastair Creamer with Fiona Lesley and Chris Higgins in three main stages in order to ensure that it will be embedded in the organisation. This will be followed by an evaluation and a new challenge. Furthermore a lot of time and energy has gone into the preparatory phases involving two people from HR regarding the contents, as the goal of this project is to engage 80% of Lever Fabergé and 50% of Ice Cream & Frozen Food. The preparation included two pilot workshops to ensure that the workshops would have the desired effects. The process is the following:

1. Live + Direct workshops (about 40 workshops with working teams)
2. 8 of these teams will have an arts associate (actor) assigned for 2-3 months
3. Live Report, a theatrical piece on what the actors have seen at Unilever, followed by feedback and discussion with the audience (Unilever employees)
4. Evaluation by an external person

5. Catalyst will issue 3 challenges to the people at Kingston and Walton

LIVE + DIRECT WORKSHOPS

The idea of the 3-hour workshops is that they should be attended by working teams, which involve around 15 people. When I was visiting Unilever, I was invited to participate in one of these workshops, so here is a first-hand account.

When I entered the room two guys from the MAP were playing ball at the centre of the room, a large open room with no tables and chairs, except for one table and a few chairs by the wall. Chris Higgins, who was in charge of the workshop, was making a few notes on a piece of paper and came over to welcome me, and I was introduced to the rest of them, Andy, Al and Dawn. When people starting coming in, they received name tags and were immediately invited to join the ball game, which was now turned into a game about keeping the ball moving and not letting it hit the floor. It was a nice way of engaging people as they entered instead of the normal sitting and waiting till everybody had arrived. When we were all there Chris said welcome and emphasised that we were now in a practice room and that there was no right way, it was merely a question of practising. After one more energiser we were invited to sit down on the floor and watch a rehearsal of a small scene from a play with 2 actors. We watched how Chris worked with the actors and noticed that Chris seemed genuinely interested, he was not domineering, instead he came up with suggestions, which were very specific, and importantly: he started by asking questions to the actors like "how do you see this character?" "What do you find interesting about him?" "What is his problem?" "How could you make him even more interesting?" "What kind of relationship do the 2 people have?" They rehearsed the scene 3 times with intermittent feedback conversations and everybody agreed that it changed a lot and got more interesting. This took us into the first conversation about feedback, based on the observations of the participants regarding what and how Chris was working and which effect it had on the actors. Chris pointed out that one of the important basics for good feedback is building trust, as this will accelerate the forming of good relationships. Therefore we tried some more energisers, one of catching each other, except when we were hugging someone (max. one minute); repeating the game but now thinking more of how we could help each other; one game standing in a circle passing around a ball of energy by clapping, etc. We also tried to tell stories in pairs, building the story word by word as each person was allowed only one word at a time. This way of telling a story would often get us to a place where we would not have gotten by ourselves.

After this we sat down again to see another scene. This was an incredibly simple scene of moving a chair. Dawn took a chair and placed it in the middle of the room and Andy sat down on it. What was interesting were the interpretations people had: One person said that Dawn was flirting, another said she was cheeky. The point of the exercise was to call people's attention to the difference between observing/noticing and interpreting/having an opinion about it. What could actually be observed? And what did we personally read into the way she smiled and made eye contact? We often do not discern between these things. The lesson was to say: I notice that ....., my opinion is ....., because I...... (the 'because I' concerned one's life experience). After a break we did a couple of exercises in pairs. The first was an invitation for people to ask someone else for work related feedback. The second task involved each person picking one sentence out of 5 (e.g. "you are going to miss me"), rehearse it while walking around the room, and make up a small story with it. The next step was to rehearse it with a partner and having your partner play your scene. The learning from this was that it is quite hard to get people to act out your idea, at least the way you imagined it. But actually they might do it in an unexpected and better way if given the freedom to do it their way.

At this point 5 styles[55]for giving feedback were explained:

- Suggest (Could you try ...)
- Enquire (I'm interested to know why ...)
- Reflect (I notice ...)
- Support (I like/appreciate how you ...)
- Challenge (I need something more ...)

After this the very first scene was played again, this time asking the participants for feedback. Five pieces of paper with the keyword for each specific style were placed on the floor, and the participants had to stand by the style they wanted to use when feeding back to the actors. The scene was played once more with a new feedback round and finally played one last time. This was rewarded with great applause. The two final questions concerned each participant's preferred way of giving and receiving feedback. People were asked to physically stand by the style they preferred, and notice that there was quite a difference between preferences in giving and receiving feedback. The team was asked to observe carefully who was standing where, in particular in relation to how they preferred to receive feedback. The session ended with giving feedback to the actors.

FEEDBACK CARETAKERS AND ARTS ASSOCIATES
After a workshop each team has to appoint a feedback caretaker, who is responsible for keeping alive the learning from the workshop. This means that about 3 weeks after the workshop the caretaker will be invited to have a chat with one of the MAP actors, and 6 weeks later the caretaker will be interviewed by an external person for evaluation purposes.

Regarding the arts associates, Alastair Creamer explained:

→ "The second level in this period was that we would pick 8 teams and once they had done the workshop we were going to place an actor in those teams, basically to embed the behaviours of giving and receiving feedback for as long as we could; as long as 3 months if we could. We called these people arts associates and we were very clear that they were not coaches, because people mean different things with that. So we said these are trained actor facilitators, but they have particular listening and questioning skills, which means they can sit in your meeting and we will work out a contract with you beforehand so you know how they are going to operate, and they are there to support you, so it is your commitment and your contract. We got teams to volunteer for that."

LIVE REPORT

Alastair Creamer continues the story on his vision for Live Report:

→ "The third aspect of the project within this timescale was that we wanted the actors to play back to us and do this piece called 'live report'. This means that they are going to provide us with half-an-hour of theatre about 'this is what we have seen'. We have been around you for almost 3 months and done nothing else, but we have a view. These are the themes that we have seen and heard. And they called it 'something is going on here', which is a quote from somebody during a workshop. But we did not want to do a bit of theatre of the actors feeding back to the business without the business allowing immediate feedback to the actors. So we structured it as half an hour of performance, a little break where the actors catch their breaths, and then we have someone to facilitate a debate. Not me, not Kathy … someone from outside. … So in a sense what it is going to be is a testament, I hope, to whether we have improved; it is like a test case of whether we have, broadly speaking, improved basic levels of giving and receiving feedback. It will be interesting, I hope, and we have been very clear that we have no idea how they are going to perform. I have not asked. So it will be as big a surprise for me as it is for anyone else."

EVALUATION AND CHALLENGE

→ "… and then 2 or 3 weeks after that they (the arts associates) have interviews for evaluation purposes with an external person, who is a brilliant writer, to get their stories about how it has been for them, so this is part of the evaluation. We are also doing video diaries and there is a lot of evaluation coming from the actors and the MAP, and there will be evaluations from the performances and the people who facilitated those. There is going to be an evaluation from the chairman of those businesses; what it felt like, what have they seen for the past 2 or 3 months. So we are going to pull all that together and issue three challenges to each of these businesses in January, February. We are going to say, as a result of this big piece of work, real challenges in Kingston are XXX, what do you want to do about it? Do you want to tackle this individually, as a team, as a business, or what? And then we are going to have the discussion and we are going to do the same over at Walton. People may say we do not believe those issues are important, or they may say yes, you have hit it on the buzz. That is what this big piece of work is about, and I think this is taking it down to a different level than what people would normally do. People will do their workshops and form the relations in teams, but I do not think they get actors being critical or having the opportunity to be critical towards the business, I think that is different."

In the above we have examined just three of the many projects of Catalyst, mainly by hearing people's own stories and experiences. We will now focus on one learning aspect from each of them. The first concerns the art of photography.

SEEING AND SAYING

When life if full of activity and information, we tend to switch on the 'automatic pilot', which means that we do not really take in the world with our senses. Life becomes dull, but actually it is not life that is to blame, but rather our outlook on life that is poor. From a gathering of statements[57], exposed as a piece of art on a staircase wall at Kingston, I have chosen a few to give the reader an idea of the individual learning that took place in the photography sessions. "The longer I looked, the more I saw." "The project made me re-appraise what I look at on a day-to-day basis. How many times did I look up above eye height?" "There is colour everywhere and some of the most exciting colours are where you're least likely to find them." "I have started listening to backing vocals, looking at shadows, watching non-speaking characters on TV. I'm looking beyond and behind things. I don't know what this means yet." "There **is** something interesting in every-thing." "For me it's been more about the experience before actually seeing any photos. Thinking, imagining, creating, anticipating." "It was great to be part of something where different views was the point not the problem." "A good coach really does help. The greatest moment came when Rut put two of my pictures together, which I had cast aside as rejects. I saw something I hadn't seen before."

Evidently the course on photography has made a lot of impact, a cognitive change, on the quality of seeing for the participants. The role of art here was to inspire, to see new forms of beauty and to provoke. How they will use their skills is not part of the story, but as we saw earlier, chairman James Hill is convinced that Unilever will directly or indirectly profit from courses like this - and judging from the above statements that seems, indeed, very likely.

PREPARATION, IMPROVISATION AND PERFORMANCE

Implicit in the notion of improvisation is a firm foundation of practice. In music you have to know the notes, the chords, the scores, etc. and you have to be able to play musical pieces more or less flawlessly before you can even begin to improvise before an audi-ence. As mentioned in chapter 3, improvisation was one of the first artistic metaphors to attract the attention of organisational researchers, and in relation to Crossan and Sor-renti's framework on organisational learning, we already introduced their definition on improvisation, that it is intuition which guides action in a spontaneous way. Intuition is "an unconscious process based on distilled experience."[58] In a world of increasingly rapid change improvisation is becoming a competency needed by leaders in particular, but in fact, also by most employees. According to the people I have interviewed preparation is essential; a singer needs to train her voice, a musician needs to practice his instrument, an actor needs to rehearse and to tune into the personality of the character, a lecturer needs to focus on the central lines of thought. And when the performance involves several persons, naturally they must practice together. In 'Sticky' people did not know each other beforehand and consequently needed to work on that in order to build relations of trust. So here we see art primarily as social, but also in many ways provocative. As Adrian Greystoke explained, the 45 minute performance was just "the top of the iceberg", but would never have been possible without all the preparation: the energisers, the conversations and the practicing. There needs to be a delicate balance between preparation and improvisation – and intuition.

FEEDBACK AND COMMUNICATION

In the workshops of 'Live & Direct', the participants were offered some interesting new ways of giving feedback by learning from theatre techniques. This learning was both experimental and anticipative, and the role of art was inspiration, provocation and social. Apparently there is a big difference between having appraisals in business settings and rehearsing for a play - and yet the purpose is the same, to improve behaviour. A theatre director, who has given this a lot of thought, is Piers Ibbotson[59]:

➤ "… an interesting thing I am doing now is talking about how directors give notes - feedback I suppose it will be called, and how very different that is in style to the way in which feedback is given in business, such as 360-degree appraisals. Appraisal and feedback are everywhere in business, but it seems to me to be a very mechanistic way of conducting relationships. The way in which good directors give notes to actors is interesting in the ways in which it is different from what I see as business practice. It is radically different, really.

The generalisations I make about directors' style come from my experience as an assistant director and as an actor, having worked with a number of different directors, working alongside some of the very best directors we have, and working on shows that were both successful and unsuccessful. Out of that I have tried to reflect back and distil what was successful practice, and that is what all my work is based on, a distillation of that experience.

It seems to me that the best directors give notes in a very interesting way. They are present and vigilant, and they observe very closely the work that is being done by the performers, and they allow the performers a massive amount of time - as much as they can bear - to try and discover their way to a solution. When they want to guide them, direct them, give them some direction to proceed in, the best ones look at the problem, make a judgment about what the difficulty or error is that the actors are making, and then they go the step further and try to frame a suggestion that will lead them out of their difficulty. But they reframe it in the terms of a positive, creative challenge or suggestion. They don't go "that is not working, because you're sitting down too early". They might give feedback of that sort, and that might be useful. But if the actor is really stuck, they will go, "why don't we just do this scene in the park? I know it says in the script that it is set in the house, but what if we set this outdoors, maybe you're walking along with an umbrella and it's raining, try that." And that reframing of the problem might unhook the actors, and they will make a discovery about a sense in which this scene can be performed without sitting down. It will break their problem, and then they can return to the furniture, but liberated from their problem. Now, what I don't see in business is managers doing that for people. They go as far as, "your problem is you sit down too soon. Don't." Feedback is almost always given in terms of prohibitions or criticisms - even when it is positive. "You sit down very, very well". Now that is nice to get occasionally, but it actually is no use at all, it doesn't advance you creatively, it doesn't develop you. The only thing that really develops you is to be constantly challenged, that is managing the creative processes, that is what the great directors do. The great directors keep you on that edge all the time, so that you are continually wrestling with the problems and with the work in a fresh way. The director is reframing you so that you are continually at that edge of creativity, so feedback in the terms of what was good and what was bad becomes redundant. When things are going well, you don't get feedback of that sort at all.

It is very interesting to me that in business there is an increasingly systematic process for doing the exact opposite, giving feedback in terms of "don't sit down on that chair". It is to do with managers either not knowing how, or not being able to give that creative-reframing sort of feedback. I have yet to find out whether this is just because people are not familiar with it as a technique or whether it is actually because managers don't see enough of what their people do, they are not in the room enough, so they don't know enough about the detail of what their people are doing. But that is a metaphor I am fiddling around with at the moment. It also connects to motivation and enthusiasm and all that stuff that people say they want, but which, it seems to me, most appraisal systems are guaranteed to eliminate. What I see at the moment is people increasingly in a state of anxiety and stress, even when they get good appraisals, they still feel anxious, more so. "Oh my God, I got a good appraisal, I have to keep up that level. How am I gonna do that again this month – how am I gonna keep my good appraisal? I mustn't be marked down next month." Whatever happens, it seems to me that this emphasis on clarity and blah, blah, blah is actually not helping anybody much. It is just making people extremely pressured, and they complain about it all the time. There are very few places I go where people go, "Oh, it's so good to have a really good appraisal system." They want appraisals, because it is an opportunity to be spoken to, and it gives them a formal structure where at least they get a conversation about their work, which is better than they had before."

This is, in fact, a very interesting observation. Obviously we have examples of two extremely different approaches here, however, both somewhat manipulative. The business appraisal is rooted in an instrumental paradigm: a rational, mechanistic management tool for improving behaviour. But would that have suggested itself to us without the comparison to this more artful paradigm: a humanistic, organic leadership process for creating a challenging atmosphere of learning?

TRAJECTORIES
"Catalyst is a programme of individual development in the areas of creativity, inspiration,

stimulation and challenge which collaborates with artists and arts organisations. It is aligned with each operating company's strategic agenda."[60] In the Arts-in-Business framework this means that Catalyst starts in the arena of 'capabilities', but as we have seen from the three projects we have just described, Catalyst has an incredible variety and a large scope and therefore conveys trajectories all through the matrix.

'Urban Fiction' applied photography as a kind of role model, creating a trajectory into the arena of 'metaphor', because as we learned, photography is really a way of seeing - just like a metaphor is. Furthermore the photos served as prototypes for creating dialogues about ways of seeing, how to tell a story and reflecting about choice. The trajectory also reached 'events' due to the interaction with the photographer and the other participants and the 'product' arena was represented by the exhibition and the postcards with the 'positives'.

'Sticky' has an almost perfect fit with the arena of 'events'. The ambiguity, the element of improvisation, the direct interaction and the teambuilding are all characteristics of this arena. Sticky, however, had a specific goal as it had to result in a live performance ('product'), which was to be seen by 15,000 people. We can thus draw a trajectory from 'capabilities' to 'events' and from there to 'products' and then back to 'capabilities' because of the learning. Evidently the people working with Sticky must have hit the 'solar plexus of learning' once or twice because of the incredibly strong experience.

At the time of writing 'Live + Direct' is still being rolled out. Its aim is to improve communication, collaboration, feedback, quality of conversations and meetings, both at the individual, team and organisational level. Therefore the trajectory starts in the two arenas of 'capabilities' and 'products' (as a product can also be a process or service) but moves into the arena of 'events' because the learning is mostly accomplished through live interaction with theatre people. Elements of the exercises do, however, move into the arena of 'metaphor', when comparing different ways of seeing (Dawn moving the chair), noticing the difference between observing and interpreting and when reflecting on the 5 different styles of giving and receiving feedback. The next stages of the project have been created in order to continue the trajectory back to the top of the matrix to embed the learning in both individuals and organisation and then to finally test this by engaging an external evaluator.

The common characteristic of these three learning-tales is that the most important learning emerged by being exposed to the artistic process: In 'Urban Fiction' it was the discovery of a different way of 'seeing' and 'saying' (expression). In 'Sticky' it was the balance between preparation, improvisation and performance. And in 'Live + Direct' it was the rehearsal technique that revealed a more energising form of feedback and communication than the usual business approach. The role of art in project Catalyst[61] has been multiple, exploring a plethora of possibilities, even art as industry – as seen in the production of postcards and children's books.

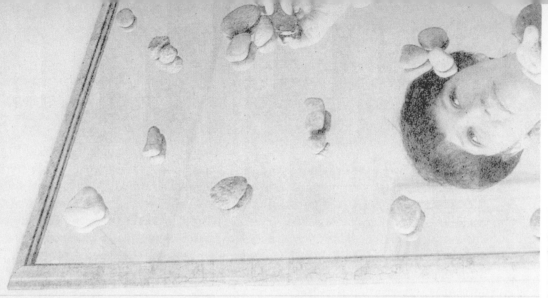

Erhvervslivet kan lære af kulturen

Et tættere
samarbejde
mellem
virksomheder og
kulturlivet er ved
at udvikle sig.
Kunstnerne taler
et sprog og har
nogle metoder,
som ledelses- og
organisationsfolk
kan lære noget af

AF PERNILLE ENGGAARD
PEDERSEN

De danske virksomheder og
kulturlivet har gennem de
seneste år fået kraftigt med
hinanden. Nu ser det ud til,
at tiltag er ved at udvikle sig
til et mere tæt og langvarigt

rammer. Det er årsagen til, at
mange virksomheder er tilba-
geholdende over for et samarbejde med kunstnerne, – for-
tæller Lotte Darsø, der ikke er
i tvivl om, at kunstnere kan
skabe den kreativitet og innovation som erhvervslivet har
hårdt brug for.

For i den nye økonomi er
kodeordet innovation. Virk-
somhederne skal satse på for-
nyelse og originalitet for at
overleve i det globale sam-
fund og kunne imødekomme
aktionærernes krav om øget
vækst og afkast. Her kan erhvervslivet drage stor nytte
af kulturlivets kompetancer.

Det er ikke alene budska-
bet fra Lotte Darsø, men også
fra blandt andre Steen Hilde-
brandt, professor ved Institut
for Organisation og Ledelse,
Handelshøjskolen i Århus.

Kunstnernes sprog

Kunsten taler et sprog og

te Darsø et af de mere
spændende projekter på vej
herhjemme. Artlab, Dansk
Musiker Forbunds Kursusaf-
deling, har i øjeblikket 19
professionelle kunstnere på
et til måneders fuldtidskur-
sus, ArtBizz, i samarbejde
med bl.a. Chr. Hansen og
Nycomed, hvor de arbejder
med nye typer konsulentop-
gaver for erhvervslivet. Et
projekt som kan udmunde
sig i et egentligt konsulent-
bureau med kunstnere.

Gode provokationer

Kunsten er fornyende og
provokerende, og det er tit
svært at tænke nye tanker
inden for virksomhedens
rammer, fordi man hurtigt
får en tendens til at tænke i
de samme baner. Kunstnere
tænker ofte længere frem,
end vi andre gør, og hvis man

mål. Og det er her, idéer til at
nyt produkt, nyt design eller
en ny markedsføringskam-
pagne opstår. Samtidig kan
kunstnerne gennem musik,
tegning eller teater få en
gruppe eller en organisation
til at kommunikere på nye
måder.

– Det kaldes social innovation, og det giver nye måder at
organisere arbejdet på eller
nye former for samspil og
samarbejde, – forklarer Lotte
Darsø, der fra 1896-2000 var
erhvervsforsker hos Novo
Nordisk og innovation coach i
Novozymes, hvor hun blandt
andet arbejdede med kunst
nere i såkaldte innovations-
cafeer.

Som innovationstræner i
erhvervslivet har hun be-
mærket, at vi iser i den vest-
lige verden lader kreativite-
ten blive hjemme, når vi går
på arbejde.

HOW GOVERNMENTS MATTER - THE SNOWBALL CASE OF DENMARK. HOW A GOVERNMENT FOCUS ON ART AND BUSINESS HAS GENERATED NEW POSSIBILITIES

In September 2000 a report was published at the request of the Danish Ministry of Culture and the Ministry of Trade and Industry. It was called "The Creative Alliance. An Analysis of the Interplay between Arts and Business".[62] This report was seminal for the current development of the Art & Business field in Denmark. It figuratively started a snowball rolling, which has evolved into a progressive and creative environment that attracts international artists, scholars and practitioners. We will start by listing the history and then return to some of the consequences.

The findings of the report were that (in 2000) only a few of the most visionary Danish companies were working with the possibilities of a 'creative alliance' and that most Danish companies kept culture and the arts at a distance, in the best case as decoration. The report concluded that a political initiative was needed in order to strengthen the interaction between the arts and business and that such an effort should aim at: 1) achieving a higher production and spread of culture, and 2) strengthening the long-term capability of business for change and development. The recommendations included competency development for the interaction between arts and business as well as some structural and political initiatives[63]. On the part of the arts the potential gain was: the development of new competencies, new arenas for artistic performance, more resources, greater freedom, a wider audience and a changed self-understanding. For business the possibilities were: being exposed to creative and artistic competencies, attracting customer attention, expressing vision, strategy and identity, development of new products, designs and services, and change in organisational culture.

➜ "When society needs an integrated political effort of industry and culture it is thus because it will by and large result in increased artistic production and, apart from that, it will supposedly have a positive effect on the competitive and developmental capability of business. In other words it is the opinion of the report that society will achieve obvious advantages by an industrial and cultural political endeavour, even though it will hardly be possible to measure this on a short-term basis on the bottom-line of the companies that seek the values of art and culture, or in the great household account of society."[64]

The report furthermore pointed out that the gap between culture and industry may be particularly large in Denmark, because culture and the arts have been subsidised by the state and because there is no tradition for business to be involved in the arts. Even business sponsorships for the arts are very traditional, i.e. they mainly involve the large museums and theatres. At the time there were no long-term, strategic, two-way relationships.

A few months later, the government presented a white paper to the Danish parliament, which resulted in the following three initiatives:

1) In 2001 the Danish government invited tenders for the creation of a national network to connect business people, artists and cultural institutions. This was to include a meeting place and a market place, as well as an exchange of sponsorships, where artists and business people could find inspiration and knowledge to strengthen partnerships and strategic sponsorships between arts and business. This was highly inspired by the work of the semi-public organisation Art & Business UK.[65] The qualification was won by NyX[66] and launched in January 2002 to be funded for three years by the Danish Ministry of Culture. In the long-term NyX will be financed by sponsorships and membership fees. The Danish 'NyX' means 'new X', indicating the birth of something new between Art and Business.

2) In August 2001 Learning Lab Denmark[67] established a research consortium, "The Creative Alliance"[68], focusing its research on exploring and accentuating the learning potentials of the interplay between Arts and Business. This was the direct result of the following findings:

➡ "Research projects/experience records: An overall observation, made in this report, is that there is a general lack of theoretical frameworks when it comes to the interplay between art and business.... There are almost no research-based studies on how the use of artistic competencies and communication forms can contribute to organisational change and product development."[69]

The consortium is the world's first research centre to conduct research on individual and organisational learning through experience, intervention and practice of the arts. Our goal is to study artistic and artful learning processes in order to produce actionable knowledge and social innovation in business and in society, and the present book is a first attempt to map and define this emerging research field. Building on the theoretical framework and the empirical findings of this book, we have developed the research method: CoLLab, The Collaborative Learning Lab, which is a safe, lab-like environment, in which we can explore and experiment with new forms of e.g. problem-solving, leadership, innovation or project management in collaboration with partners from both the arts and business (see also chapter 6).

3) In 2001 the government invited tenders for the establishment of a cultural entrepreneurial incubator to be placed in the vicinity of the schools of architecture, theatre and film. This was won by LOUIZ[70], which opened in May 2002 with two types of ventures; one is the innovation environment for newly started entrepreneurs focusing on business development; the other is the Louiz Saloons for cultural entrepreneurs, which is supported by 9 public organisations, including the EU Social Fund. The target group includes artists, designers, musicians, cultural communicators, computer game developers and

concept developers. The saloons run twice a week over a period of 3-4 months and cover themes such as networking, business, sales, strategic business development, idea development, competency development, customer and market focus, etc.

Another institution, Artlab[71], a laboratory for art, creativity and business, has existed since 1998 as the educational part of the Danish Musicians' Union. The goal is to improve the qualifications of artists as well as their job possibilities and to encourage collaboration between artists of various kinds. Inspired by the government white paper, in 2001 Artlab created a 9-month pilot education, Artbizz, for out-of-work musicians, dancers and theatre people. The vision was to transfer artistic competencies into new types of jobs or niches for artistsIn order to ensure concrete practical experience, Artlab initiated collaboration with two companies, and in 2002 Artbizz Consult was conceived in order to sell and market the services of the new artistic consultants. In 2003, upon receiving new funding from the EU Social Fund, they developed two new course streams, one for artists and one for business people. The artist stream and the business stream cross several times during the course in order to learn from the interaction with each other.

In 2002 Danish Centre for Management[72] started a course of exploration in the field of Arts-in-Business as part of the present research. The idea was to introduce the research project, the theory and findings to the business people, who were members of the Centre, and to start a dialogue with the artists involved and, of course, to explore the potential of the arts. During the 5 main explorations, starting in Oct. 2002 and ending in March 2003, the participants were exposed to many concrete learning experiences and various artistic methods. The course involved a full day of working with theatrical methods and actors, a full day of exploring painting processes[73] and the fine arts, and a full day of musical experience including sitting in the middle of the Radio Concert Orchestra in a session with Miha Pogacnik. The participants also experienced singing as a chorus, 'singing themselves',[74] non-verbal communication and different types of expressions by the Royal Danish ballet and non-verbal leadership by conductinglxxv a professional chorus. From this project several networks were created, including X-border[75].

In 2003 the Copenhagen Business School opened The Centre for Art & Leadership. Its foundation is philosophy, which is, according to their motto, "the core of genuine leadership".[77] The idea is for philosophers and artists to work together in order to develop performances and new knowledge and hopefully to influence leaders and organisations towards a better world through "the revolutionising, uncompromising and sensitive powers of Art".

Apart from the six recent initiatives listed above, which are, of course, complementary to the more traditional arts institutions, many new entrepreneurs and companies saw the light of day. The initial report and the government initiatives of 2000 hit fertile ground. The invitation for tenders to the Art & Business network spurred a lot of meetings, conferences and numerous events involving the arts. Far from all of these meetings were successful, as many were being planned and executed by people with little experience and little time. This resulted in some people regarding the field as full of 'hot air', a label, which was in some cases probably deserved. Regionally, counties and municipalities started their own projects and a lot of free agents and small creative companies were born. Some have survived, others have not. All in all, Denmark has very quickly acquired a lot of experience and many advantages in this field.

In 2003 the present government came with a follow-up document "Denmark in the Cultural and Experiential Economy", which pointed out four main areas of interest: architecture and design; interaction between cultural institutions and business; cultural and sporting events; sports and business. This means that the focus and funding have taken a different direction.

On my travels around the world, among others at the 2004 Davos meeting of the World Economic Forum[78], I have realised that many people regard Denmark as an exemplar for advancing Arts-in-Business – and at that, one they would like to learn from. Upon their request I have added this brief account. The Danish challenge is to grant the creative environment and the government initiatives the time needed to prove itself. It would be a shame to cut the tree before it gets a chance to bloom and bear fruit, in particular when the tree has an initial advantage and is seen by many as worthy of imitation. In the creative economy of the future, this type of environment is exactly what can supposedly attract the most inventive and creative minds. Richard Florida's book[79] on 'creative societies' demonstrates that culture is an important attractor to people's choice of a place to live – to such a degree that this affects business. Only a decade ago the location of corporations would attract people to come to them, now it is almost the opposite; corporations have to consider where to find the best people - and locate their business accordingly. Obviously, there are many opportunities here.

TRAJECTORIES

If we try to understand the three government initiatives in the light of the Arts-in-Business matrix, the initial analysis emphasised developing competencies ('capabilities'), research and language ('metaphor'), and structures to enhance meetings ('events') as well as cultural start-ups ('products'). The government initiatives focused on building the basic infrastructure for interaction, through the Art & Business network of NyX ('events') and by procuring LOUIZ with a building and funding for entrepreneurial cultural start-ups ('products'). The research consortium, The Creative Alliance, was started as an initiative working on developing models and theoretical frameworks ('metaphor') for understanding and creating a language to bridge mutual understanding. All three initiatives have trajectories towards 'capabilities' for the organisers as well as the participants. In building something entirely new it is, of course, necessary to learn from past experience, but in fact, maybe even more important to learn from the future as it emerges, which we shall look at in the next chapter.

As we are trying to describe a field in the making, we cannot fully discuss the learning aspects yet. Evidently, what a government chooses to focus on attracts people's attention. Secondly, when a government takes the step to invite tenders involving funding, this spurs a lot of activity and helps the field advance by opening new opportunities. The projects are not far enough in their development to be evaluated. NyX has discovered that it is difficult to get business involved when there are still only few documented effects of Arts-in-Business. And the lack of economical optimism after 9/11 2001 has not made it any easier. Fortunately they have had more luck in getting municipalities and counties interested, and a new regional initiative on innovation alliances between artists and business was launched in the fall of 2003. The first big project of The Creative Alliance concerns this research project and book, which will form the basis for our work with CoLLabs (see chapter 6). At the time of writing LOUIZ has housed 70 small cultural entrepreneurial companies or persons. Of necessity all these initiatives have to be regarded as long-term projects – at least if we want to harvest the fruit of this new area of research and practice.

1   Interview with Jill Chappell, programme coordinator at George Washington University, Washington DC

2   Interview with Herbert Tillery, Deputy Mayor for Operations in Washington DC

3   Seely Brown, 1999, xi, in Craig Harris (ed.) (1999): Art and Innovation. The Xerox Parc Artist-in-Residence Program, The MIT Press

4   Interview with Rich Gold, Delft, Holland, November, 2002

5   Ibid.

6   Ibid.

7   The Technical University, Delft, Holland, November, 2002

8   Interview with Rich Gold, Delft, Holland, November, 2002

9   Ibid.

10 www.bang-olufsen.com

11 www.beo.com go to "Vision & Legend"

12 This whole paragraph builds on "The Beauty and the Machine" by Camilla Mehlsen, 2003, Copenhagen University

13 Per Arnoldi, a Danish artist, who makes a lot of industrial art

14 Mogens Stiller Kjärgaard, a Danish philosopher

15 Camilla Mehlsen (2003): "The Beauty and the Machine", Appendices, p. 16-26, Copenhagen University

16 "Bang & Olufsen Business Theatre", brochure by director Thomas Asger Hansen, Department for International Training and Human Resource Development, Bang & Olufsen, 2000

17 Camilla Mehlsen (2003): "The Beauty and the Machine", Appendices, p. 16-26, Copenhagen University

18 Lotte Darsø (2001:172): "Innovation in the Making", Samfundslitteratur

19 Chris Argyris and Donald Schön (1996): "Organizational Learning II: Theory, Method, and Practice", Addison-Wesley Publishing Company

20 Ironically under the paragraph of "Telling Bang & Olufsen", the 'Bang & Olufsen Business Theatre' brochure mixes different discourses and does include war language, as it talks about "being intellectually dressed to *kill* in every

conversation with prospects or customers" (my italics).

21   David Barry (1997): "Telling changes: From narrative family therapy to organizational change & development". Journal of Organizational Change Management, Volume 10, #1:32-48

22   In the CoLLab "Project Management as a Work of Art", Sept. 2003

23   Margaret Wheatley (2002): "Turning to one Another", Berrett-Kohler Publishers

24   Stefan Meisek & Michael Dawids (2004): "Organization Theatre – A Serious Play". The case study is part of a larger research project conducted at Learning Lab Denmark. The data was collected using interviews with two managers at the municipal level, five managers at the district level and four representatives from Dacapo Theatre. Further, eleven theatrical performances and the audience receptions to them were videotaped and analysed. Finally, a questionnaire comprising qualitative and quantitative elements was sent to the audience members about a week after they had participated in the organisation theatre event.

25   Augusto Boal (2000:122): Theater of the Oppressed, Pluto Press

26   www.dacapoteatret.dk

27   Stefan Meisek & Michael Dawids (2004): "Organization Theatre – A Serious Play", Learning Lab Denmark

28   Ibid. 2004:24

29   Augusto Boal (2000:122): Theater of the Oppressed, Pluto Press

30   David Barry & E. Palmer (2001): "Serious questions about serious play: Problems and prospects in the study of mediated innovation". Proceedings of the ANZAM Conference, Auckland, New Zealand

31   Teresa Balough (1996:0): "May Human Beings Hear it! IDRIART", published by CIRCME, School of Music The University of Western Australia in association with IDRIART

32   www.miha.mihavision.com

33   Heide Tawil, Gundula Piene and Andreas Henning, *Idriart celebrated its tenth anniversary, 1991*, in Teresa Balough (1996:21): "May Human Beings Hear it! IDRIART"

34   Teresa Balough (1996:25): "May Human Beings Hear it! IDRIART"

35   Miha Pogacnik in Idriart USA, Newsletter No. 1, in: "May Human Beings Hear it! IDRIART", by Teresa Balough, published by CIRCME, 1996

36   Interview with Miha Pogacnik, Borl, Slovenia, June 2002

37   Miha Pogacnik plays selected fragments ('dissects') of the whole in order to illustrate and demonstrate certain features and developments

38   Teresa Balough (1996:15): "May Human Beings Hear it! IDRIART"

39   Ibid.

40   Anne von Lange: *"Man, Music and Cosmos"*, Sussex, Rudolf Steiner Press, 1992, in Teresa Balough (1996:15): "May Human Beings Hear it! IDRIART"

41   www.musicmindspirit.org/interview.htm

42   Don Campbell (2001): "The Mozart Effect. Tapping the Power of Music to Heal the Body, Strengthen the Mind, and Unlock the Creative Spirit, Quill

43   Interview with Miha Pogacnik, Borl, Slovenia, June 2002

44   Interview with Michael Brammer, Copenhagen, November 26, 2002

45   In her thesis, "Oh Thou Beautiful Management", Lykke Ricard did two case studies, one of them on Michael Brammer. In the English summary p. 115-116 she writes: "My case studies point to the fact that these two artists are indeed businessmen, they do have to sell themselves and keep accounts, but the best way to sell themselves is not by acting as businessmen – quite the opposite. They sell themselves by living up to the image of being a self-centered, creative and artistic bastard type."

46   Lotte Darsø (2001:278-281): "Innovation in the Making", Samfundslitteratur

47 Design DK, Nanna Schacht: "Not the Emperor's new clothes", 4:2002 December, p. 19

48 www.AandB.org

49 Børsen, Anne Louise Houmann: "Controversial artist to inspire Volvo", June 29, 2001

50 Interview with Alastair Creamer, Catalyst producer, Unilever Fabergé, London, November 2003

51 www.unilever.com

52 Quoted from a Lever Fabergé Catalyst brochure from 2002

53 In his interview, Milo Shapiro, CEO (Creative Energy Officer) of ImproVentures, explained how he deliberately works with failure. He emphasiesed: "We have to be willing to fail a certain percent of the time and we have to respect that our staff will do that if we are ever going to expect them to be brilliant and innovative."

54 rutb.lux@virgin.net

55 Sticky Diary, Monday 8th – Saturday 13th of September 2003, by Eileen McLennan, Ice Cream Brand Development, Unilever Ice Cream & Frozen Food

56 Catalyst and the MAP consortium: "The Book. Live + Direct 2", p. 18-21

57 These sentences are the same as the 'positives' (instead of film 'negatives') from the set of postcards.

58 Crossan, M.M. & Sorrenti, Marc (2002:31): "Making Sense of Improvisation", in Kamoche, Pina e Cunha, & Vieira da Cunha (Eds.) (2002): "Organizational Improvisation", chapter 3, p. 29 - 51

59 Interview with Piers Ibbotson, actor and assistant director, The Royal Shakespeare Company, London, April 2002

60 The language of Catalyst", p. 1

61 For further examples from Unilever and Babson College see Ted Buswick, Alastair Creamer, and Mary Pinard (2004): "(Re)Educating for Leadership: How the Arts Can Improve Business", forthcoming

62 "Den kreative alliance. Analyse af samspillet mellem kultur og erhverv", udarbejdet af Advice Analyse A/S for Kulturministeriet og Erhvervsministeriet, september 2000

63 Ibid. Chapter 8

64 Ibid. Page 90

65 www.AandB.org.uk

66 NyX, www.nyxforum.dk is a consortium formed by the KaosPilots, www.kaospilot.dk; Copenhagen Eventures, www.woco.dk; K-fab, see www.louiz.dk; and Deloitte & Touche, www.deloitte.com . Why the name NyX? "Greek mythology tells how Nyx, the goddess of the night, was the child of Chaos. She in turn gave birth to the atmosphere, the day, fate and dreams. In the reflective silence of the night, she creates dreams and new visions to the sound of the Muses' poetic chants. In the light of day and the hours of reality, she transforms these dreams into action."

67 www.lld.dk

68 www.lld.dk/creativealliance

69 "Den kreative alliance. Analyse af samspillet mellem kultur og erhverv", udarbejdet af Advice Analyse A/S for Kulturministeriet og Erhvervsministeriet, september 2000:92

70 A consortium formed by K-fab between The Danish Ministry of Culture, Deloitte & Touche and Lokdam, Kjellund & Partners

71 www.artlab.dk

72 www.cfl.dk

73 "Painting as teambuilding" with artists from CreaLab, www.CreaLab.dk

74 A way of singing on a single note, inspired by Indian singing. Githa Ben-David (2002): "Tonen fra himlen. At synge sig selv" (ed."The tone from heaven. Singing yourself"), Borgen

75 A concept developed by Peter Hanke, www.exart.dk

76 www.xborder.dk

77 www.cbs.dk/cal

78 I was invited as a Forum Fellow to the annual Davos meeting of the World Economic Forum in January 2004 to moderate the workshop "If an Artist ran your business ..." and to participate as a panellist and discussant leader in the session "Creativity as Comparative Advantage", www.weforum.org

79 Richard Florida (2002): "The Rise of the Creative Class", Basic Books

CHAPTER 5

TRANSCENDENCE AND TRANSFORMATION

How can we make sense of what happens when we apply artistic processes to organisations? What kind of learning took place in the tales told in chapter 4? And what kind of learning should we aim at if we want these processes to become genuinely effective?

Until now we have used the Arts-in-Business matrix for classifying the case studies and for studying the trajectories between the four types: metaphors, capabilities, events and products. The purpose of this chapter is to develop further understanding of these tales and trajectories by relating them to relevant theory. We will introduce Otto Scharmer's presencing model and analyse the findings by working through its seven steps. At the end of the chapter we will examine the zones of transition at the centre of the Arts-in-Business model, the 'solar plexus of learning', and redefine it as 'artful creation'.

PRESENCING AND LEARNING FROM THE FUTURE

A way of understanding transformation is through Otto Scharmer's presencing model (Scharmer, 2002, 2004). Scharmer argues that there are basically two kinds of learning:

learning from the past (reflecting on experience) and learning from the future that wants to emerge. The latter is further developed through the concept of presencing, which refers to tuning in to future possibilities and bringing them into the present. The concept blends the two words 'pre-sensing' (sense before) and 'presence' (being totally present). Scharmer (2002:7) describes transformation as a threshold:

➔ "The point of presencing theory is that, for a social system to go through a profound process of transformation, the process must cross a subtle threshold, a threshold that throughout the book is referred to as the eye of the needle. The eye of the needle is the Self – our highest future possibility, both individually and collectively."

As illustrated below, the model is shaped as an U-curve and has seven steps:
1. Downloading
2. Seeing (from outside)
3. Sensing (from inside)
4. Presencing
5. Crystallising
6. Prototyping
7. Embodying

In the following we will compare the trajectories and learning aspects from chapter 4 with the seven steps of the presencing model by including data from the interviews as well as relevant theory.

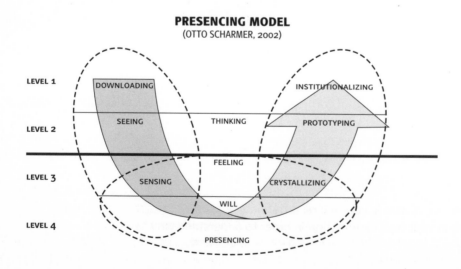

PRESENCING MODEL
(OTTO SCHARMER, 2002)

DOWNLOADING

Downloading is the normal 'mode of operation' in today's institutions. We think within the limits of habit, switching on the 'automatic pilot' and accepting the given boundaries. We simply repeat the past and do as we have always done. Downloading is what the business world does all the time. Due to the increasing workload most business people experience, there is simply no time for going deeply into anything. When, for instance, a strategy is presented to the employees, the CEO will typically go through a PowerPoint presentation, which at the most activates the left hemisphere of the brain. The demands of efficiency leave time for only one-way information. There is no time for dialogue, no time for reflection. Conversations consist of collective monologues[1], meaning that people in most meetings are so busy preparing their own input that they don't listen at all to what the others say. When this mode becomes 'business as usual' it can be difficult to penetrate the facade. People, who feel comfortable in this mode, will avoid being moved and will withdraw from the arts. They throw a quick glance at paintings but are not moved. They have the television on most of the time to fill the empty space with voices and music (or musac), maybe in order not to feel, not to reflect. To them art is merely entertainment and is best if kept safely at a distance. This is one of the barriers the arts meet when working with business. The first step is therefore to *suspend* downloading by sharpening our quality of attention.

SEEING

Seeing involves careful observation of what is going on. What are the facts? What can be seen? In how many different ways can we look at the subject in order to get a better understanding? This involves identifying the problem through careful observation of data by looking at what is actually going on – without judging or evaluating or forming any opinion. In a group this involves using the many different perspectives inherent to the individuals of the group and trying to connect these into a whole picture. The photography course at Unilever is a good example of observing from without and the learning gained from using the photographs, which had originally been discarded because they did not come out as intended, said something important about preconceptions and judgment. Martin Best, musician and specialist in the art of the troubadour, uses observation as his major approach when coaching leaders through poetry. He says:

→ "What we are doing is helping them (leaders) understand how to see themselves in their world, through the eyes of the poet. If you are going to see the world through the eyes of William Blake, you have to understand how he sees. Why does he use these words, why is tiger spelt with a y (tyger)? Could it be a metaphor? Blake is asking you, he is sitting with you and asking you to look differently at things through his eyes. What do you have to see in your own imagination in order to understand why he wrote that? Once you start to try and answer that question, then you begin to look at everything differently, including people. ... If a line in a poem like that is not as it appears, but is far more profound and complex, then it stands to reason that other things are far more profound and complex too.

Including people. This initially begins to lead to an ability to understand diversity. ... *It is a learning process. We are not just teaching these people about art. They are involved in personal change.*"

In other instances artists are used as role models. In the case of Creative Leaps, the participants noticed the kind of leadership that took place during the concert, how different people took over leadership whenever it was needed. They described it as shared leadership, which arose out of the awareness of what was needed in each situation. Using observation is also applied by the conductor Roger Niehrenburg (The Music Paradigm) from Stamford, USA. Working with big symphony orchestras in such a way that the audience is placed in between the musicians, he asks the audience to look closely at the performing musicians and note something about them. The audience comes up with words like discipline, precision, concentration and hard work. This leads to an understanding of the artistic capabilities. Roger Niehrenburg repeats this approach in relation to conducting, as he demonstrates different ways of conducting (leading) and how this affects the orchestra, their motivation and their energy. His method is observation from without (a trajectory from 'event' towards 'capabilities' in the Arts-in-Business matrix). Ben Zander (Boston Philharmonic), another well-known conductor, uses musical performances in his particular way to develop new thinking and insights in a variety of audiences.

Forum Theatre involves seeing, starting with a play on stage that is carefully observed by the audience. Gradually the spectators become involved in the play, first by giving advice to the actors, then by becoming actors themselves in trying out different ways of solving the 'problem'. While giving advice is very much based on seeing from without, getting involved crosses the 'threshold' into Sensing.

Careful observation is also applied by Miha Pogacnik, who starts his masterclass by urging the participants to observe while he draws on paper and explains the elements of the masterpiece. He urges people not to get carried away – just observe. Later, however, he asks the participants to become one with the music (Sensing).

Observing is a mental capacity correlated with thinking (left brain) and verbalisation. We can easily communicate our observations through verbal language. The next level, however, concerns feelings and more holistic (right brain) thinking. Consequently it is mostly non-verbal. Thus, after seeing the problem area from without, observation is *redirected* to sensing it from within.

SENSING

Sensing turns the focus into becoming one with the world. In this stage the most important aspect is to open up for the world that was just observed from outside and to sense it from within. Each individual needs to find his/her own sources of inspiration and to reflect upon the impressions from the former observations. Groups can become collective organs of reflection that immerse themselves in co-sensing. The social boundaries collapse and the group feels as 'one'. When successful, this feels like true bonding or the creation of 'common ground'[2]. This is 'the heart of art'. Sensing from within concerns both the individual aspect of immersing oneself in the experience, thus becoming one with the play or the music or the dance, *and* the bonding between people, the connectedness, the relations. Music, in particular, opens up for this space. Music can in an instant set a mood or change a mood. It creates atmosphere and climate – even magic. This is evident in the case of Creative Leaps, as well as in the master classes by Miha Pogacnik. But whereas Creative Leaps take people quickly into this mode and invite them to dream, recall and watch their own inner images, Miha Pogacnik urges people not to dream but rather to sharpen their listening skills and become one with the music. He asks people not to get carried away in their own memories, but to awaken their senses. His intention is for people to get into the core of themselves in order to sense deeply what it means to be human. Both paths, however, can carry people into the fourth step of presencing, even though the paths are different, the first being entirely personal, the second being more archetypal.

As for Forum Theatre, the play engages people, not just in their ways of thinking, but also emotionally. Paul Levy, change facilitator and director, UK, strongly recommends organisational theatre for change processes:

➡ "What I find interesting is that a year later, if you talk to people about that workshop, they remember that piece just like their best film or movie. It was a critical incident because it is drama and an incident of the heart. And seeing with the heart, Steiner says, penetrates our reality much more than just seeing with the eyes of the head. And it is more likely to lead to change because it was a dramatic event."

People are moved, disturbed, enjoyed, inspired and even frightened when being involved in organisational theatre. Most often bonding will form through the social interaction and the experiential learning that takes place. In 'Mythodrama', another form of theatre, which is a combination of mythological stories and drama techniques, the approach is more personal. Richard Olivier, actor and director, UK, who applies Shakespeare plays for leadership development, recalls:

➡ "I had been asked to direct Henry 5th for the opening of the Globe Theatre in 1997 and so we decided that we would use this workshop as a way of exploring the subject, what does this 400-year-old play have to say to modern leaders of public management? We got a group of public service leaders into a room for two days and we gave them all the text of the play, read scenes, did a few exercises, talked through it. And at the end of the two days, they said that they had learned more from Henry 5th about leadership than they had from the management courses that they had been sent to for the last ten years."

Today selected Shakespeare plays are combined in leadership development programs with the four Jungian archetypes of leadership: the medicine woman, the great mother, the warrior and the good king[3]. An important difference between Mythodrama and Forum Theatre is that Mythodrama involves personal development and can thereby more easily access the zone of presencing, whereas Forum Theatre is collective, which makes it more difficult.

The Sensing mode is also present during social painting events, mainly because the process is non-verbal. Collective painting can be used for team building, relation building, communication training, and appreciation of diversity as well as for purposes of envisioning. Some artists have developed specialised processes for teambuilding. In one hour artists from CreaLab[4], for instance, can transform any auditorium or meeting facility into a studio, wrapping everything in plastic and bringing in all kinds of equipment from aprons to easels, canvas, paint, rinsing buckets, brushes etc. The planning of the session secures that the size of each canvas fits the exact number of participants who will be painting on it in such a way that collaboration is almost inevitable, and the process is designed in such a way that in certain periods people paint and are not allowed to talk (accompanied by selected music), and in other phases the music stops and people are asked to step away from the painting to talk about the progression. After having alternated several times between these two types of processes, the painting is finished. Finally there is a debriefing on both the painting process and the teambuilding. Painting is a very subtle form of communication and of 'sensing' others and it often reveals new facets of people that have not been noticed by the others in the group before. The form of team building that takes place through a painting process is different from other forms as it is cohesive rather than competitive. Linda Naiman, Canadian catalyst for creativity and innovation, led a US-based Research & Development team of a multi-national food company through several painting activities involving communication and collaboration:

➤ "A small miracle happened in this particular session. One of the activities was for pairs to paint (non-verbal) visual conversations with each other, then discuss and analyse the experience afterward. One of the pairs (a man and a woman) were also team-mates in their work, and never had gotten along with each other. After this exercise they reported to the group, they had unleashed all their passion and hostility in their painting and had fun in the process. When they discussed the picture they had created they came to a new understanding and appreciation of each other and how they could work together."

One major advantage of a painting process is that the 'minutes' are highly visible, even aesthetic, and continually remind the group of the process. The painting process in a group has certain similarities with art therapy, but the aim and focus are different. Art therapy is deeply psychological and therapeutic and concerns bringing hidden knowledge forward to consciousness through painting[5]. Art therapy is a personal process, which can go into the depth of the Self (into the presencing zone), and then onward towards releasing some of the old tension and finding new ways of coping with the world. In a relation-building group the aim is simply the *experience* of the painting process in a team, whereas art therapy is interested primarily in analysing the *content*.

   In order to get to the next step, the bottom of the U, which is presencing, it is necessary to *let go* of all former impressions.

PRESENCING

Presencing means opening up to our interior in order to become one with our deepest source of potential. Seen from the outside, time slows down towards stillness. The purpose is to let the inner knowledge emerge and to reflect upon it. The questions that are important here are: Who is my Self?[6] What is my work? What is my purpose? Depending on which kind of process is created, this can be a very deep experience resulting in the birth of a new Self. When these deep reflections and revelations are shared in a group this zone can best be described as co-inspiration.

In order to transcend into the zone of presencing, it is necessary to let go of all control and to be still. For most people this is a very private zone, and for many this is completely unknown. Why should we then access this field? And why on earth should we do so in a business setting? Some would say that presencing should not happen in business or in an organisational context as it belongs to the private sphere. But the underlying assumption of such an argument is that work and privacy are and should be separated, and the question is whether this separation makes sense any longer? Author and poet David Whyte maintains that it is important to nourish the soul - also at work (2002:224): "... we cannot split off the vitality we ardently wish for in our work from the same vitality that gives the world its awe-inspiring and destructive mutability. To meet the fiery qualities of the world we must be able to live with a little fire in the belly ourselves. Like athletic or artistic endeavor, taking the reins of responsibility in an organization at whatever level takes some education and experience, but without a vital ability to tackle the fiery qualities of the present, neither education or experience is of much use." Entering the zone of presencing is the door to our inner motivation, it is our zone of passion and here we come into contact with our will. Being in the zone of presencing means rethinking our values and concerns, possibly renewing ourselves, and rekindling our spirit. This is, in fact, the zone of personal development and of inner transformation, the 'solar plexus of learning'. People who want to experience their authentic self and Self must enter this space. In an interview Dianne Legro, a professional vocalist and principal artist from Creative Leaps, emphasised the difference between presence and performance:

➡ "The focus of my work, and many other singers' as well, is to not be presentational but as you are with people, and you are doing your art to be in the process of allowing the music to teach you in the moment. To authentically not know where you are going, to go emotionally on the journey of that piece of music. It is going to be a new discovery each time. And when you do that, when you allow that, then the audience that you are working with takes their journey... To authentically let it happen means something new to you and to discover it in the moment is a very, very powerful thing for all. And what is interesting is that after a performance of this kind, people will come back and say "You sang exactly what I was feeling, how did you know my exact song?" And the answer to that is that I don't know how I knew. But that is the best description I can give you of being fully present. They experience you, yes, but largely they are having their own experience and you authentically have to be in that state in order for that to work. And it goes right into the workplace because many, many people come to me and the first thing they tell me is about when they put away their passion to take this job, to support their family, to have this child, to buy this house, to have this lifestyle. And that's the first thing that comes out. Amazing stories. ... But the main thing is how they understand that they have to have that (passion) back in their life in order to be a complete person. ... Your passion informs everything you do."

It seems evident that Dianne is talking about the zone of presencing. She also indicates that through her authenticity as an artist she can bring people into that space. A similar state is described by Miha Pogacnik regarding his experience in the Cathedral of Chartres in 1980:

➜ "While I was playing I suddenly felt that I did not play the violin –*I played the cathedral!* I played from the periphery, I was completely present in all these far spaces and I played out there. It slowed me down, it slowed me down. My arms grew into infinity."

This sense of timelessness, total absorption in the process and the loss of ego, was labeled 'flow' by Mihalyi Csikszentmihalyi (1990), and presencing has, indeed, a lot of similarity to flow. Other expressions are: being in the 'zone' or in the 'groove', both well-known phenomena from jazz improvisation. In the east the concept of zen expresses a similar state of high absorption, a total surrender to the process. Once you start thinking, it evaporates. Miha Pogacnik explains it this way:

➜ "The highest moment in the creative experience of music is in the sphere of inspiration, which has a different time quality than the usual experience of time. What meets us in such precious moments is new and gives vision and the strength to pursue the vision."[7]

When the process of presencing succeeds people feel drawn towards expressing future possibilities, which means *letting come*.

CRYSTALLISING

Crystallising concerns the vision that is born out of the former process. Having observed what is going on carefully from without, having sensed it from within, and having been in contact with the higher Self, deep values and personal will form the foundation for co-creating the new vision and intent. Crystallising concerns the emerging vision or intent, growing out of the future field of potential. In my earlier studies on innovation processes (Darsø, 2001:169-170) I described it as follows: "The ideal type of crystallisation is the moment when everything falls into place, when opportunities emerge, when the strategy or the solution becomes clear, when the problem can finally be formulated and when the group breathes a sigh of relief or shouts 'AHA'." When that happens the energy is soaring.

We indirectly witnessed a process of crystallisation in the creation and discussion of 'Business Theatre' at Bang & Olufsen, as this had a very concrete outcome. Other examples of crystallisation were Rich Gold's two ideas, which sprang out of the interaction between scientists and artists. Also personal crystallisations may have emerged. The participants of the leadership programme that started out with the concert of ideas may have had inner visions, even decisions, on how they would do things differently in the future, and so may the participants in Miha Pogacnik's sessions, but inner crystallisations naturally cannot be recognised from without. The process of crystallisation can be personal, but it also happens in good conversations and can be enhanced through metaphors, questions and 'conversation pieces'. When working with creativity and innovation, the crystallisation of a concept or a prototype is the first important outcome and milestone. In strategy sessions and scenario planning, painting and graphic facilitation[8] can be very helpful for envisioning the future. This can, in fact, encourage the next step of *concretising* it into a prototype.

PROTOTYPING

Prototyping means manifesting our thoughts into a physical context and presenting a concept before it is done[9]. This makes it possible to elicit feedback early in the process and to come up with different ideas. By making the concept concrete, prototyping can bring out totally different trajectories of possibilities. Verbal language has certain limitations. Groups can talk for a long time and believe that they agree on a concept. But just ask each person to make a prototype of the concept, and they will be totally different! Still it depends on the kind of discussion the group has. Real dialogue is important during this step as it calls for a common search and discovery. In his book "Serious Play" from 2001, Michael Scrage describes how prototyping encourages, facilitates and speeds up communication and thus increases the potential for innovative outcomes.

Prototyping is used by many of the artists I have interviewed (even if they may not call it prototyping). Prototyping is what Forum Theatre does, when the actors and spectators seek new solutions together by trying out different approaches. Through acting it is possible to see what could happen. In real life we cannot 'rewind' situations and start all over again - unfortunately. Sometimes we wish we could do that. In Forum Theatre we can, and that is one of the major strengths of this method.

A different way of prototyping is through painting or drawing. During an all-day session we have had an artist follow the process by painting what he experienced.[10] At the end of the day we used his paintings as a leverage point for reflection and dialogue. Having something concrete to use as our basis for understanding what went on during the day facilitated the evaluation process and made the process a lot more tangible. This method can likewise be turned around so that the participants each try to draw a small picture or a symbol of what the day meant to them. Also Miha Pogacnik uses prototypes in his icons and drawings for communicating important messages and metaphors. Metaphors are, indeed, perfect prototypes for dialogue, as we saw in chapter 4. The actualisation of the prototype is, however, still the most difficult step to complete because when the prototype has been elaborated and created, the last step concerns *institutionalising*.

EMBODYING

Embodying means actualising or making real. This involves bringing the prototype into new practices, new routines, new infrastructures. This is by far the hardest challenge, and it takes a lot of courage, will and perseverance. Implementation takes acceptance and use by the stakeholders, whether they are internal or external 'customers'. Only when the process of creation includes this last step of institutionalising the new practices or new processes, can we talk about real transformation. "The real challenge is the organisational issue, the interface between individual and organisation." [11] This is where most individuals and organisations give up.

Thus, embodying the new prototypes or practices in the organisation is the institutional 'eye of the needle'. How can the process of creation, which is arduous work, be embodied in such a way that it will have transformative impact on the organisation? Would it be enough if a certain number of individuals experienced personal transformation? If that is the case, then a lot of the cases described in this book have succeeded. From the viewpoint of the organisation, however, it is hardly enough. Interestingly, according to my investigation, it is often the organisations that prefer one event only, whereas many artists would prefer more continuous processes. But when organisations arrange one event only, they run into one of the oldest organisational challenges, the 'Monday morning' syndrome: What happens when you get back to work? How will you embody your new knowledge and skills from the seminar you just attended? How will you change when everything around you seems to want to remain the same? Often your own colleagues will want to hold on to your earlier way of being. You are not to disturb their certainty. Business as usual, please! We brought this up in chapter 3 when introducing Crossan & Sorrenti's framework as the difficulty of moving from 'anticipatory learning' towards 'integrated learning' (instead of 'blocked learning'). Thus step number seven is the main challenge for Arts-in-Business. Business has always looked at the results, and business still likes to measure things. And because this field is new, business obviously does not realise that the learning process must be continued and 'anchored'. We will revert to this in chapter 7, which concerns the practical recommendations.

A final challenge is to harvest the learning through reflection, which completes the cycle by linking it back into the arena of 'capabilities'. Otto Scharmer put it this way: "You need to create a reflective space that allows people to become aware of what they experienced and learnt and also offer them a little space to apply it and link it to their own situation." This type of reflection can be individual as well as collective. And it sounds so easy, but in actual fact how many organisations leave time and space for reflection?

AN EXAMPLE OF THE WHOLE PROCESS

In order to make sense of this entire process of creation, it was necessary to break it down into bits and pieces. Now let us examine one specific case study as a whole, Creative Leaps and their Concert of Ideas, which was followed by a debriefing. At the beginning when the participants of the leadership programme came into the big hall, they were most likely in the mode of 'downloading' as the morning had contained a lot of information about the programme. It is also fair to say that they started by 'seeing', watching and listening to Creative Leaps from 'outside'. Assisted by John Cimino, the audience gave their full attention to the concert. They were taken into 'sensing' when asked to find their inner images and stories and in particular when they were asked about which feelings the music evoked inside them. At the same time the music affected the atmosphere in such a way that bonding took place between people. People felt connected through the music, smiled to each other and were playfully engaged. Music has great power to set moods, and, as we can see from the debriefing that followed, music has a subtle way (maybe combined with poetry and questions) of making us pass the threshold into 'presencing'. A lot of the people said afterwards that the experience had touched them deeply, it had rekindled their spirit, it had influenced their intrinsic motivation, and it had reminded them of the real purpose for being leaders – something larger than themselves. It had also affected their will. They suddenly found that they made or could make a difference to a lot of people. In that sense we can talk about individual transformation for at least part of the participants. The last three steps of 'crystallising', 'prototyping' and 'embodying' were not covered in depth. You could say that the debrief and the group discussions tried to connect the experiences to leadership and change, but from the present data it is still difficult to judge whether it will have real impact on their future leadership. There is, however, no doubt that some of the participants have been touched deeply in ways that could very well induce change. Herbert Tillery, deputy Mayor for Operations in Washington D.C., states that this programme has had a lasting effect on municipal leadership in the capital of the United States since about 300 people have been through the programme. His main message is powerful: "Transformational leadership, out-of-the-box thinking, are the kinds of things that transform governments".

TRANSCENDENCE AND TRANSFORMATION
By applying Scharmer's presencing model as a framework for our analysis, we are now more able to define transcendence and transformation. Transcendence literally means to pass through and beyond, and would therefore, in Scharmer's framework, indicate a transition into the deepest level of the U-curve, i.e. into the field of presencing. But presencing takes stillness, allowing time to slow down and almost stop, and it is rare that 'time' will allow this to happen in organisations, in particular because, on the surface, this looks entirely like the opposite of business efficiency. In Margaret Wheatley's words, "the real need is presently to find the speed of life." Presencing can happen only at the 'speed of life' and it is not possible to 'transcend' if you have only five minutes at your disposal. Genuine organisational transformation takes all seven steps of the U-process – with emphasis on the seventh step of embodying and institutionalising the vision. Thus special attention should be given to the fourth and the seventh steps, as they seem to represent the thresholds for transformation.

BUILDING THE NEW MODEL

Scharmer's framework has enlightened our understanding of the learning processes acquired through artistic experiences, and we are now ready to construct the new Arts-in-Business matrix. In the illustration below the model has been provisionally emptied of the earlier contents in order to make room for Scharmer's U-curve.

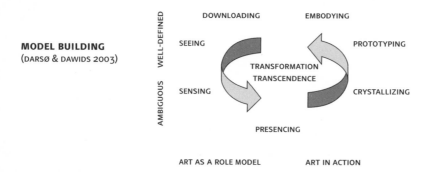

We start by zooming in on the centre of the model, previously described as the 'solar plexus of learning' to indicate that emotions are involved in real transformation. With the new insight derived from Otto Scharmer's model, the overall process can be understood as transcendence (moving downwards through step 4) and transformation (moving upwards through step 7). We call this a learning process of 'artful creation', 'artful' because of a heightened awareness and a changed consciousness based on direct experience, 'creation' because this is combined with vision, passion and will.

When people go through the different levels of the U-curve, they are moved and they are ready to move - if the organisation will let them fulfil their artful creation process. It takes will and perseverance from the group that created it, but it also takes receptivity and support from the top managers and the organisation. The new model will be presented in the next chapter, where we will sum up the findings regarding what business can learn from the arts.

1   Lotte Darsø (2001): "Innovation in the Making", Samfundslitteratur
2   Ibid.
3   Richard Olivier (2001): "Inspirational Leadership. Henry V and the Muse of Fire", The Industrial Society
4   www.CreaLab.dk
5   Interview with Ellen Speert, director of Art Therapy programmes at the University of California, San Diego, USA, September 2002, London
6   In general, literature discerns between the self and the Self. The first concerns the ego and is related to egoism and to concerns of making the world better for 'me'. The Self, on the other hand, means quite the opposite. It concerns the altruistic regard for the common good and for something larger than yourself.
7   Teresa Balough (1996:9): "May Human Beings Hear it! IDRIART", published by CIRCME, School of Music The University

of Western Australia in association with IDRIART

8   E.g. the work of Kuchenmüller and Dr. Stifel at www.visuelle-protokolle.de

9   Interview with Otto Scharmer, September 2002, Copenhagen

10 Karsten Auerbach, at an Arts-in-Business session at Danish Centre for Management in 2002, fam.auerbach@post.tele.dk

11 Interview with Otto Scharmer, September 2002, Copenhagen

CHAPTER 6

WHAT CAN BUSINESS LEARN FROM THE ARTS?

Global society is evolving into a different type of economy with new characteristics, but which? And how will we measure success? If the people, who predict that creativity[1] and 'soft power'[2] will be the most important currency of the future are right, what will replace bottom-line thinking? I will argue that business will also have to pay attention to qualities such as energy, imagination, sensitivity and expression, which can all be learned from the arts. In this chapter we will try to answer the research question 'What can business learn from the arts?' by summarising the main insights and findings in the adjusted Arts-in-Business framework, and secondly by using Ken Wilber's framework, introduced earlier.

THE NEW MATRIX
The revised arenas are: Conceptualising and prototyping; Artful capabilities and competencies; CoLLabs and practice spheres; Social innovation and product innovation. Each will be discussed in the following.

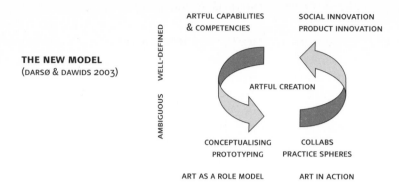

THE NEW MODEL
(DARSØ & DAWIDS 2003)

ARTFUL CAPABILITIES & COMPETENCIES

SOCIAL INNOVATION PRODUCT INNOVATION

WELL-DEFINED

AMBIGUOUS

ARTFUL CREATION

CONCEPTUALISING PROTOTYPING

COLLABS PRACTICE SPHERES

ART AS A ROLE MODEL

ART IN ACTION

CONCEPTUALISING AND PROTOTYPING

The purpose of this arena, previously called 'metaphor', is conceptualisation, communication and expression through any kind of 'language'. Metaphors are essentially tools for making shifts of focus and of mind, both as a way of conceptualising something that is difficult to describe and articulate, and as a way of noticing new aspects of what is well known. Prototyping is basically externalising a mental image or a feeling, putting thoughts into matter. This arena is thus a playfield for rehearsing mental images, thoughts or hunches through dialogue, drawing, painting, modeling, sculpting and working with other creative approaches (e.g. Lego blocks).

Apart from the importance of gymnastics for the imagination, a second aspect, which is just as important, concerns prototyping as advancing human communication. Applying new approaches for starting conversations, e.g. 'conversation pieces', fragments, drama or images, increase the quality and depth of communication between people. The arts include many types of 'language' ('visual speech') and expression (dance and miming), which could inspire and renew business. Looking at leadership through Shakespeare's eyes and seeing through the eyes of a poet illustrate new trends in business. One of the pioneers in bringing poetry into business is David Whyte[3], who today coaches management groups and individual leaders. Interestingly, poetry seems to combine the essence of this arena, as it is a special kind of language, a way of seeing and a vehicle for inner mind shifts. We will therefore voice three different perspectives on poetry and conclude with a fourth role of poetry, namely as a social process. Ted Buswick from Boston Consulting Group, who is working with Clare Morgan of Oxford University on a book for business people about expanding your thinking through reading poetry, says:

➤ "Intensive work in any of the arts is likely to improve emotional and intuitive abilities. Poetry in particular also helps you develop your language skills. Poetry is the most precise and concise use of language that you can find ... There are so many skills - such as language being used for associative rather than logical connections - that you should be able to learn if you really continue to read poetry. It's not just a quick lesson, it's not a workshop, reading and thinking about poetry is something that has to be done continually to build these skills."

Martin Best[4], specialist in the art of the troubadour, has his own particular approach:

➜ "So for example, if we have two faculty members in a symposium, and the subject of the symposium is T.S. Eliot, they will discourage discussion about T.S. Eliot as a poet or artist. My team try not to talk about art, because talking about art is really a waste of time, you either do it or you don't. What we are doing is helping people understand how to see the world through the eyes of the poet. All the facilitation is towards that direction. They are learning from T.S. Eliot to see through the eyes of T.S. Eliot. That's it!"

Judy Sorum Brown, poet and organisational developer, emphasises the inner shifts:

➜ "The essence of poetry is its ability to create inner shifts of understanding by offering an image or a turning or another angle without pushing it. Therefore it does not call forth our defences. Poetry changes us profoundly, but in a way that we will have to be reminded about from time to time. We lose track, and a poem can bring us back."

Finally poetry can also have a social function according to William Ayot, poet and associate director from Olivier Mythodrama, London:

➜ "My aim and my hope is to be accessible, to make something real, and to fill the gap in poetry that has been left out for about a hundred years of modernism. My ultimate desire is to recreate the conversation between poet and audience. This has been very important to our cultures over the millennium. In the north tradition it is called the skaldic tradition. I have been asked to marry people, and to hold meetings in groups, and to find the sense of a meeting in a group and to hold that. I believe that that is also the function of an artist."

In the case studies from chapter 4 we found examples from this arena in Bang & Olufsen's use of the "Business Theatre" metaphor that gave birth to a new training concept and also in the photography sessions at Unilever that brought about important mind shifts. Miha Pogacnik's icons illustrate the application of conversation fragments and the organisational theatre for the home care workers can be understood both as a way of prototyping problem solving and as a conversation starter.

ARTFUL CAPABILITIES AND COMPETENCIES

In the new model we have added 'competencies', which stands for the ability to know when, how and with whom to bring one's capabilities into play. In the case studies we have identified not only some specific – almost tangible – capabilities from the arts, which business can draw directly on, but also capabilities and competencies, which are a lot less tangible, in fact, rather elusive. Evidently business people do not need to become painters or actors or musicians or dancers – not for business purposes, anyway. But, as pointed out by the Catalyst project, business sometimes overlooks the fact that many employees have not had any formal training in reading or writing since they went to school – and yet 90% of their jobs might involve reading and writing. Courses in creative writing, advertising, journalism and business writing as well as reading groups and poetry recitals can improve these skills. Actors and consultants work in different ways with communication and presentation skills, as they include voice, posture, body language and gesture also. Oral skills like storytelling and new approaches to feedback can add value to people's capabilities.

The less tangible capabilities are e.g. sharpening the senses for deep listening and being exposed to new ways of seeing. This implies a higher awareness and a greater sensitivity to signals from the environment and, of course, a greater empathy in relation to people, which again feeds the potential for using intuition and improvisation competently. Other features that business can pick up from the arts are an emphasis on more precise forms of expression, perhaps through new types of 'language'.

Finally, what stand out as unique are some new qualities that business can pick up from the arts. The most important is the concept of *energy*, which was one of the surprising concepts that came up in the interviews. Business people are greatly attracted to the energy that surrounds most artists. Where does it come from? According to Miha Pogacnik this is the core of art and is simply due to *loving what you do*. Artists are passionate about their work and most artists know how to motivate themselves and are good at finding their own passion. "Engagement occurs when we experience a deep sense of caring about the work, a sense that what we are doing is worthwhile in and for itself."[5] Arts director Eric Booth, Juilliard School of New York, explains the difference between motivation in arts and business: "That may be one of the key pieces for the arts that intrinsic motivation is placed in extremely high priority, whereas in most other situations extrinsic motivation really rules the day." Not only do artists work devotedly with their own motivation, they are also able to touch and inspire people in such a way that people feel energised and rekindled after participating in sessions that invite them to transcendence and 'presencing'. This quality is most important to business people, as motivating oneself intrinsically gives more energy and satisfaction than motivating oneself extrinsically through bonus and prestige, and it is important for productivity that leaders are able to inspire and motivate their people. So far energy is only a spin-off effect from working with artists, but it could be interesting to examine it more thoroughly. Most business people would acknowledge that energy is of extreme importance for any type of meeting, any type of organisation, any type of society. Other new qualities, which could become important for business, are practising conscious mental shifts, exercising people's fantasy and imagination, and training intuition and presencing, in short, developing people's potential for artful creation.

Much of the material presented in this book documents the large potential for business in this arena. Project Catalyst is outstanding in its bold vision and its long-term strategy. Unilever (Fabergé and Ice Cream and Frozen Food) strongly believe that they will prosper and grow by developing and training the capabilities and skills of their employees through the arts. And because capabilities and learning are so deeply intertwined, in fact, all the case studies, directly or indirectly, involve this arena.

COLLABS AND PRACTICE SPHERES

The term 'event' was the best we could find at the time we started this research project, but it never quite covered what could take place in this arena. During the investigation of the field, we found two more appropriate labels. The practice sphere is inspired by the hard and disciplined practice of artists. Why does business not have such a space? Otto Scharmer argues:

"It is the notion of practice spheres. An orchestra needs practice spheres before you get the performance. You must create practice spheres in which you can encounter these archetypes of shifts in a safe environment. Because if you do the real thing here it is a high-stake, high-risk environment and what art can offer to us is to do the same thing but in a safer environment."

EXPLORATION
- JOINTLY IDENTIFY PROBLEMS/INTERESTS/QUESTIONS
- REVIEW APPLICABLE FRAMEWORKS/APPROACHES/THEORIES
- DESIGN POSSIBLE EXPERIMENTS AND "LABORATORY SPACE"
- CONSIDER POSSIBLE OUTCOMES AND USES

APPLICATION
- CONSOLIDATE LEARNING
- DEVELOP COMPANY-BASED CHANGE INITIATIVES
- PROMOTE AND DISTRIBUTE FINDINGS
- INVESTIGATE OTHER OUTLETS AND OPPORTUNITIES

EXPERIMENTATION
- ESTABLISH A COMMON GROUND FOR EXPERIMENTATION
- SEEK UNCONVENTIONAL INSPIRATION & PROVOCATION
- PROTOTYPE AND CONTINOUSLY EXPERIMENT
- INVITE OUTSIDERS TO REVEAL BLIND SPOTS

In the industrial age laboratories were created as safe spaces for research and development of new products, but where can we explore and experiment with the social aspects of business? As Stefan Thomke[6], Harvard Business School put it: "We have well-tested, scientific methods for developing and refining manufactured goods – methods that date back to the industrial laboratories of Thomas Edison – but many of them don't seem applicable to the world of services." As a response to this challenge, we developed the CoLLab, a special kind of practice sphere, a Collaborative Learning Lab, which is an invitation for organisations to develop social innovation together with professionals (e.g. artists) and researchers in socially safe spaces. It is "a safe space for organisational discovery, experimentation, and innovation".[7] The idea is to minimise the fear of failure and to make surprise welcome by designing experiments for creating useful and actionable knowledge. The organisation and the professionals will gain new knowledge, the intention being to gradually integrate the learning as it emerges, and the researchers will generate findings to be distributed to a wider public. In the model below, the three phases are outlined.

Whereas the arena of conceptualisation and prototyping is a playground for rehearsing mental images, this arena is a physical playground for human interaction. This concerns relationships between the business people as a group as well as between the participating artists and business people. The first type concerns bonding, creating common ground and connectivity because the focus is on shared experience. The second type concerns the rehearsal and 'experimental learning' involved in a new practice. In some cases the performance of the artist is physical and the involvement of the participants is more mental or verbal, e.g. with Miha Pogacnik's sessions, whereas in others all participants are involved, e.g. in a masterclass, a painting process or in producing music[8]. Forum Theatre is somewhere in between, involving some spectators directly in the play, while the rest are emotionally and mentally engaged. When looking at the case material of this book, most of the case studies take their point of departure in this arena, Forum Theatre and Miha Pogacnik's sessions as mentioned above, but also the concert of ideas starts here and the PAIR project was about interaction between scientists and artists, even if on a smaller scale.

Business can learn a lot from this arena, because it involves many issues related to organisational culture, such as value discussions, storytelling, problem solving (e.g. by Forum Theatre), changes in culture, etc. The arena can also serve as a training field for social innovation, discovering new ways of interacting and new interesting constellations between artists and business people.

SOCIAL INNOVATION AND PRODUCT INNOVATION

This arena is focused on the concrete creation of an innovative product, a new type of service or an organisational change process. Therefore it also includes entrepreneurial start-ups and creative industries. Often the process preceding the creation will start from either the arena of prototyping or practice spheres. The point here is that there is a much better opportunity for innovation if the process involves the arts. As discussed in chapter 3, the building blocks for social innovation are relations of trust and respect, because these grant people the courage to access their own ignorance and what is generally unknown. Interestingly, when I recently asked the Indian film instructor, Shekhar Kapur[9], about his role as an artist, he said: "I can give you an answer to 'What is my role as an artist?' in just three words - 'I don't know'." Obviously Kapur regarded accessing what he does not know as his main role. Thus artists are in general better equipped for participating in the early chaotic processes of innovation than business people. Business people in general prefer certainty, goals, plans – all the things that point towards the well-defined. The implications of 'ignorance' (the diamond of innovation, see chapter 3) are uncertainty, search, trial and error – a lot of complexity and ambiguity. In the arts we find distinct complementary categories, such as scripts, scores, choreographies on one hand, and improvisation, rehearsal and performance on the other. Apparently artists are skilled at handling scripts as well as improvisation, scores as well as rehearsal, etc. What could business learn by being exposed to an artistic working model? Business is skilled at the well-defined, which has been the focus of the industrial age, but not very good at handling the ignorance and uncertainty part of their daily work, which is greatly needed today. As for the two other parameters needed for innovative crystallisation, relations and concepts, relation building is not taken seriously by business people, and yet this is the foundation for any social practice. As for concepts, communication, in most business settings, consists of 'downloading' and 'collective monologues', mainly because of time pressure, but also because of old habits rooted in 'scientific management'.

In the case studies of this book we have described several outcomes, which belong to this arena. An extraordinary example was Volvo Car Corporation, who bought the services of an artist as a product. They hired an artistic mind-set, because they wanted inspiration and provocation. Other examples were artists being given specific tasks, such as encouraging resolution in the decision-making process or giving new inspiration to a team, whose members were stuck in their habitual thinking. Also the B&O new training concept, 'business theatre', is an example of an innovative product that was developed through an artistic metaphor. Another outcome was the improvised performance of 'Sticky', and an example of a change process was Unilever's 'Live & Direct' project of rehearsal for improved feedback processes.

Thus, the application of artistic and artful processes can move business forward to make better business in two interdependent ways: one towards innovation and profit, the other towards more humane and energetic organisations. Evidently, this organisational hybrid will attract top talent.

WHAT CAN BUSINESS LEARN FROM THE ARTS? APPLYING KEN WILBER'S FOUR QUADRANTS

We will end this chapter by applying Ken Wilber's four-quadrant framework, introduced in chapter 2. This means answering the question from four different viewpoints: the subjective individual (I), the objective singular (it), the intersubjective collective (we), and the interobjective collective (its).

WHAT CAN THE INDIVIDUAL BUSINESS PERSON LEARN FROM THE ARTS? (I)

This quadrant concerns the personal and individual I. The keywords are experiencing, seeing, sensing, listening, feeling, touching, moving, imagining, thinking, trying, exploring, wondering, reflecting, voicing, expressing, challenging, presencing - and learning. Throughout the book it seems evident that artistic and artful processes can have strong impact on personal development, self-management and leadership development. The quest for personal and spiritual development is increasing in Western society ("the Revolution from Within"[10]), as apparently a lot of people desire to explore self-realisation, the top of Maslow's pyramid. The arts are often gateways towards spiritual growth, because the arts touch people's hearts. We saw the power of music in the description of Miha Pogacnik's Brahms' Sonata and in the Concert of Ideas by Creative Leaps, when people talked about being rekindled and having re-found the core of leadership. Becoming

FRAMEWORK BY KEN WILBER, 2000

	SUBJECTIVE	OBJECTIVE
INDIVIDUAL	I	IT
COLLECTIVE	WE	ITS
	INTERSUBJECTIVE	INTEROBJECTIVE

more artful involves a different level of consciousness, based on practice and experience of the heart. The arts thus have a strong potential for individual learning and transformation.

Furthermore, personal development has become an important aspect of people's working life. People want to work for companies that give them the benefits of challenging tasks and self-development[11] - as seen in the quotes from the people from Unilever ("I want to experience life at the maximum"; "My aim is to bring the colour, daring, contrast and innovation that is 'Sticky' into my work and my life"; "The opportunity, the potential, the atmosphere and that buzziness, the vibrancy, I love that feeling of opportunity"). Unilever (Fabergé and Ice Cream & Frozen Food) has realised that by developing these competencies of self-management and creativity, the company will have motivated, creative and highly effective employees. But oddly, few companies have yet realised that this is really a win-win situation.

WHAT OUTCOMES DO WE SEE OBJECTIVELY FROM ARTS-IN-BUSINESS? (IT)

This quadrant concerns facts. Looking at the case studies of this book we can see that the Washington leadership programme continues with Concerts of Ideas, not because of habit, but because of the personal development that results from it. The Xerox PARC PAIR project resulted in various artistic products, a book, in which the outcomes have been described and analysed, and two interesting ideas by Rich Gold, the first concerning artists keeping projects alive so as to fill the gap between research and marketing, and the second concerning the development of EKO's (Evocative Knowledge Objects) to bridge the communication gap between scientists and engineers. At Bang & Olufsen the "Business Theatre" metaphor resulted in a brochure and a training concept for sales people. In the case of the domestic helpers participating in Forum Theatre, their social working conditions improved after the sessions. Miha Pogacnik has, in collaboration with others, manifested 180 IDRIART festivals around the world, and his business consulting workshops are growing. The involvement of an artist at Volvo Cars, apart from what happened internally, resulted in a lot of publicity and media interest in Volvo Cars. At Unilever Fabergé and Ice Cream and Frozen Food project Catalyst has added many fingerprints. Physically, in both places there are small creative islands with 'artsy' furniture (e.g. huge arm chairs with built-in loud-speakers), an inspirational library based on the employee's recommendations and favourite books, colourful walls and bright office ornaments, art exhibitions, e.g. a stairwell art collection, selected by the employees, touring photo exhibitions from 'Sticky' and from 'Urban Fiction' (the photography project) together with the postcard series of the photos in mini-format, and the children's book, "A Freak Food Accident and other stories"[12]. For the last couple of years Unilever Fabergé has consistently posted double-digit profit growth in a mature market[13], and, when asked about why they have taken on a project like Catalyst, the chairman, Keith Weed, emphasises:

➤ " At the end of the day, I am a hard-nosed businessman who wants to sell more washing powder. This is not a soft issue, it's a very hard issue of how you motivate and inspire people. We are a mass-market consumer goods company. We sell more than a million and a half units a day. And if I didn't think this programme was pulling its weight I would cut it in a second."[14]

In Denmark several initiatives were launched by the Danish government: NyX (a network of Art & Business people), LOUIZ (cultural entrepreneurs), and The Creative Alliance at Learning Lab Denmark (doing research on artful approaches for organisational transformation).

The above outcomes are, of course, far from exhaustive. They derive from the cases and people I have chosen to focus on. Within the last few years the numbers of artists working in business have greatly increased, so we will surely see many more results in the future.

WHAT CAN ORGANISATIONS LEARN FROM THE ARTS? (WE)

This quadrant concerns the subjective 'we'. Here the most important feature is the connectedness and togetherness that can be created and enhanced through the arts. We have seen that relations of trust and respect are fundamental to innovation, but they are, in fact, also important for organisational culture in general. The idea of starting vital conversations in organisations is not new, e.g. David Bohm started 'dialogue' sessions in the 1970s because he saw participation as essential not only for organisations but for the world: "The general view I have is that participation is fundamental. That means we must have dialogue. We must share our thoughts. We must be able to think together. If we can't think together and talk together, then we can do nothing together. But in fact that is the hardest thing in the world."[15] Because of the increased time pressure on work and output in business, the need is so much bigger today. Conversation starters, conversation pieces, Forum Theatre and storytelling are new attempts to create and recreate organisational identity and mutual understanding. Margaret Wheatley has said that the sustainability of a company, in particular in times of crisis, rests on the quality of its relationships. And as pointed out before, shared experiences that involve feelings build strong relationships. On the department level or project group level, the arts can inspire new approaches to working as a team or as an ensemble[16], which again is fundamental for effectiveness and efficiency.

WHAT IMPACT DOES ARTS-IN-BUSINESS HAVE ON SOCIETY? (ITS)

This quadrant concerns the objective impact on a larger collective scale. Obviously, because the field is new at this point in time we have more questions than answers. Going through the case studies of this book, we can start with the powerful words of Herb Tillery, Deputy Mayer of Washington D.C.: "Leadership transforms governments". It is not within the scope of this study to put this statement to the test, but it could be investigated. As for the teachers in Norwalk, if this experiment is successful, it will have wider implications for the school system of Connecticut. Regarding the Xerox PARC PAIR project, apart from being a pioneering adventure, it has involved many local stakeholders and is, according to Craig Harris[17], a "portable" project that others can learn from, especially because of the book. It remains to be seen whether Bang & Olufsen's strategy of 'Business Theatre' will influence the strategies of their competitors, as the HR training director proposed. Will it have a lasting impact, could it be a new social type of disruptive technology[18] - or will it be replaced by something else?

Has Miha Pogacnik initiated the societal and cultural transformation that he thinks is so incredibly urgent and important? What is the impact of all the IDRIART festivals, making cultural meetings in order to get inspiration from the outside world in areas on the planet where people are oppressed and cannot leave their country? History has demonstrated that single individuals like Nelson Mandela, Mother Teresa, Mahatma Ghandi or Adolf Hitler can influence, for good or for bad, the development of society. History also shows how groups of people who start important conversations, like the 'solidarity' movement in Poland or Greenpeace, can become waves that influence nations and our increasingly global society. Volvo Car's Peter Rask[19] ponders: "Art has always reacted to the surrounding world, and if anything has an impact on society today, it's companies. It is natural for art to relate to the business world. It is strange that we don't see more activity in this area." Unilever receives a lot of attention from the media, which could help inspire other companies to follow their example. The government initiatives in Denmark influence government initiatives in other countries (e.g. the Nordic countries). And hopefully this book will inspire and influence people around the world in business, arts and society. In the chapter that follows we will outline some practical recommendations.

1   Richard Florida (2002): "The rise of the creative class", Basic Books

2   Joseph Nye (2004): "Soft Power: The Means to Success in World Politics", Public Affairs

3   David Whyte (2002): "The Heart Aroused: Poetry and the Preservation of the Soul in Corporate America", Currency, a division of Random House

4   Martin Best is also founder of The Corporate Theatre, London, www.thecorporatetheatre.com

5   Dick Richards (1995:31): "Artful Work. Awakening, Joy, Meaning, and Commitment in the Workplace", Berrett-Kohler Publishers

6   Stefan Thomke (2003:71): "R&D Comes to Services. Bank of America's Pathbreaking Experiments", Harvard Business Review, April 2003, p. 71-79

7   The Creative Alliance, Learning Lab Denmark: CoLLab www.lld.dk/creativealliance

8   E.g. Art in Rhythm, Holland, see www.artinrhythm.com

9   This took place at the World Economic Forum in Davos, in the workshop "If an Artist ran your Business", January 2004

10 Otto Scharmer, presentation at Learning Lab Denmark, November 6, 2000

11 Ian I. Mitroff & Elizabeth A. Denton (1999): "A Spiritual Audit of Corporate America. A Hard Look at Spirituality, Religion, and Values in the Workplace", Jossey-Bass Publishers

12 Margot Rose, John Simpson & Nik Wilkinson (2003): "A Freak Food Accident and other stories", published by Unilever Ice Cream & Frozen Food, Walton

13 David Butcher (2003:41): "A Fruitful Union", article in Management Today, August 2003

14 Ibid.

15 David Bohm (1998:111): "On Creativity", edited by Lee Nichol, Routledge

16 According to Piers Ibbotson: "An ensemble is engaged in co-creation, and a team is more focused on external goals", from interview, April 2002, London

17 Craig Harris (ed) (1999:34): "Art and Innovation: The Xerox PARC Artist-in-Residence Program", MIT Press

18 This concept was developed by Clayton Christensen (1997) in "The Innovator's dilemma", Harvard Business School Press

19 Nanna Schacht: "Not the Emperor's new clothes", Design DK: 4, 2002 December, p. 20

CHAPTER 7

RECOMMENDATIONS FOR ARTS-IN-BUSINESS

REARRANGEMENT OR DEEP CHANGE?

If we apply Scharmer's learning cycle for understanding different levels of change that can be reached in organisations, we can identify four levels. The first level, consisting of steps 1 and 7, only scratches the surface. Many top-down change programmes have no real effect, as they are merely 'forced learning' or rearrangements. People obey orders by pretending and paying lip service, while they silently resent the change and wait for it to 'pass' until the next 'change initiative' is launched. The next level, steps 2 and 6, involves thinking and discussion. This would happen typically on an off-site meeting of a management team, where there is time to think and talk. The subject could be strategy and goals, solving a critical problem or other management issues that need to be decided upon. By and large the discussion would be rational and factual, and the result could be a change programme for the organisation or important decisions on strategy. Generally these are the two levels applied by business. According to Scharmer, the two first levels are only reactions and reflections on the experiences of the past. Because feelings are considered irrational in business and therefore illegitimate, the door to the next level is kept mostly closed. In addition to that, feelings are often too complex and difficult to handle with the available business tools.

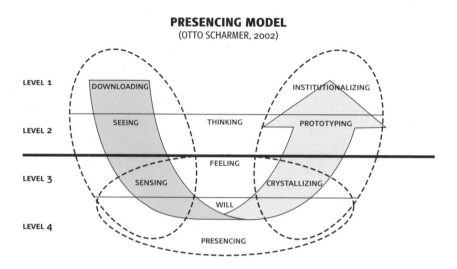

Taking the step of accessing the next level, steps 3 and 5, involves feelings, and there the arts, as we have seen earlier, have proven to be powerful. On important matters, such as value discussions, teambuilding or culture building, it is natural to include both sides of the brain, intellect and feelings. A value discussion, which involves only the intellect, is not a real value discussion. Thus, involving people's feelings in relevant matters is acceptable as long as the process is respectful, but it must be emphasised that this takes good process and facilitation skills, which is something that artists do not always have. Finally, step 4, the deepest level, enable contact with people's higher Self, which means their passion, commitment and will. Real transformation happens only when these last two levels are reached. We must, however, imprint these levels with 'handle with care'. Only healthy and honest organisations should attempt to work with all levels. Most companies are better off with only the first two levels of 'business as usual'.

APPROACHES TO ARTS-IN-BUSINESS
In the first chapter we outlined four possibilities regarding Arts-in-Business:

1. The arts as *decoration*
2. The arts as *entertainment*
3. The arts as *an instrument*
4. The arts as a *strategic process of transformation*

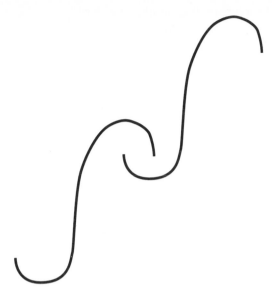

The first two approaches are mainstream, and in the following we will focus on numbers 3 and 4. Let us start off the discussion with one of Miha Pogacnik's 'icons'.

According to Miha Pogacnik, this icon symbolizes a development in classical music, where the lower figure denotes the development of a theme. The music builds up, nicely at first (when the figure is rising), but then (the curve going down) becomes chaotic or violent or harsh (or all of this together) – but out of this chaotic mess the new and transformed theme (symbolised by the higher figure) is born. At the 2001 Arts & Business conference in Borl, Slovenia, this particular icon started several deep conversations; first a conversation involving all the participants regarding the future of the arts, business and society; later a more private conversation of five people over lunch, refining the discussion. Probably each person has his/her own interpretation.[1] The following is mine.

To me this 'icon', metaphor or conversation fragment symbolises the dying out of the old instrumental paradigm of the industrial age. While the dinosaurs are struggling to stay alive (being aggressive and immoral) or are starving themselves (by firing people) in order to last a bit longer, the new pioneers and entrepreneurs are struggling to breathe, clinging to hopes for a better world, carried by the paradigm of 'artful creation'. Many companies and people are caught in between these two paradigms, they sense that one is dying, but in crisis and moments of doubt they cling to the old and well-known, they dare not invest wholeheartedly in the new, as it is barely being born and still mostly unknown. This elusiveness is symbolised in the somewhat misty quality of the top figure.

To use Arts-in-Business for real transformation, belongs to the new paradigm. But the new, of course, builds on and incorporates the old. It is not an either – or. It is *more*: body,

THE DEATH AND BIRTH OF PARADIGMS

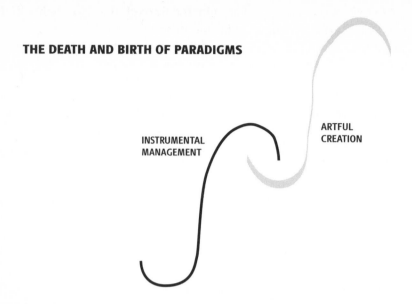

INSTRUMENTAL
MANAGEMENT

ARTFUL
CREATION

mind, heart and spirit. Therefore, let us start by depicting the contours of artful creation. When artful thinking becomes part of strategic thinking, the vision for business becomes more whole and encompassing. Business will realise that it is not enough to work with only the 'true', business also needs the 'good' and the 'beautiful' – in particular on the long run. The following is an image of the future business organisation: the artful organisation has a higher purpose and works for something noble, e.g. to cure diseases, to make functional and beautiful houses, to find new ways of growing and distributing food to the large part of the population that needs it, to create intelligent machines or robots that can relieve people of hard physical work – there are numerous possibilities for solving the pertinent problems of our global society. The artful company does not have a fixed growth rate to make stockholders happy, it could be owned by the employees, at any rate it is happy with a small, reasonable profit. The company genuinely cares for its employees, the managers do not only say "our people are the most important asset" - they act on it. Personal and professional development is an important part of the agenda, as this is what gives the people their passion for continuous creativity and innovation. The investment in people pays off in a high loyalty and in a playful, compassionate and artful culture. The image may seem rosy, but it is far from unobtainable. Unilever is taking that road.

Regarding the instrumental approach, where business applies the arts as tools for team-building, communication training, leadership development, problem solving and innovation processes, there are some pitfalls that should be avoided. The greatest trap can be phrased very bluntly. Do not use the arts to 'stir the pot'. Artistic processes are powerful beyond measure, which is good, of course, but they also make people think and feel, which is both good and bad, because if the business is a 'flatland'[2] business without real purpose or the organisation is highly political, which unfortunately applies to many organisations today, these features are illuminated through the sharp lights of the arts - because basically the arts disturb, provoke and mirror behaviour. The result of 'stirring the pot' in an unhealthy organisation is often that the people who stay become cynical and the others (the best) leave the organisation, because people who think and feel do not put up with bad organisations - or governments or societies for that matter. A highly political or unethical corporation will be wise to stay away from the arts – or use it only for entertainment and decoration.

If we go back to the icon and assume that the logic of the icon is plausible, corporations that do not renew themselves and do not take their global, social and ethical responsibility seriously will die out (the end of the figure symbolising instrumental management). At the same time there are numerous examples of social entrepreneurs and groups who decide to make a difference. Naturally some will succeed and some will fail, but hopefully they use what they learn and try again. In the icon the trying and failing is symbolised in the downward curve at the beginning of the top figure. Corporations of the future will be artful creators, which means that they have integrated instrumental management with the new paradigm of artful creation. And for the corporations that are in between the old and the new, a small bridge has been constructed to get them across to the future. It is a bridge of hope, a bridge of practice, a bridge of connectivity, a bridge of energetic and important conversations – an artistic bridge towards artful creation.

THE DEATH AND BIRTH OF PARADIGMS

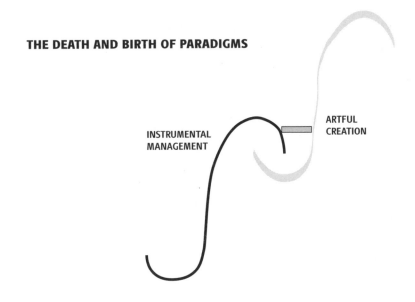

INSTRUMENTAL
MANAGEMENT

ARTFUL
CREATION

RECOMMENDATIONS FOR ARTS-IN-BUSINESS

The following suggestions are for people who are considering applying the arts to business:

1. Be clear about the purpose and objectives
2. Consider short-term or long-term
3. Consider the timing in relation to the organisation
4. Select excellent artists
5. Consider the type and potential of an Artist-Business relationship
6. Prepare well by asking relevant questions
7. Start small

BE CLEAR ABOUT THE PURPOSE AND OBJECTIVES

Ask yourself *why* you want to bring in the arts. Is it for a well-defined task or is it for a process? Try to use the Arts-in-Business matrix to help clarify the purpose and objectives. Then consider whether the process or the result could be obtained in any other way? What would be the difference? What are the consequences of bringing in the arts? What could possibly go wrong?

I can give you an example from my own work to illustrate some of the deliberations and difficulties involved. As a consultant I was recently asked to conduct a one-day seminar for a company of about 50 people. I intuitively sensed that something was wrong, as my contact persons seemed nervous, and I did ask and got an evasive answer, but I did not follow my intuition, so I accepted. There had been some difficulties in this young company, because, for the first time in the company's history, about 20% of the employees had been sacked a month earlier. Apparently this was causing some doubts regarding the future of the company, and some of the best people were leaving for new jobs. The goal of the seminar was to restore hope and to reassure that everything would be fine. The day was full of pep-talks, creative group work and appreciative leadership, and the artistic surprise of the afternoon was that they would all sing as a chorus, helped by a wonderful energetic team of two young people, a woman singing and conducting and a man accompanying on the piano. This was my idea and at the time it seemed right – and it looked like a success then. A month or two later I heard that the company had had to dismiss another large group of people and that there were problems in the management group. I felt regretful, because I *had* sensed that something was wrong. How would the employees feel when they looked back on the seminar and their singing together? I would assume that they would feel betrayed – maybe even violated, because this, in retrospect, seemed as a show put on to manipulate them, to calm them down, and to make them stay. In that way, retrospectively, this exercise might have had the opposite effect than that intended. Furthermore, if we ask the question, 'Could it have gone wrong?' Yes, the atmosphere underneath the fun must have been more or less explosive. Had one person voiced the doubts that they all felt, then singing together might not have been an option. And to answer the above question, we should probably have done something else and have saved the singing for a better occasion.

The thing *not* to do is to exploit the arts in order to be able to say to the media "we have tried this and done that", meaning, "we are so much at the front edge". That is counter-productive and a shame. It is important, like Keith Weed of Unilever Fabergé, to have a clear purpose, as was the case when he and his management team took the strategic decision to invest resources in the company culture:

→ "I wanted to create a business that really valued creativity and innovation and embraced change. Art's a great way to bring that sort of inspiration into the business. It's not sponsorship; we don't sign cheques to support things. It's an exchange. We put funding in, but in return for something. We start with 'What's the business issue we're trying to address?' Then we find an artist to help us tackle it."[3]

SHORT-TERM OR LONG-TERM?

This question is important in relation to the desired effect, which brings us back to the purpose and the objectives. Short-term works very well with artists in well-defined tasks (the upper part of the Arts-in-Business matrix). Example: a project group is working on an innovation task with a special kind of plaster for feet. They feel stuck and uninspired and therefore ask an artist for inspiration. The project manager meets with the artist and explains their situation and their needs. Two weeks later the artist meets with the group and shows them a short-film he has produced on feet. Through this film, the project group suddenly sees feet from a totally different perspective and the work continues with a lot of new energy. This was a perfect short-term success[4], because it was a small, well-defined task ('product'). There are many successes of this type. Alejandra Mørk, senior vice-president of Nycomed, has engaged artists for several small well-defined jobs in the company's project work. Every time it was a matter of business tasks and it was never just for fun – but it was often great fun to work that way. She believes that artists will become a new type of consultants, both because consultancy and business in general need renewal, and because business will come to value more aesthetic approaches. Other well-defined tasks could be in the arena of capabilities, e.g. training presentation and communication skills.

It is when organisations move into the area of process (the bottom part of the Arts-in-Business matrix) that long-term continuity seems preferable. This includes change processes, culture development, problem solving, important conversations, leadership development, and creativity and innovation processes. Paradoxically, according to the interviews, it is often the organisations themselves that do not want a follow-up or a continuous process. It is an often-articulated wish from the side of the artists that they would prefer processes that were more continuous. This is the missing link in most one-time events. Even with a debriefing afterwards, the process tends to evaporate – which in reality means no real learning ('blocked learning'). It will be remembered, certainly, but the long-lasting effects remain to be seen. Therefore it is recommended that an experienced facilitator, e.g. a HR consultant from the company, works closely with the artists in order to draft a continuous process, which is followed closely and adapted according to what emerges. According to Eric Booth, artistic director at the Juilliard School, New York City, the planning itself can be a good learning process:

➤ "In the conversations I have had, where we are trying to plan out what a program might look like, they almost don't know how to participate in the conversation, because they don't know what the outcome looks like. So, it is a very awkward planning dance; it takes a long time to really plan in a way that is going to be more than just a quick explosive high, like a scud-missile event, in which everyone is all shaken up and then settles, and nothing lasting happened. Too often that is what they have in mind. In the cases where people have been willing to think beyond that model towards something that is really looking at changing the way people do business, changing the way they relate to ideas in the workplace, the planning takes at least as much time as the actual events themselves. ... I took several lessons away from that, number one was the importance of the planning and how in fact the deepest issues of values come up in that planning. Probably the educational process of the planning is the single most important element for long-term success."

It is important to note that when moving downwards in the Arts-in-Business matrix into the field of ambiguity, the outcome cannot be defined and specified beforehand. The overall purpose can, but the outcome itself cannot be controlled, as it will be emergent. Obviously, this calls for questions like: Is the organisation geared for long-term processes? Does management really want change of this emergent kind? And will they support it?

CONSIDER THE TIMING IN RELATION TO THE ORGANISATION
The above questions are important as they point towards the context and the history of the organisation. We will not go into the line of thought on the developmental phases of an organisation (e.g. Greiner[5]), but rather focus on the current situation of an organisation. Where is the organisation right now? What kind of change processes has the organisation been through within the last couple of years? What are the immediate challenges? What are the long-term needs of the organisation?

When Unilever Fabergé started the Catalyst program, it took place around the merger of Elida Fabergé and Lever Brothers. Alastair Creamer happened to enter the stage at the right time, saw the potential and seized the opportunity. Bobby Brittain, Innovation Director, Unilever Ice Cream, recalls:

➤ " ... I think we can see some tangible benefits from the programme, and doing it at the right time is also important, guessing the timing right within a business. It is one of the things I have noticed in Kingston when Catalyst started, that it was at a time when, within Lever Fabergé, the whole climate was ready, the business as a whole was mature enough to take on something like Catalyst. Similarly with ice cream, we did not do Catalyst when I first turned up 2 years ago because there were other things we needed to fix. We actually had to get the business into a good enough shape, and we were making lots of big structural changes to the business, which inevitably meant redundancies and it was not appropriate to have the Catalyst programme there. Now we have got a much more stable business where people are looking for new ways to tackle the problems they face because they know they are going to have them. There is a feeling of certainty and security about the business that now needs to be injected with a bit of passion and creativity."

Brittain thus recommends starting long-term processes involving the arts in business when things are somewhat stable. Large and mature organisations need injections of energy and renewal much more than small young companies. Involving the arts in connection with an important change, like a merger, is also recommendable, as it is important to work on creating a new common culture, instead of having cultural 'wars' and create a win-loose situation. And the arts are perfectly suited for bonding and developing good relations, as we have seen in so many examples already.

But when change processes are taking place, which involve difficult challenges, e.g. redundancies, involving the arts is not a good idea, as this will only make the process more thorny and painful.

SELECT EXCELLENT ARTISTS

Most of the artists I have interviewed have been artists all their life and are excellent, and excellence penetrates the many barriers that business people put up against the arts. People immediately recognise quality when they see it, and this creates respect. The danger is, of course, that people who call themselves artists, but who are far from excellent, look at business as a new opportunity for making 'fast' money. That could cause a lot of damage in this dew-fresh field. Therefore it is important to get the artists' credentials, CV's or talk to people who have tried the process earlier. Senior vice-president Alejandra Mørk from Nycomed raises this whole question of professionalism as the 'Achilles heal' for business, both in relation to the difficulty in judging the quality of artistic capabilities and in relation to ensuring specific 'consultancy skills', such as being professional in communication and facilitation. The way Unilever solved this problem was to employ an experienced artist to be in charge of project Catalyst. Other options are to form joint ventures between artists and consultants. Professional organisations like Art & Business, UK and many organisations from CEREC[6], have created networks, banks and web-based exchanges. Surely new types of consultancies that can guarantee the quality and skills needed will arise.

CONSIDER THE TYPE AND POTENTIAL OF AN ARTIST-BUSINESS RELATIONSHIP

Another recommendation is to consider various types of relationships with artists. Should it be a short-term relationship or preferably long-term? Should the artist remain an outsider or would the effect be stronger with an artist-in-residence? Of course, it depends on the purpose, but it is important to keep in mind. At Unilever several relationships have become long-term.

Karl James, actor and co-director of Trade Secrets, started with Catalyst already in 1999 and is still working with Unilever. He and his team have had various tasks, among others leadership development, and they still coach some of the top managers. Karl James expressed the dilemma this way:

➜ "And I think it is both a curse and a blessing that an organisation builds and creates and supports and sustains Catalyst, whose job is to challenge and change and provoke and educate and inspire and yet, of course, by being in the cage, you know, the danger is always that you are going to lose your edge, but then you seem to address that because you are constantly inviting in edge"...

The danger of being inside an organisation ("being in the cage") is, of course, that the artist loses his edge, because he gets socialised and tends to become part of the culture. The advantage, on the other hand, is that the artist gets to know the organisation better, can speak and understand the 'language' and has good relationships – and a good reputation. Through Alastair Creamer Unilever has developed several types of relationships with artists. The MAP consortium of actors and facilitators have been artists-in-residence for a three-month period and the relationship with Rut Luxemburg, the German photographer, has developed into a mutually fruitful collaboration. At Nycomed they have developed a fancy for scenography, which they use to create a different 'feel' and atmosphere at meetings. Thus they have developed a good relationship with a scenographer. In fact, this is comparable to good consultancy; if consultants do a good job, people tend to invite them back. As for artists-in-residence, this is a model often used in the United States, but mostly in the educational sector. Inviting artists into a research laboratory, as done in Xerox Parc, is unusual, but some interesting ideas and experiences have come out of that. Other examples are the London Musici being a 'chamber orchestra in-residence' at Clifford Chance, and companies having 'in-house authors'[7]. A different type of relationship is to invite a group of artists into the organisation to make art with the production materials in collaboration with the employees.[8] Surely the future will bring many new types of artists-in-residence and artists-ex-residence.

CATALOGUE OF QUESTIONS

What is the purpose and what are the objectives?
- Why do you want to bring in the arts?
- Using the Arts-in-Business matrix, where is your focus and what do you hope for?
- Could the process or the result be obtained any other way? What would be the difference?
- What are the consequences of bringing in the arts?
- How will you inform and communicate about this?[9]

- What could possibly go wrong?

Short-term or long-term?
- Is it for a well-defined task or is it for a process?
- In what ways is the organisation geared for long-term processes?
- Can you find an experienced facilitator to be part of the planning team?
- Will management let go of control and allow emergent change?
- Will management support processes involving the arts?

What is the timing in relation to the organisation?
- What is the situation of the organisation right now?
- Is it a young or more mature organisation?
- What kind of change processes has the organisation been through recently?
- What are the immediate challenges of the organisation?
- What are the long-term needs?

How will you select excellent artists?
- What are your criteria for selection?
- How will you verify the credentials of the artists?
- How will you introduce the artists?
- Which barriers do you foresee from the participants?
- And how will you deal with them?

Which Artist-Business relationship would benefit the organisation?
- What would be the benefits of a short-term versus a long-term relationship with artists?
- What would be the benefits of an artist-ex-residence versus an artist-in-residence?
- New types of sponsorships, collaborations, exhibitions?

START SMALL

Even if you have great visions, it is recommendable to start small. Begin with small well-defined tasks. It could be to bring a spark of inspiration into a project, to bring provocation and challenge into a meeting, to change the atmosphere of a course, to encourage motivation, to improve relationships, to inspire important conversations, to develop new skills, to build a team in a new way, etc.

It may sound like Unilever saw the potential of the arts, set out with a vision and a strategy, immediately hired an experienced artist, gave him a huge budget and launched project Catalyst. But that is not quite what happened. Unilever had a vision and a strategy for creating an 'enterprise culture'[10]. James Hill and Keeth Weed, CEO's of Unilever Fabergé and Ice Cream & Frozen Food, ran into Alastair Creamer, who happened to be finishing a working commitment elsewhere, so they asked Alastair to join Unilever Fabergé for three months to come up with a project. One thing led to another, one success led to another, and so the ground became fertile for suggesting a project like Catalyst. Catalyst is now an important asset, but its reputation was earned through a lot of hard work and through a massive variety of small successes.

Working on the strategic level with the arts is a complex affair, which can be recommended only to courageous organisations and corporations that honestly want to transform themselves; organisations, which are ready to go on a hero's journey including uncertainty, anxiety, crisis and pain in order to give birth to a renewed and transformed, artful organisation. Still, it will be wise to start the journey with small trips to the nearest hamlets in order to see if the travellers and the vehicle can hold together and carry through successfully, before setting out on the real journey.

1   E.g. Margaret J. Wheatley (2002): "Supporting Pioneering Leaders as Communities of Practice. How to Rapidly Develop New Leaders in Great Numbers", www.margaretwheatley.com

2   This concept is borrowed from Ken Wilber, 2000

3   David Butcher (2003): "A Fruitful Union", article in Management Today, August 2003

4   This was part of the Danish Art-Lab project in 2002, see chapter 4, 'How Governments Matter'

5   E.g. Larry Greiner's model of organisational life cycles from 1972, in Mary Jo Hatch (1997:174): Organisation Theory, Oxford University Press

6   CEREC, the European Committee for Business, Arts and Culture, www.cerec-network.org

7   Marianne Gade was employed for 6 months as inspirational author-in-residence at the company Klingspor, Denmark (sales of metal milling and grinding machines) www.labcom.dk

8   "Visionsindustri" udgivet af Vestsjællands Kunstmuseum og Informations Forlag (ed. "Vision Industry", an exhibition and catalogue by the Museum of Western Zealand and Information Publishing)

9   A lesson was learnt about the importance of information and communication in the case study "Why not catapult a brand new Volvo?" (chapter 4)

10 A few years earlier Dutch Unilever went through a different, but very interesting learning journey of transformation, see Philip Mirvis, Karen Ayas & George Roth (2003): "To the Desert and Back. The Story of One of the Most Dramatic Business Transformations on Record", Jossey-Bass

CHAPTER 8

ARTFUL SOCIETY

THE FUTURE OF CAPITALISM

What is the future role of business in a global economy? What is the future of capitalism? In the following I will list some of the fears and hopes in order to envision 'artful' business and 'artful' society. Margaret Wheatley pointed towards some of the dark sides of global capitalism:

→ "Well, capitalism is in deep trouble, and it is not just capitalism. I appreciate it when it is described not as simple capitalism, but as global capitalism, because that is a different animal. Global capitalism is all about the flow of money and about the complete disconnection between the people, who are producing the products and the owners - with so many levels of removal from people's communities and their lives. Decisions are made only on behalf of very short-term profit, or how we can make money in this instant. So global capitalism has no long-term perspective, and has no really human face; and it DOES operate at just about the speed of light, because it is all electronic transactions. Even calling it a short-term focus is not appropriate, because it can be a moment-to-moment focus on how you make money. It is not about sustainability, it is not about building for the long term, and it has been completely disruptive and destructive for human communities everywhere. I have not the least bit of patience for anyone who any longer believes that global capitalism has improved a lot of people. It has ONLY made a VERY few people and nations extraordinarily wealthy - and created increased poverty in the world....

So I do not see any future for capitalism in its current form. I believe in the older form, the early form of capitalism, which for a while in Europe was being promoted under this wonderful phrase; capitalism with a human face. We have really got to focus on the human side of it now, if we are going to make any changes. But when I look at it into the future, it almost does not matter what happens to business, because the pressure of population growth, disease and poverty is overwhelming. You know half of the world lives on less than 2 dollars a day. Half of the world! And 800 million people live in abject poverty and starvation."

How did it get this far? When we hear about these massive challenges of global society, of politics and business, we know this is 'true', and we also know that this is definitely neither 'good' nor 'beautiful'. The problems of this planet are enormous and complex and, of course, we cannot blame it on business alone, but the fact is that corporations are becoming increasingly influential – maybe even more powerful than politicians. Rightly a lot of people's attention is drawn towards the possible directions that business could take. Will business continue to be "only in it for the money"?[1] Or will business assume a social responsibility for our global future?

ART AND BUSINESS – THE HEART OF BUSINESS?
How can the arts influence business? In my interview with Ted Buswick, director of publications at BCG, he emphasised an important feature regarding the question of impact:

➜ "You do not necessarily have to reach a majority to have an impact. What you have to do is reach the right person, and you don't even know if you are reaching that person, once you send your books out into the world or however you are communicating, whether it is a lecture or whatever it may be. But if you reach a few of the right people and then through those people, what you are doing affects a larger number, then you are doing your job, and it is all worth it."

At times business is seen as a monster – and sometimes rightfully so – but let us not forget that there are people behind business, human beings with hearts. Reaching the people with influence and power is important for many of the artists I have interviewed, and the way to reach these people is through their hearts. "To connect on the level of our humanity is the most important thing", says John Cimino, Creative Leaps. And Margaret Wheatley adds: "Whatever happens, I want people to understand the goodness of human beings, and the strengths we have that we could call upon." Otto Scharmer believes in art as the transformative power of the future: "Because the world is driven by business, we need *an art that is transforming the heart of today's society, that is, the social relationships, in particular business."* In the following paragraph seven artists express their intentions and hopes for influencing business towards more heart:

→ Richard Olivier, actor and director, London: "I did some work for Nokia, which now turns over more in a year than Finland, an entire nation. Nations and governments are no longer able to have the control. So if you look fifty years into the future, where is that oversight going to come from? It is going to have to come from the business. I know some people who may be flirting with the field rather than have stepped into it, who think that their purpose is to get people out of business, but then, who is going to be left in? I think the real sacrifice for people is to say - *this is where I can do the most good in my life, this company, on the ethical part - and maintaining a sustainable future for itself and the communities in which it works.* ... One of the guys from BP, who is in charge of 115,000 people worldwide, said that he was meeting with some of the other CEO's and HR directors of a world company after September 11th, and he said that the conversation had changed. People really started to question what right they had to go into a third world country company, the whole thing with unbalances and disagreements. ... *And he said he had never heard anyone in the world talk like that before. I think that is something that artists can help, to sustain those conversations*, they might all have happened on September 12th, but often by December the 12th, they would have been forgotten, *and I think artists can help to set the agenda. 'Agent for change', that is something, I think, artists are doing.* Tomorrow people are preparing for May Day riots, anti-capitalist protests in the city, throwing bricks at McDonalds - so, that is one way, and I think that this is probably very important. But the other way is to get in. No one will listen to you when you are throwing a brick through their window. They will say okay, maybe we need to do something else so that our customers don't get upset, but they won't actually listen to what those people are trying to say. We (the artists) are like the Trojan horse."

→ Bruce Copley, didgeridoo player and director from South Africa: "So I don't only think that it is the arts that can be a benefit to business. I think everything can be a benefit to business. We see arts being of benefit particularly to business in that the arts are very rich in emotion. *The arts are about heart stuff.* I mean we go to the theatres because we want to be moved, we listen to music because we want to be moved. There is a spiritual, emotional intuitive essence to it. And because that is so missing in business it is almost like that is the medicine business needs. But business can also get that medicine from many other things."

→ Ashley Ramsden, actor and storyteller, London: "I think business can learn a new language. Clearly, business people are very tired of the sort of bullet-point acronyms, that kind of dry head language. When you bring in the picture language of storytelling, when you actually tell a story, and leave that story behind like a kind of seed, there is imaginative language that people can refer back to and engage in – not just with their heads, but *also with their hearts*. And because there is no one interpretation to a story, the story lives on and keeps on revealing different levels of truth, so it is not just a dry thing, a dead thing. It is something that actually speaks to the imagination. When you are working with story, you are in the room of potential. You are in the room of the future; it is not something that is fixed. And that is one of the things that storytelling does."

➤ Steve Taylor, assistant professor and organisational playwright, USA: "During that time I was reading something that Athol Fugard had written, where Fugard said that when he was 30 he realized what he wanted to do in life. He wanted to change the situation in his country, South Africa, and he wrote plays with the intention of basically getting rid of apartheid. I think he was a big part of why that happened over there. I think his work was very critical there and I think, like Vaclav Havel in Czechoslovakia, *theatre was important in social change*. I like writing plays, *but social change is what I was really interested in. But I decided that in the US social change wasn't going to happen through theatre. In fact the place this was going to happen, the place where people live sort of an emotional life was in organisations*."

➤ Oliver MacDonald, self-taught percussionist and community builder, London and South Africa: "Something that we see very clearly, because of the nature of our work, is that we work *with corporations, great enablers, that can create a lot of change due to the backing that they have*, and that affects us all in very different ways in terms of having weight behind them, as you have your company or organisation to back you on this project. It makes it easier and makes it more credible, because they have contacts. Corporations have a large and fairly bad name, but the way we see it is the possible good that can come of it. ...We have done some projects with companies where they have worked in the community; they have sponsored projects and have actually taken part in them, because what goes on in such a project is very much two-way. They go away feeling amazing, because they have made this connection. It brings a spark into their lives and that relationship is balanced. The challenge is to challenge the perception that if a business gives something to a community it is a one-way charity to these needy people. In fact, it is perceived as a two-way thing, *businesses will become involved in charities because it is good for them, and they seem to be doing something good. We like to make it explicit that the relationship that can be built on, is a two way process, which is mutual and beneficial*. That is a challenge. An aspiration that I have is to bring some of the great community leaders that I have worked with together for a week with some of the great corporation leaders and actually share experiences, share understanding and really see how they can help each other out."

➤ David Pearl, opera singer turned 'business arts pioneer', London: "A lot of artists want to change the world. They want to be loved and appreciated, sure, but they also want to make a difference. There are many who feel 'corporate work' compromises their artistic ideas. For myself, I feel the work serves our ideals. A good deal more than a lot of conventional performing does. The people we work with are very senior. We are tapping into the corporate reservoir of power. If you make a small incremental difference in their thinking or in their structure or processes, it can amount to a big collective shift. It is not always easy to see that shift but if you pull out and see the whole mosaic – all the people working internationally in this area with thousands of companies every day – it starts to look more like a compelling movement."

➤ Miha Pogacnik, violinist and business consultant, Slovenia: "In the 1990s it suddenly became obvious that economy is at the centre of all questions. It was not just ideology; the ideology went out of the window in 1989, and suddenly it was gone. But economy and the question of poverty and wealth had to be looked at from another angle and acted upon. ... *How do you bring the world of artistic process into organisational development and personal development, because that was really at the heart of the problem for the whole world.* We live in economic society, and those who run economic society have difficulties in becoming whole human beings. As a leader, art really is inclusive in all that it takes to compose human society. *Yet the power is there, so we felt that from the point of view of the business or the economy the traditional perception of art is to help artists. This is totally wrong; it has to be turned around. Artists are supposed to help economy. Because artists are at the gateway of advancing worlds of capacity, which we need in these turbulent economic times in order to be responsible.*"

Will business take this invitation to dance with the arts? Will business recognise its responsibility for improving the global economic balance? Will the artists succeed in humanising business? Only the future will tell. New concepts of 'corporate giving' and 'corporate philanthropy' have seen the light of day, and the fact is that many large corporations support educational and technological projects around the world. The root meaning of "economy" is, according to David Bohm, "household management". Bohm further suggests[2]: "So the first step in economics is to say: 'The earth is one household. It is all one.'" It *would* make a difference if business would think in wholes as well as in global balance and long-term effects. And here business could get inspiration from the Native Americans, who have made a habit of considering seven generations to come when making important decisions.

THE DOUBLE CAREER PATH OF THE FUTURE

Many of the artists I have interviewed turned out to have interesting career paths. As a routine I would ask them about their background and much to my surprise it turned out that a lot of them had had two separate career paths, or one career and one very time consuming hobby, until at a certain point in their life these suddenly merged into one - their current occupation. And most often this was catalysed by a consultant, as we saw with Miha Pogacnik. Each tale was slightly different, for some it seemed quite natural, as John Kao, who describes how this happened early in his life:

➤ "When I was growing up, my first career goal was to be a musician. I actually began to study music when I was four. And my mother was a musician, so she started to teach me even before I was four. So I played music pretty intensively from that age on, and it wasn't really until the age 18 that I realized that I wasn't going to be a full time musician. That was a high level of commitment. But at the same time, I was also acting as an entrepreneur, except I didn't really know that it was business. So I started my first business when I was 10 years old. I started my first venture, which was I had an idea, and I figured out how to do it, I figured out how to get the resources and to promote it. I didn't know that that was business, I just thought that it was things that you did, to take your idea and make your idea come true. So, in a way I have always had this kind of dual task – with arts on the one hand and starting new businesses on the other. I have always been very attached to the process of creation."

For others it happened later. Marijke Broekhuijsen kept two career paths going for many years, one in cultural pedagogies and one in theatre. On the first one she was active in adult education and as the curator of a museum, on the second path she worked on the stage and for TV. By working for Shell as an independent management trainer the two paths came together: using the knowledge and skills gained from professional theatre in management development. At present she is programme director at the EMDC Nyenrode University, responsible for designing and executing programmes for senior managers. Although arts in the strict sense is only one of the many methods in this function, she maintains that the most important source for her professional activities originates from her acting and directing rather than her university studies of pedagogy.

Karl James, musician and co-director, Trade Secrets, UK, expresses it in few words:
➔ "As a child my passion and one of my instinctive skills was music, and I was good at music and I was good at math and I was good at English. And actually those three strangely are with me in this kind of work" ...

Michael Jones, pianist, teacher and consultant, used to have two separate careers until a seminal conference:

➔ "This was the first time I had actually been invited in to a conference to play the piano in the conference and not after hours. So I went to the conference and a number of people, who were part of this newly formed MIT dialogue project, were there, and this was the first point when these two things in my life, of leadership and organisation on one hand and the artistic and creating and imagining on the other, began to converge."

Could this incidence of double paths signal the emergence of new and more encompassing careers? Could these be indications of the third revolution, "the revolution from within", which, according to Otto Scharmer[3], concerns spirituality and self-development? Some facts point in that direction. If we look at the types of books that make the bestseller lists, a lot of them are on personal and spiritual development. In fact, most people in the Western world practice some kind of artistic endeavour in their leisure time, a trend that can be seen from the increased sales of arts 'equipment'. As we see boundaries melting between work and leisure, our mental boundaries of what constitutes 'work' and 'productivity' may soften too and allow new insights to emerge.

→ Paul Audley, member of the board of Creative Leaps: "Arts in a business community or a business organisation changes productivity, it changes sick patterns, it changes a lot in the lives of the people, because it allows them to tap into themselves, vent their emotions. They may not be singing but the singing may drive them to tears and they have released something that somebody just doesn't get the opportunity to do anymore. And I think that it does create a lot more energetic thinking, a lot more creativity. There is value in stimulating the brain and the soul of people who have become treadmill runners. It makes a difference in our lives and it certainly makes a difference in a business culture."

Interestingly, one of the 'side-effects' of bringing the arts into business is that it surfaces the (hidden) talent, which is already present in the organisations. Seeing professional artists at work and seeing the effects of that work inspires people with similar interests and talents to try new things. *It gives them permission*. This is evident both at Unilever and in Nycomed. A lot of employees have talents that are never used at work, because, as a relic of the industrial age, these are not considered productive. According to Margaret Wheatley it is well documented that most businesses use very little of what people have to offer. In her interview she gave an example of a CEO from a telecommunication company (and this was before the industry became crazy), who admitted that they only used 10% of what their workers had to offer (and he added that the problem was that they actually succeeded in using only 10%). Her real question was, however: "How could we expect people to fully contribute to an organisation if they cannot bring their whole souls to work? " Thus, we need to reconsider 'productivity'. The suggestion of this book is that the productivity of the future is 'artful creation'.

WHAT CAN THE ARTS LEARN FROM BUSINESS?

All through this book we have focused on what business can learn from the arts. Let us now in one small paragraph reverse that question.

→ Rich Gold, director of PAIR at Xerox Parc: "We live in the era of business. We don't need to help business. They are running the planet. The problem is in the other direction, how do you help the arts? So the question in my mind is: how can the arts learn from business? In the PAIR programme the artists learned far more. It radically altered the artists. The artists came out with their eyes wide open."

→ Martin Best, founder of The Corporate Theatre: "The artist must understand that business is also an art, because both imply a search for structure. I do not believe in this attitude that art is good and business is dirty. I believe that human beings are good, and that those that are in business are doing good things, just as those that are in the arts are doing good things. It is not to say, that you can't get bad artists and bad art and bad business and bad business people. Of course you can. We have confused popular art with real art, or to put it another way: We have confused mood with feeling. We have substituted beat for rhythm. We have tunes instead of melodies. I find that the globalisation of pop culture is a very dangerous thing. Conversely, I think business is moving into a new paradigm of inspiration. That is why I think business could actually teach more to art, than art to business."

At the beginning of this book we raised the important question whether the arts have come to a crossroads. According to the above quotations, this seems the case. Artists' general (mis)conception of business is that business is a monster and business people are evil, and conversely business' general (mis)conception of artists is that art is soft stuff, touchy-feely, and cannot add anything to business. Both are, of course, misconceptions and wrong. Some artists will never want to approach business and with all respect, nobody would want them to compromise their art. But some artists are keen on renewing their artwork and their own understanding of it. They see a new potential, a new playing field, and a new source of income. The guidance from the artists, who are already in this field, is for the new artists to remember to keep practising their art also. Their own art must remain their pool of inspiration. The artists in business generally have a lot of respect for people working in organisations.

➜ David Pearl, opera singer and director: "It is a question which presupposes the arts and business are very different. I like to think of business and arts, not as different fields, but as different aspects of the creative process. Shakespeare, remember, was a manager *and* an artist. He ran a company and wrote the plays. If the two fields weren't separate for someone like him, why then for us normal mortals?

For me, working with organisations has been as revealing and valuable as all the hours I have spent rehearsing and performing. Specifically I have learned about how to make things happen – how to be an entrepreneur I suppose. And to do it artfully, so it is not painful or effortful. I also have picked up a lot more compassion and respect for people who do something different but are, in essence, very similar. Boal said something like " All of us act, some of us are actors". Some of the most beautiful things I have seen theatrically have been created by people who are not actors or trained artists and despite (or perhaps because of this) produce amazing moments of discovery.

Again, speaking for myself, I love to bring things to life. I think there is just as much opportunity in the arts as in business. When you see how sleepy and fixed many arts organisations are it can be a shock. Just because your output is 'artistic' it doesn't justify being Neanderthal in the way you treat people or think about enterprise. Put it another way, if you want to be a healthy creative enterprise, then you need to be creative about everything; how you operate, organise yourself, nurture people, create wealth, run your paperwork. All of it.

A lot of the transformation work we do involves taking 'non-theatre' people into theatres. I sense the suspicion that theatre staff has when 'business people' start invading their territory. I love to watch that melt as they see we are honouring the deep traditions but in a fresh way. As one theatre director said to me recently when we were working with civil servants in his house, 'This is how theatre used to be when I got into it'. And in a way, I think people are now coming to workshops for the transformational experience that theatre used to give them. Maybe it is the theatre of the future."

THE NEW ROLE OF THE ARTS

In an artful society everybody will have the freedom to develop multiple intelligences and artistic skills. This will contribute to business and society with an abundance of productivity, but the measurement will be of quality and artfulness instead of quantity and price. The value added will be energy, beauty and magic, often developed in co-creation. This new type of productivity calls for new types of intelligences, capabilities and competencies. The higher the education the more important it will be to develop extra non-formal and artful competencies. We are already seeing new varieties of academic research that reflect more artful and aesthetic[4] qualities as well as new forms of representation. An outstanding example of artful research and representation is the work of Dr Laura Brearley[5] from RMIT University, Victoria, Australia. In one of her studies she gathered data by having post-graduate students draw images of their experience of undertaking post-graduate research. This was followed by an interview where the drawings were explained and thereby used as a conversation piece. Laura then used creative modalities to analyse the data and wrote up her findings both as research publications and as lyrics. In fact, Laura has presented her findings at several academic conferences[6], singing them live, accompanied by her guitar. Incorporating emotional, aesthetic and artful qualities in research is an interesting example of new types of integration. As proposed by Ken Wilber, integration follows a period of differentiation and tends to weave together the old and the new, the individual and the collective, the mind and the heart, the past and the future, knowledge and wisdom - but on a higher level of evolution. According to professor David Cowan[7], both knowledge and wisdom are needed for 'artistic intelligence':

➡ "Artistic intelligence promotes full expression of one's potential in ways that meaningfully affect the world around us. Thus, artistic intelligence is not detached, head-in-the-clouds fantasising, but it is also not taking existing ideas and merely forcing them into place like a template. Within this juncture, artistic intelligence connects with the past yet reveals fresh inroads to the future. Knowledge is a prerequisite but only in terms of its principles and patterns. The wisdom side of the equation brings fresh awareness and playful responses because it is not constrained by the past."

Due to increased competition companies have for several decades recognised an urgent need for creativity and innovation in their organisations. In an industrial paradigm the natural approach is to take training courses in techniques and tools for creative problem solving. The difficulty is, however, the 'Monday Morning' syndrome of 'no learning', as the new tools rarely fit into the existing company culture and procedures. In the new paradigm of 'artful creation' creativity becomes an attitude or a mind-set, which is integrated into the organisational culture. The ability to change perspective, appreciate diversity and look at opportunities from new angles is a vital value, which penetrates the 'products' from conception to marketing. James Hill, CEO of Unilever Ice Cream & Frozen Food, refers to the magic ingredient Unilever aims at creating to give them competitive advantage. John Kao, musician, entrepreneur and author, explicitly explains how magic can be artfully designed:

➡ "What's the best thing you say about a movie, a play or a ballet? That is "that was magical". But the magic is actually designed; it is not an accident. Producers know how to create that intense magic performance, maybe it's the way the lights shine on people or something about the costumes or what comes before something else. Most people in business don't even understand magic, except maybe they understand it intuitively, so some CEOs, for instance, are very good at communication, because they have an intuitive sense of what it means to be a good communicator. But because business is mostly a child of the industrial revolution, magic is not important, efficiency is important. But that's why being in business in this period of time, where we are in the middle of going from the industrial economy to the idea economy or the dream economy or the new economy, whatever you want to call it, is so exciting, because it involves a whole set of new skills. And artists have a lot of those skills, except the problem with artists is that they don't necessarily have the language for talking with business people."

Artists can use these new types of skills for specific tasks, which, as we saw in chapter 7, is a recommendable approach for companies when beginning an Arts-in-Business track. This means using the arts instrumentally. If this approach is successful and attracts focus and recognition from key people in top management, the journey - apart from solving a few immediate problems - will also generate important spin-off effects in the longer term. It will permit the existing hidden artistic capabilities of the employees to surface, which may again encourage a new strategic direction for personal development and transformation, as we have seen in the Catalyst programme of Unilever. One of the important challenges of leadership today is the increasing complexity of business. Consequently there is a need to develop competency for planning *and* improvising as well as capacity for control *and* release. The difficulty is, of course, deciding when to plan and when to improvise. In an artful paradigm authenticity and presence is paramount, but interestingly this must be founded on preparation and disciplined practice. Professor and artist Nancy Adler phrased it like this:

➡ "One of the things I increasingly realise, when I paint a painting, is that the best paintings are born. It happens when I get quiet and I do not get in the way of the painting. It still means that I need all the technique and every bit of knowledge that I can get whether it is colour, composition, texture, you know the various tools, all of that stuff. Little by little I have recognised that when I get the absolutely best talk, this is exactly the same thing, I do my homework very well beforehand, I plan, some of my friends laugh because I will do this whole outline; I will have the quotes I want to use, I will have the examples I want to use and they go "You will be totally rigid", but that has nothing to do with being rigid. If I am that well prepared then it allows me to set it aside so that I am totally confident that whatever moment questions strike, there is in me what wants to come out of that moment..."

This is an excellent example of combining knowledge with wisdom and also of learning from the future. In artful society art reverts to becoming integrated in human life, whether in business or in the private sphere. The idea of extending the notion of art to everyday life was important to Joseph Beuys, the German artist, who maintained that art should play a wider role in shaping the content of our daily lives, "whether in painting, music, engineering, caring for the sick, the economy or whatever"[8]. According to Beuys the art form of the 20th century is the "social sculpture", and as we have seen throughout the pages of this book the real difference in relation to the role of art is that the new type of artists are engaging not so much in their own artistic process of creation, but rather in a social process of artful co-creation. The new type of artwork is joy, energy, magic, relationships, learning and innovation – and heightened sensitivity, increased awareness and widened consciousness. Evidently, we need to examine these phenomena more closely. In this book we have only scratched the surface.

We will conclude with a message from the great composer, Johan Sebastian Bach, whose music has accompanied much of my writing. Bach accentuated the social role of art with the message of his own music:

"In the architecture of my music
I want to demonstrate to the world
the architecture of a new and beautiful social commonwealth.
The secret of my harmony?
I alone know it.
Each instrument in counterpoint,
and as many contrapuntal parts as there are instruments.
It is the enlightened self discipline of the various parts,
each voluntarily imposing on itself the limits of its individual freedom
for the well-being of the community.
That is my message.
Not the autocracy of a single stubborn melody on the one hand,
nor the anarchy of the unchecked noise on the other.
No, a delicate balance between the two:
an enlightened freedom.
The science of my art.
The art of my science.
The harmony of the stars in the heavens,
the yearning for brotherhood in the heart of man.
This is the secret of my music."[9]

1 This was the title of an album with Frank Zappa and The Mothers of Invention in the 1970s

2 David Bohm (1998:110) (edited by Lee Nichol): "On Creativity", Routledge

3 Lecture with Otto Scharmer, Borl, Slovenia, July 2002,

4 ACORN stands for Aesthetics, Creativity, and Organization Research Network and consists of about 100 organization, management, and work-life researchers united by a common interest in creatively advancing research into aesthetics, creativity, and arts-based learning in organizational settings, www.acorn.lld.dk

5 Senior Lecturer and Manager, Organisational Development, RMIT University, Faculty of Education, Language and Community Services, Bundoora, Victoria, Australia

6 E.g. at the Academy of Management 2003 in Seattle, USA

7 David A. Cowan (2002:7): "Artistic Intelligence and Leadership Framing: Employing the Wisdom of Envisioning, Improvisation, Introspection, and Inclusion", The Art of Management and Organization conference, London

8 http://members.aol.com/mindwebart2/page183.htm

9 Johann Sebastian Bach quoted in Idriart 10th Anniversary Report, Summer 1991, in: Teresa Balough (1996:14): "May Human Beings Hear it! IDRIART", published by CIRCME, School of Music The University of Western Australia in association with IDRIART

LIST OF INTERVIEWEES

Nancy Adler, professor of International Management, McGill University, Montreal, Canada
Nancy consults and conducts research on global leadership, cross-cultural management, strategic international human resource management and women as global leaders. She has authored more than 100 articles and produced the film "A Portable Life". Her "International Dimensions of Organizational Behavior" (4th edition, 2002) book has over a quarter million copies in print in many languages. Recently Nancy has also revealed her talent as an artist working with watercolours.
www.mcgill.ca
Interview: December 2003, Copenhagen, Denmark

Richard Albagli, principal percussionist and timpanist, Creative Leaps International, NY, USA
Richard is founding Vice President and Treasurer of Associated Solo Artists Inc (1972). He holds Bachelor's and Master's degrees in physics from Rensselaer Polytechnic Institute. His dual background in physics and music has been the basis of dozens of projects linking the arts, sciences and humanities. As principal percussionist Richard has performed with the Berkshire Symphony and the Albany Symphony. He is Musical Director of the Empire State

Youth Percussion Ensemble and holds teaching posts at SUNY-Albany and Rensselaer Poly-technic Institute.
www.creativeleaps.org
Interview: August 2002, Washington DC, USA

Paul Audley, member of the board of Creative Leaps Inc., NY, USA
Paul Audley holds a Bachelor's degree in Social Science and English from the University of Bridgeport and a Juris Doctorate from Quinnipiac College School of Law. He has been an international speaker on strategic planning, re-engineering, change management, and performance measurement, most recently as a consultant with JMC Industries.
www.creativeleaps.org
Interview: August 2002, Washington DC, USA

William Ayot, poet, playwright and associate director, Olivier Mythodrama, London, UK
William worked closely with Richard Olivier on the development of Mythodrama. His special interests are creativity and access to the imagination in the workplace. William's writing includes the play 'Bengal Lancer' and two collections of poetry. He is a past winner of the Piccadilly Poets Competition for spoken poetry and was commissioned by Shakespeare's Globe Theatre to write/read a poem for the 400th anniversary of Julius Caesar. Other writing includes television, film and radio work, and numerous articles.
www.oliviermythodrama.com
Interview: July 2002, Borl, Slovenia

Martin Best, musician and specialist in the art of the troubadour. Founder of The Corporate Theatre, London, UK
The Corporate Theatre is structured as a core team of four people plus a highly networked faculty of leading trainers, facilitators, performing artists, political scientists, philosophers, historians and organisational psychologists. All are highly successful in their fields and are hand-picked for their powers of empathy and communication. The Corporate Theatre uses performance skills, intensive study, and team-working to open people to new freedoms of expression, new modes of thought, new powers of engagement and co-operation, and new levels of self-awareness.
www.thecorporatetheatre.com
Interview: April 2002, London, UK

Debbie Bird, senior brand manager, Unilever Ice Cream & Frozen Food, Walton-on-Thames, UK. Interview: November 2003, Walton-on-Thames, London, UK

Victor Bischoff, actor, mime and specialist in masks, Hamburg and London
Victor has a background in mime and body-oriented training, but has also studied clowning and Comedia in Paris and Italy. His main interest is the neutral mask, which can help uncover stereotyped ways of behaving, moving and acting. Victor spent 18 years with an Indian Yogi, working with meditation and presence. He has done corporate work with sticks and masks and is associated with the Cranfield School of Management, UK.

Interview: May 2002, Copenhagen, Denmark

Eric Booth, artistic director of the Mentoring Program at The Juilliard School, NYC, USA
The Mentoring Program was established to help Juilliard art students adapt to an arts world that has changed, demanding a wider range and repertoire of personal skills in young artists. Eric Booth is on the faculty of Lincoln Center Institute, The Kennedy Center, is Founding Editor of the Teaching Artist Journal, and is a consultant and frequent keynote speaker on the arts to the general public, business groups, arts and governmental organisations, and schools.
www.juilliard.edu/college/mentoring.html
Interview: August 2002, New York City, USA

Michael Brammer, artist, Copenhagen, Denmark
Michael Brammer works with conceptual art and installations. With roots in the punk environment of the 1980s Brammer deliberately wants to disturb and provoke. In 1994 he included 4 stuffed Labrador puppies in an art exhibition, 'Love', in Copenhagen. Brammer has worked thematically with the business world in various artworks and exhibitions, and in 2001 he secured a one-year collaboration with Volvo Cars Corporation.
Interview: November 2002, Copenhagen, Denmark

Marijke Broekhuijsen, actor and programme director, the Executive and Management Development Centre, Universiteit Nyenrode, Breukelen, The Netherlands.
Marijke Broekhuijsen trained as a performing artist and has performed in many professional productions on stage and for television. She studied Cultural Pedagogy and has an M.A. in Arts & Media Management. She has been active in a wide range of adult education and development programmes as museum curator and project manager in theatres, and since 1980 in management development where she often uses theatre techniques and approaches. She also works as an independent trainer/consultant and since 1991 as a faculty member of Nyenrode University.
www.nijenrode.nl/
Interview: November 2002, Breukelen, The Netherlands

Bobby Brittain, innovation director, Unilever Ice Cream & Frozen Food, Walton-on-Thames, UK
Interview: November 2003, Walton-on-Thames, London, UK

Judy Sorum Brown, independent educator, consultant and author doing work in organisations on leadership, change, learning, dialogue, diversity and renewal, Hyattsville, MD, USA
Judy holds a Ph.D. in Comparative Literature from Michigan State University, and has served as a White House Fellow. She teaches leadership at the School of Public Affairs at the University of Maryland, where she is also a senior fellow of the James MacGregor Burns Academy of Leadership. An author, poet, and public speaker she works with leaders and leadership teams across all sectors. Her most recent book of poetry "The sea accepts all rivers and other poems" was published by Miles River Press (2000).

www.judysorumbrown.com
Interview: July 2002, Borl, Slovenia

Ted Buswick, director of publications for The Strategy Institute, oral historian for The Innovation, Marketing and Communications Group, BCG, USA
The Boston Consulting Group is an international strategy and general management consulting firm whose mission is to help leading corporations create and sustain competitive advantage. The Strategy Institute was created to enrich strategic thinking by collecting insights into the nature of strategy from various fields and transferring them to strategy in business and society. Ted currently heads an institute project relating the reading of poetry to strategic thinking.
www.bcg.com
Interview: February 2003, Copenhagen, Denmark

Jill Chappell, programme coordinator, George Washington University, Washington DC, USA
Interview: August 2002, Washington DC, USA

John Cimino, singer & composer, director, Creative Leaps International, founding president of its parent company Associated Solo Artists Inc., NY, USA
Educated at Rensselaer Polytechnic Institute (biology & physics), the State University of New York at Albany (learning theory), and the Manhattan and Juilliard Schools of Music (music & voice), John holds a uniquely interdisciplinary perspective and works both creatively and interpretively across the arts, sciences and studies of the learning process. He is the winner of 24 international awards for singing and has performed throughout the USA and Europe including opposite tenor Luciano Pavarotti.
www.creativeleaps.org
Interview: June 2002, Borl, Slovenia

Bruce Copley, director, AAHA Learning, Cape Town, South Africa
For the past 15 years Bruce has immersed himself in the art and science of informal education. He has pioneered and developed a revolutionary holistic method of education and training known as COGMOTICS. Utilising a remarkable array of activities and skills such as storytelling through a didgeridoo, vocal harmonics, commusication, drama, poetry, comedy, edutainment, holoprinting, etc., Bruce transforms boring conventional messages and topics into vibrant and captivating learning adventures.
www.aahalearning.com
Interview: July 2002, Borl, Slovenia

Alastair Creamer, producer, Catalyst, Lever Fabergé and Unilever Ice cream & Frozen Food, Kingston and Walton-on-Thames, UK
Alastair studied music throughout his education and has worked in arts management for 20 years. He worked at the BBC, the Aldeburgh Festival, ran the Blackheath Concert Halls, Chicken Shed Theatre Company, was Dean of Faculty at the London College of Music and Media and ran a private arts foundation. He also worked in business, as arts sponsorship manager

for Sainsbury's in the early 1990s. In 1999 he created the Catalyst programme at Unilever, which was the amalgam of all these experiences - sharing artistic and business processes as a source of inspiration.
Interview: November 2003, Kingston and Walton-on-Thames, London, UK

Janet de Merode, member of the board of Creative Leaps Inc., NY, USA
Janet's first career was as an economist and manager at the World Bank. During her twenty years there, assisting the economic development of poor countries, she worked extensively in Africa, Asia and Europe. Janet subsequently founded GlobalMed, a company providing procurement services for buyers and suppliers of basic medicines in developing countries. Janet is also a piano accompanist and cellist.
www.creativeleaps.org
Interview: August 2002, Washington DC, USA

Lily Donagh, brand manager, Unilever Ice Cream & Frozen Food, Walton-on-Thames, UK
Interview: November 2003, Walton-on-Thames, London, UK

Annemarie Ehrlich, eurhythmy trainer, teacher and consultant, The Netherlands
Annemarie studied eurhythmy in Den Haag and was a eurhythmy teacher in a Steiner school in The Netherlands. She was co-creator of "Academie voor Eurythmie" in Den Haag and in 1986 founder of "Institute for Eurhythmy in Working Life", The Netherlands.
Annemarie has used eurhythmy in leadership courses and many types of courses in companies, and she has also developed advanced courses for eurhythmy trainers. She has recently started an educational business project in Holland and Egypt.
Interview: July 2002, Borl, Slovenia

Rich Gold, digital artist, inventor, cartoonist, composer, lecturer and interdisciplinary researcher, CA, USA
Rich Gold co-founded the League of Automatic Music Composers, the first network computer band, he invented the field of Algorithmic Symbolism and worked as a consultant in Virtual Reality. In 1991 he joined Xerox PARC and in 1993 he created the PARC Artist-In-Residence program (PAIR). Rich Gold was a provocative speaker who lectured throughout the world, from corporations to art organisations, on the future of the book, the nature of engineering, creativity, innovation and Evocative Knowledge Objects. Rich Gold died in his sleep on January 9, 2003.
www.richgold.org/
Interview: November 2002, Delft, The Netherlands

Adrian Greystoke, marketing trainee, Unilever Ice Cream & Frozen Food, Walton-on-Thames, UK
Interview: November 2003, Walton-on-Thames, London, UK

Stanley S. Gryskiewicz, Ph.D, member of the board of Creative Leaps Inc., NY, USA
Stan is an international authority in creativity, leadership, and innovation with over thirty

years of experience. He is currently the Vice President of Global Initiatives and Senior Fellow of Creativity and Innovation at the Center for Creative Leadership in Greensboro, North Carolina. The Center for Creative Leadership is an international non-profit organisation aiming at expanding the leadership capabilities of individuals and organisations from across the public, private, non-profit, government and education sectors.
www.creativeleaps.org/ and www.ccl.org
Interview: August 2002, Washington DC, USA

David M. Guss, author and associate professor of anthropology, Tufts University, Medford, MA, USA
As an anthropologist, David's main scholarly focus has been Latin America, with research projects in the Amazon and Bolivia. Also interested in local cultural history, he headed "The Lost Theatres of Somerville", an exhibit that ran at the Somerville Museum. David sits on the Somerville Historic Preservation Commission. David has written several books, including "To Weave and Sing. Art, Symbol and Narrative in the South American Rain Forest", 1989, and "The Festive State: Race, Ethnicity, and Nationalism as Cultural Performance", 2003, University of California Press.
http://www.tufts.edu
Interview: August 2002, Boston, USA

Hollis Headrick, executive director of The Center for Arts Education, NYC, USA
Hollis is a musician and an anthropologist by training. He has taught in public schools and is a performing jazz musician and producer of contemporary music concerts. Hollis worked in an arts agency, where he was responsible for an arts education programme and in 1996 he started The Center for Arts Education in New York City on a 12 million dollar challenge grant from the Annenberg Foundation in Philadelphia. The mission was to address the issues of school reform and improvement.
www.cae-nyc.org
Interview: August 2002, New York City, USA

James Hill, chairman, Unilever Ice Cream & Frozen Food, Walton-on-Thames, UK
James Hill obtained a M.A. in Economics and Accountancy from the University of Glasgow in 1980 and started the same year in Unilever as a personnel trainee. Later he switched to marketing as brand manager and as senior brand manager. During 10 years he worked in Spain, Greece and Belgium before returning to the UK, first as chairman of the Fabric Conditioners Category for Europe, and in 2003 as chairman of Unilever Ice Cream & Frozen Food. James is a member of the Royal National Theatre Board and of the Food Policy and Resources committee of the UK Food and Drink Federation.
www.unilever.com
Interview: November 2003, Walton-on-Thames, London, UK

Piers Ibbotson, actor and assistant director of The Directing Creativity Programme at the Royal Shakespeare Company (RSC), London, UK
Piers trained originally as a scientist and worked in the oil industry before entering the

theatre in 1980. He had a successful career as a performer, working at the Royal National Theatre and the RSC as well as making appearances in TV and film. In 1990 he became an assistant director with the Royal Shakespeare Company and started The Directing Creativity Programme, which was developed with the support of Allied Domecq plc. The programme provides management development and consultancy for business using techniques and approaches from the world of theatre.
Interview: April 2002, London, UK

Karl James, actor and co-director, Trade Secrets, London, UK
Karl started playing music from early age, but discovered theatre, went to drama school and became an actor. He later started directing in a professional theatre environment, but his work with a children's play about the Bosnian war led him into educational theatre, sponsored by the British government and various foundations. He was introduced to the corporate world through his work with a management consultancy, which inspired him to start the company Trade Secrets. Karl was one of the first artists to start working with project Catalyst at Unilever.
www.tradesecrets-uk.com
Interview: November 2003, Walton-on-Thames, London, UK

Michael Jones, pianist, author, recording artist, seminar leader and speaker, Canada
Since Michael's solo debut album Pianoscapes (1983) he has produced and sold over 2 million recordings and performed throughout North America as well as in Japan and Korea. Michael has also had a successful career in organisational consulting, teacher education and leadership development. In 1994 his experience in music improvisation was integrated as part of "The Dialogue Project", an innovative exploration into the art of generative conversation, funded by the Kellogg Foundation and located within the Organisational Learning Centre at MIT.
www.pianoscapes.com
Interview: June 2002, Borl, Slovenia

Mathilda Joubert, musician and creativity consultant, London, UK
Mathilda was originally trained as a musician and became a teacher in classical music. She also did a postgraduate diploma in choral conducting. Later she became a research officer at the National Advisory Committee on Creative and Cultural Education. She has worked with art education projects at the Royal Society of Arts. Mathilda also took a degree in neuropsychology and did a thesis on music and the brain. She recently did some work on creativity with the company Synectics.
Interview: April 2002, London, UK

John Kao, entrepreneur and business pioneer, author and speaker, San Francisco, USA.
John Kao is an authority on corporate innovation and transformation, digital media, design strategy, and the future of business. Both a psychiatrist and Harvard MBA, he taught at Harvard Business School for 14 years and was also a visiting professor at the MIT Media Lab. He is author of the best seller "Jamming: The Art and Discipline of Business Creativity". From

1997-2001 John was founder and CEO of The idea Factory. He is founder and director of several venture companies, honorary Vice President of Arts & Business, UK and a Fellow of the Royal Society of Art.
www.gbn.org/PersonBioDisplayServlet.srv?pi=23555
Interview: April 2002, London, UK

Bernard Kelly, storyteller and training development consultant in Storytelling in Organisations, Crowborough, UK.
Bernard is co-founder of Storytelling in Organisations, a consultancy company founded in 1995 with Sue Hollingsworth and Ashley Ramsden. Since the start they have worked together as storytellers and consultants exploring the transformational power of stories to address some of the key issues at the heart of business today.
Interview: April 2002, London, UK

Isabelle King, assistant producer, Catalyst, Unilever Ice Cream & Frozen Food, Walton-on-Thames, UK
Interview: November 2003, Walton-on-Thames, London, UK

Elmar Lampson, conductor, composer and professor of phenomenology of music, dean at the Facultät für das Studium Fundamentale, Universität Witten/Herdecke, Witten, Germany
Elmar was a free-lance conductor and composer for many years and was one of the first persons to work with Miha Pogacnik around the IDRIART festivals. Later Elmar started teaching and became the dean of the Faculty of Fundamental Studies at Witten-Herdecke University, which covers philosophy, history, sociology, cultural management, cultural politics, cultural science and arts studies. At the university reflection, communication and the arts are an important part of all studies, including dental medicine, human medicine, economics, management and life sciences.
www.uni-wh.de/
Interview: July 2002, Borl, Slovenia

Dianne Legro, vocalist and principal artist of Creative Leaps International, artist council representative on the board of Associated Solo Artists Inc., NY, USA
A graduate of the New England Conservatory and The Juilliard School, Dianne has starred in countless musical theatre productions including the Broadway revival of My Fair Lady. She is also an accomplished recitalist, cabaret artist and opera singer. Paralleling her work on stage, Dianne completed advanced studies in Bioenergetics, Alexander Technique and Yoga applying these competencies to peak performance training, stress management and leadership development in the business sector.
www.diannelegro.com
Interview: August 2002, Washington DC, USA

Paul Levy, actor, researcher and director, CATS3000, Brighton, UK
Paul Levy is a writer on management, a change facilitator and director of CATS3000, a theatre company and a training/development organisation that helps individuals, groups

and societies to be more creative and innovative. Paul facilitates workshops all over the world and has long experience in developing managers using a creative and hands-on approach. He is the author of several books including "E:Quality" and "Technosophy". He is also a theatre director and is involved in research, which is attempting to measure the link between art, creativity and innovation.
http://www.cats3000.com
Interview: November 2003, Copenhagen, Denmark

Oliver MacDonald, percussionist and partner, RedZebra, UK and South Africa
Oliver is a self-taught percussionist and co-founder of RedZebra. Since 1995 Redzebra has operated in Brighton, UK and from 1999 in Cape Town, Soweto and Johannesburg, South Africa. Its aim is to encourage a world community through transforming the way people communicate and by celebrating difference. Their work is 80% community work and 20% corporate. Projects include the "Omniculture Carnival" at Brighton, the "Unified Rhythm" in UK, The "Rumble in the Jungle" samba band of street youths and a partnership with "Street Universe" in South Africa.
www.redzebra.org.uk
Interview: April 2002, London, UK

Alexander Mackenzie, storyteller and consultant, London, UK
Alexander comes from Northern Ireland, where storytelling is a natural part of the community. Alexander became conscious of his storytelling skills when running a home for maladapted children of 7-11 years. One evening, when the children were behaving very badly, he sat down in frustration and started telling a story. To his surprise the children stopped misbehaving and sat down to listen, and every night for a whole year he continued the story, making it up all along. Today Alexander applies storytelling to leadership development and communication training.
Interview: April 2002, London, UK

Alejandra Mørk, senior vice-president, International Product Development, Nycomed, Roskilde, Denmark
Alejandra has a Master of Science and a Ph.D. in Pharmacy from the Royal Danish School of Pharmacy, Copenhagen. She has worked in Nycomed since 1989 in several different functions, both with regulatory affairs, strategic portfolio management and project management. As vice-president of Project Management, Alejandra came into contact with the artists from ArtLab, which made Nycomed one of the pioneering corporations to work with arts in business in Denmark. Alejandra is chairman of The Pharmaceutical Society of Denmark and is on the board of NyX Innovation Alliances.
www.nycomed.dk
Interview: December 2003, Roskilde, Denmark

Linda Naiman, catalyst for creativity and innovation, director, Linda Naiman & Associates Inc., Vancouver, Canada
Linda Naiman & Associates' training and consultation services aim to draw out brilliance in

organisations through the art and science of applying creativity, innovation and visionary thinking to business strategy. Linda Naiman, who calls herself a corporate alchemist, uses visual arts as a means of encouraging creativity, collaboration and diversity in organisations. She is co-author (with Arthur VanGundy) of "Orchestrating Collaboration at Work", published by Wiley/Jossey-Bass, and her essays on creativity have been published in numerous business journals.
http://www.creativityatwork.com/
Interview (written): December 2003

Robert A. Nalewajek, member of the board of Creative Leaps International and chair of Associated Solo Artists Business Committee, NY, USA
Bob holds a B.A. from Niagara University and an M.A. from the University of Southern California. He spent 22 years with Pfizer, Inc., where he was responsible for HR strategic business support in Europe, Asia, Africa, the Middle East, Russia, and Australia. He has headed several other departments, including Pfizer International's Management Development, Executive Development, Succession Planning and Manpower Planning. Bob has served on several boards, including the Greenwich Library, Catholic Charities of Fairfield Count and the Global Leadership Institute.
www.creativeleaps.org
Interview: August 2002, Norwalk, USA

Richard Olivier, director of Olivier Mythodrama, London, UK
Richard has been a leading theatre director for over ten years and is the founding voice within Mythodrama, aiming at developing authentic leaders through a synthesis of theatre skills, psychology, mythology and organisational development. Richard is an Associate Fellow of Templeton College, Oxford, and Master of Mythodrama at Shakespeare's Globe Theatre. Richard also works internationally as an independent consultant, conference speaker and workshop leader. He is the author of 'Inspirational Leadership - Henry V and the Muse of Fire', Spiro Press, 2001.
www.oliviermythodrama.com
Interview: April 2002, London, UK

David Pearl, opera singer turned business arts pioneer, director of the Corporate !nspiration Agency (C!A), London, UK.
For over a decade, David has been pioneering the use of creative disciplines in business. Based in London, the C!A has been set up to help organisations become more inspiring places for creating extraordinary results. The last decade of radical work includes over 600 projects internationally. C!A brings together extraordinary long-term colleagues in the field of organisational and personal transformation, who are hugely experienced and have a knack of making their hard-won insights easily accessible to the companies served.
www.theothercia.co.uk
Interview: April 2002, London, UK

Miha Pogacnik, violinist, entrepreneur and cultural ambassador for Slovenia, Hamburg, Germany

Miha communicates new ways of thinking via his violin. Through music and art, he is able to demonstrate the underlying principles of renewal and change, transforming core thinking and removing the barriers that traditionally limit a company's visionary capabilities. Miha is the founding director of IDRIART (Initiative for the Development of Intercultural Relations through the Arts) and has also conceived the idea of the European Identity Cultural Caravan, taking artists and organisational scholars on a train throughout the new EU member states to the 2004 summit in Prague.
http://www.borl.org/eng/index.php
http://www.european-identity.net/index_02.html
Interview: July 2002, Borl, Slovenia

Ashley Ramsden, actor and storyteller from Storytelling in Organisations, Crowborough, UK. Founding director of the School of Storytelling at Emerson, East Sussex, UK
Ashley performs in Europe and America, running workshops and international symposia. He is co-founder of Storytelling in Organisations, a consultancy working with the transformational power of stories to address some of the key issues at the heart of business today. Emerson College, founded in 1962 by the educational pioneer Francis Edmunds, converges on the fields of education, environment, and social and artistic renewal, drawing their inspiration from anthroposophy and the work of Rudolf Steiner.
www.emerson.org.uk
Interview: April 2002, London, UK

Paul Robertson, first violin and leader of The Medici Quartet, London, UK
Formed in 1971, The Medici Quartet is widely regarded as one of Britain's leading international ensembles, having appeared in more than thirty countries across five continents. Paul is very interested in the powerful effect that music has on the human brain. The growing awareness of the role that music plays in the healing process has led to links with the Amsterdam Medical Centre and the Karolinska Institute Stockholm, as well as Chelsea & Westminster, Geneva University, Guy's, Royal London, Michigan University and St Thomas' Hospitals.
www.musicmindspirit.org
Interview: July 2003, Borl, Slovenia

C. Otto Scharmer, co-founder and lecturer, Leadership Lab for Corporate Social Innovation at MIT Sloan, Boston, USA
Otto studies leadership, organisational learning, and the dynamics of multi-stakeholder dialogue, collaboration and change. Otto is co-founder of the Society for Organisational Learning and the Global Institute for Responsible Leadership. He is a co-author, with Senge, Jaworski and Flowers, of the book "Presence: Human Purpose and the Field of the Future", SOL press. He is the sole author of a forthcoming book, "THEORY U: Leading and Learning from the Future As It Emerges". Otto is on the Advisory Board of The Creative Alliance Consortium at Learning Lab Denmark.
http://www.ottoscharmer.com
Interview: September, 2002, Copenhagen, Denmark

Milo Shapiro, speaker, workshop leader and entertainer, CEO (Creative Energy Officer) ImproVentures, San Diego, CA, USA
Milo has a Bachelor of Science in Computer Science and worked for 15 years in both state government and utilities. He pursued an interest for theatre, joined the international theatre alliance, Theatre Sports, and became the business manager of the San Diego Troupe for many years. In 2000 he founded ImproVentures, a training and consultancy company offering interactive events with improvisation to organisations, e.g. communication and teambuilding workshops, interactive motivation speeches, and business presentations loaded with entertainment.
www.improVentures.com
Interview: May 2003, San Diego, California, USA

Ellen Speert, director of the Art Therapy Center of North County, and director of Art Therapy Programs, University of California, San Diego, USA
Ellen is a Board Certified and Registered Art Therapist as well as a Registered Expressive Arts Therapist. She is a founding member and past president of the San Diego Art Therapy Association. Ellen teaches art therapy at the University of California, where she coordinates the Expressive Therapies Certificate Program. She is an internationally known writer and lecturer, teaching and presenting workshops in Switzerland, Germany and Canada. She has served as consultant in many clinical settings including UCSD Medical Center, San Diego Hospice and Grossmont Hospice.
www.artRETREATS.com
Interview: September 2002, London, UK

Steven S. Taylor, assistant professor, Department of Management, Worcester Polytechnic Institute, Worcester, MA, USA.
Steve's research focuses on the aesthetics of organisational action. In particular, he has been focusing on the intersection of aesthetic forms with traditional management topics. Examples of this are his dissertation research into leadership storytelling, and his use of theatre as a presentational form within academia.
www.mgt.wpi.edu and http://acorn.lld.dk/Members/Steve%20Taylor
Interview: September 2002, London, UK

Herbert R. Tillery, deputy mayor for Operations and interim director, Department of Health, Government of the District of Columbia, former executive director at Center for Excellence in Municipal Management (CEMM), The George Washington University, Washington DC, USA
Herbert has progressive experience in senior-executive-level human-resource management and development. He has a proven track record of success in training and leadership positions requiring solid organisational skills. He is known by his reputation for innovation, vision and tenacity. At CEMM, a training and research centre focusing on leadership and management in the public sector, Herbert was primarily responsible for the design, development and implementation of the Program for Excellence in Municipal Management.
http://www.gwu.edu/~cemm/
Interview: August 2002, Washington DC, USA

Margaret J. Wheatley, consultant, speaker, best-selling author and founding president of The Berkana Institute, Provo, Utah, USA
Margaret has a Ph.D. from Harvard's programme in administration, planning and social policy, with a focus on organisational behaviour and change. She has lectured at numerous universities and has been a consultant and speaker since 1973. She is the author of the bestseller "Leadership and the New Science" and co-authored "A Simpler Way". Her latest book is "Turning to One Another: Simple conversations to Restore Hope to the Future". The Berkana Institute is a global charitable foundation founded in 1991 dedicated to serving local leaders, currently in over 30 countries.
http://www.margaretwheatley.com and http://www.berkana.org/
Interview: April 2003, Copenhagen, Denmark

Mads Øvlisen, chairman of the board of directors, Novo Nordisk A/S, Bagsværd, Denmark
Former president and CEO of Novo Nordisk, Mads Øvlisen became chairman of the board in November 2000. Øvlisen is also chairman of the board of the Danish Royal Theatre (2000), and chairman of the board of LEGO A/S and a member of the board of the Wanås Foundation, Sweden. Mads Øvlisen was made Knight of first degree of the Dannebrog in 1997 and holds the Italian Order of Merit (It.F.3). He is adjunct professor of corporate social responsibility at the Copenhagen Business School.
www.novonordisk.com
Interview: November 2002, Bagsværd, Denmark

BIBLIOGRAPHY

Knud Aunstrup (editor) (2000): "You do not have to like the art... ", Novo Nordisk

Chris Argyris (1992): "Organizational Learning", Blackwell Business

Chris Argyris and Donald Schön (1996): "Organizational Learning II: Theory, Method, and Practice", Addison-Wesley Publishing Company

Rob Austin & Lee Devin (2003): "Artful Making. What Managers Need to Know About How Artists Work", FT Prentice Hall.

Teresa Balough (1996): "May Human Beings Hear it! IDRIART", published by CIRCME, School of Music The University of Western Australia in association with IDRIART.

David Barry & E. Palmer (2001): "Serious questions about serious play: Problems and prospects in the study of mediated innovation". Proceedings of the ANZAM Conference, Auckland, New Zealand

David Barry (1997): "Telling changes: From narrative family therapy to organizational change & development". Journal of Organizational Change Management, Volume 10, #1:32-48

Peter Bastian (1987): "Ind i Musikken. En Bog om Musik og Bevidsthed" (ed. "Into the Music. A Book about Music and Consciousness"), Gyldendals Bogklub

Githa Ben-David (2002): "Tonen fra himlen. At synge sig selv" (ed. "The tone from heaven. Singing yourself"), Borgen

Augusto Boal (2000): "Theater of the Oppressed", Pluto Press

David Bohm (1998): "On Creativity", edited by Lee Nichol, Routledge

Tom Burns & George M. Stalker (1961): "The Management of Innovation", London: Tavistock

Ted Buswick, Alastair Creamer and Mary Pinard (2004): "(Re)Educating for Leadership: How the Arts Can Improve Business", forthcoming

David Butcher (2003): "A Fruitful Union", article in Management Today (www.clickMT.com), August 2003

Julia Cameron (1992): "The Artist's Way. A Spiritual Path to Higher Creativity", Jeremy P. Tarcher/Putnam.

Don Campbell (2001): "The Mozart Effect. Tapping the Power of Music to Heal the Body, Strengthen the Mind, and Unlock the Creative Spirit", Quill

Mihalyi Csikszentmihalyi (1990): "Flow. The Psychology of Optimal Experience", Harper Perennial

David A. Cowan (2002): "Artistic Intelligence and Leadership Framing: Employing the Wisdom of Envisioning, Improvisation, Introspection, and Inclusion", The Art of Management and Organization conference, London.

David A. Cowan (1995): "Rhythms of Learning. Patterns that Bridge Individuals and Organizations", Journal of Management Inquiry, Vol. 4 No. 3, 222-246.

M.M. Crossan & Marc Sorrenti (2002): "Making Sense of Improvisation", in Kamoche, Pina e Cunha & Vieira da Cunha (Eds.) (2002): "Organizational Improvisation".

Lotte Darsø (2001): "Innovation in the Making", Samfundslitteratur.

Lotte Darsø & Michael Dawids (2002): "Arts-in-Business – Proposing a theoretical Framework", presented at EURAM Stockholm, May 2002, at The 5th Art & Business Conference, Borl, Slovenia, June 2002, and at The Art of Management and Organisation, London, Sept. 2002.

Peter F. Drucker (1993): "Post-Capitalist Society", Butterworth-Heinemann

Betty Edwards (1986): "Drawing on the Artist Within", Simon and Schuster

Richard Florida (2002): "The rise of the creative class", Basic Books.

Frederiksen, Siggaard & Dawids (2002): "Speculations on organization, capabilities and learning in the creative industries", presented at the Third European Conference on Organizational Knowledge, Learning, and Capabilities, ALBA, Athens, Greece, 5-6 April 2002.

Craig Harris (ed) (1999): "Art and Innovation: The Xerox PARC Artist-in-Residence Program", MIT Press.

John Kao (1996): "Jamming. The Art and Discipline of Business Creativity", HarperBusiness

Shaun McNiff (1998): "Trust the Process. An Artist's Guide to Letting Go", Shambhala.

Camilla Mehlsen (2003): "The Beauty and the Machine", Master dissertation at Copenhagen University

Philip Mirvis, Karen Ayas & George Roth (2003): "To the Desert and Back. The Story of One of the Most Dramatic Business Transformations on Record", Jossey-Bass

Ian I. Mitroff & Elizabeth A. Denton (1999): "A Spiritual Audit of Corporate America. A Hard Look at Spirituality, Religion, and Values in the Workplace", Jossey-Bass Publishers

Gareth Morgan (1997): "Images of Organization", Sage Publications

Joseph Nye (2004): "Soft Power: The Means to Success in World Politics", Public Affairs

Richard Olivier (2001): "Inspirational Leadership. Henry V and the Muse of Fire", The Industrial Society

B. Joseph Pine II & James H. Gilmore (1999): "The Experience Economy. Work is Theatre & Every Business a Stage," Harvard Business School Press

Plato, "Politicus" (Statesman), written 360 BCE.

Dick Richards (1995): "Artful Work. Awakening, Joy, Meaning, and Commitment in the Workplace", Berrett-Kohler Publishers

Donald Schön (1986): "Generative Metaphor: A Perspective on Problem-Setting in Social Policy", in Andrew Ortony (ed): "Metaphor and Thought", Cambridge University Press

Hyemeyohsts Storm (1994): "Lightningbolt", Ballantine Books.

Lykke Ricard (2003): "Oh Thou Beautiful Management", Master dissertation at Copenhagen Business School

Margot Rose, John Simpson & Nik Wilkinson (2003): "A Freak Food Accident and other stories", published by Unilever Ice Cream & Frozen Food, Walton.

Nanna Schacht (2002), "Not the Emperor's new clothes", Design DK: 4, 2002 December.

C. Otto Scharmer (2004 forthcoming): "THEORY U: Leading and Learning from the Future As It Emerges", Berrett-Koehler Publishers

Michael Schrage (2000): "Serious Play. How the world's best companies simulate to innovate", Harvard Business School Press

Peter Senge, C. Otto Scharmer, Joseph Jaworski and Betty Sue Flowers (2004): "Presence: Human Purpose and the Field of the Future", SOL Press

Peter Senge et al. (1994): "The Fifth Discipline Fieldbook; Strategies and Tools for building a Learning Organization", Necholas Brealey Publishing

Antonio Strati (2000): "The Aesthetic Approach in Organization Studies", in Stephen Linstead & Heather Höpfl: "The Aesthetics of Organization", Sage publications.

Steven S. Taylor & Hans Hansen (2004) "Finding form: Looking at the field of organizational aesthetics", (work-in-progress)

Stefan Thomke (2003): "R&D Comes to Services. Bank of America's Pathbreaking Experiments", Harvard Business Review, April 2003, p. 71-79

Arthur B. VanGundy and Linda Naiman (2003) "Orchestrating Collaboration at Work: Using Music, Improv, Storytelling, and Other Arts to Improve Teamwork", Wiley/Jossey-Bass

"Visionsindustri", udgivet af Vestsjællands Kunstmuseum og Informations Forlag (2001) (ed. Vision Industry, an exhibition and catalogue by the Museum of Western Zealand and Information Publishing)

Margaret J. Wheatley (2002): "Turning to one another. Simple conversations to restore hope to the future", Berrett-Koehler Publishers

Margaret J. Wheatley (2002): "Supporting Pioneering Leaders as Communities of Practice. How to Rapidly Develop New Leaders in Great Numbers" (www.margaretwheatley.com)

Margaret J. Wheatley (1999): "Leadership and the New Science", Berrett-Koehler Publishers

Ken Wilber (2001): "The Eye of Spirit. An integral vision for a world gone slightly mad", Shambhala

Ken Wilber (2000): "A Brief History of Everything", Shambhala

David Whyte (2002): "The Heart Aroused: Poetry and the Preservation of the Soul in Corporate America", Currency, a division of Random House

Rosamund Stone Zander & Benjamin Zander (2000): "The Art of Possibility. Transforming Professional and Personal Life", Harvard Business School Press

INDEX